IMAGES
of America

Skiing in Southern California

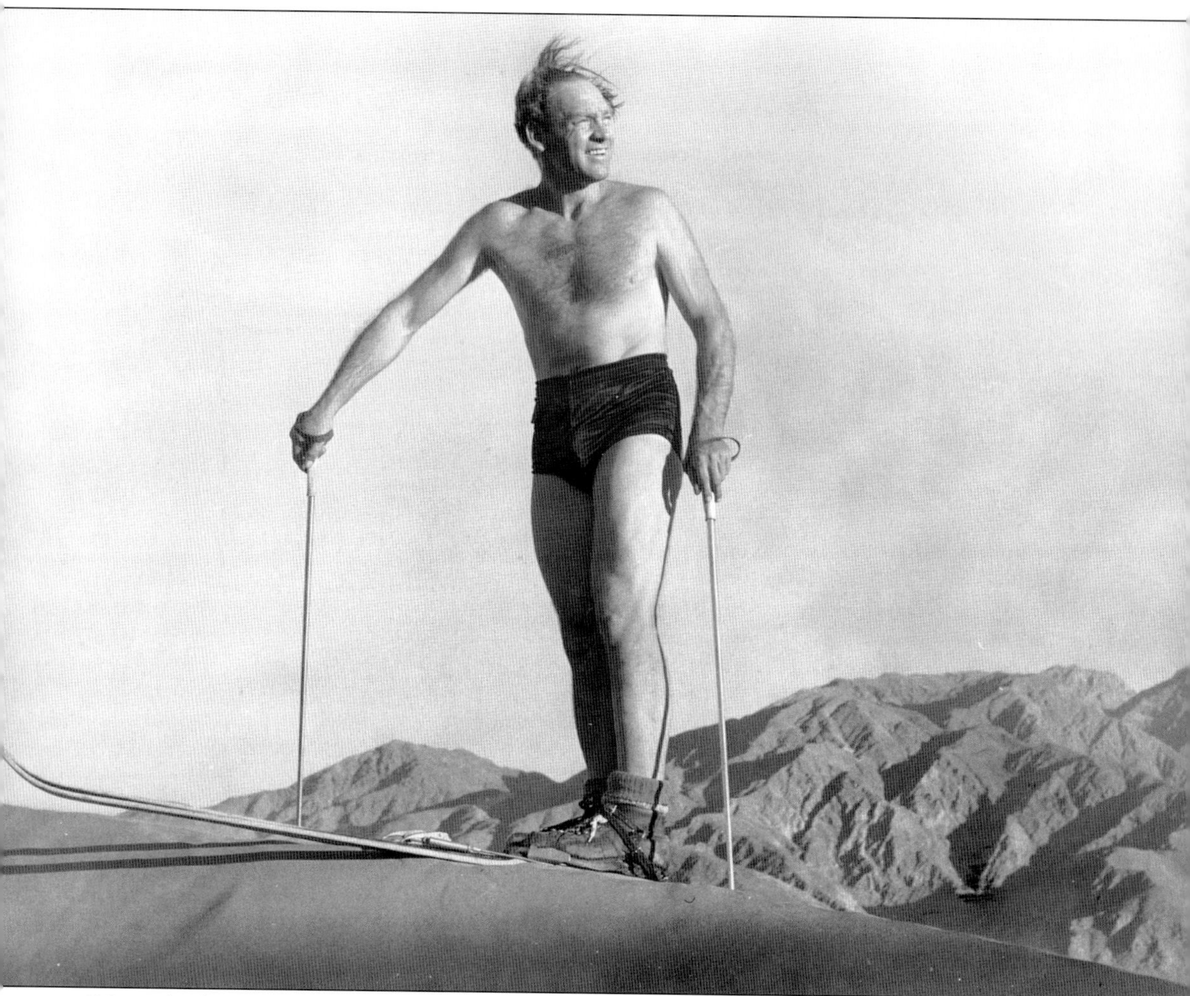

Often the brunt of jokes about snowfall or the lack thereof, Southern California ski pioneers nevertheless forged ahead to promote and develop the sport. Progressing from pine needles and straw to summer snow and innovations in snowmaking, the Southland became one of the most popular centers of skiing in the United States, despite its unlikely location and warm temperatures. Here Sepp Benedikter takes in a view of his surroundings while sand skiing in Death Valley in the 1930s. (Courtesy Claudia Benedikter Pedersen.)

ON THE COVER: In the 1930s, skiers flocked to Big Pines, near Wrightwood, where they could take in a weekend winter carnival or partake in winter sports on their own. Noted Southern California ski pioneer Ethel Severson Van Degrift, second from right, visits Table Mountain at Big Pines with a group of her cohorts in March 1935. Ethel noted that this was her fifth ski trip. Her first was in January 1935 to Harwood Lodge in the Mount Baldy area. She went on to promote and influence Southern California skiing for more than 20 years. (Courtesy Craig Van Degrift.)

IMAGES *of America*

SKIING IN SOUTHERN CALIFORNIA

Ingrid P. Wicken

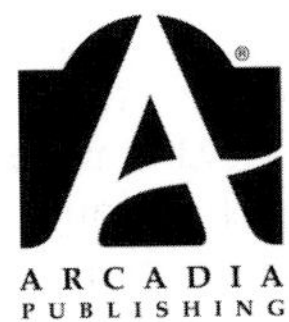

ISBN 978-0-7385-5568-3

Published by Arcadia Publishing
Charleston SC, Chicago IL, Portsmouth NH, San Francisco CA

Printed in the United States of America

Library of Congress Catalog Card Number: 2007928966

For all general information contact Arcadia Publishing at:
Telephone 843-853-2070
Fax 843-853-0044
E-mail sales@arcadiapublishing.com
For customer service and orders:
Toll-Free 1-888-313-2665

Visit us on the Internet at www.arcadiapublishing.com

In memory of my parents, John and Pauline Wicken

CONTENTS

Acknowledgments 6

Introduction 7

1. Leading the Way 9
2. Sierra Club Skiing 25
3. Ski Jumping 39
4. No Snow, No Problem 55
5. Ski Clubs and the Far West Ski Association 63
6. Skiing in the San Bernardinos 77
7. Skiing in the San Gabriels 91
8. San Gorgonio 107
9. Eastern Sierra Skiing 115

Acknowledgments

Several individuals merit credit and thanks for the images included herein. First, thank you to Aileen Spiller, Wolfgang Lert, Craig Van Degrift, Vi White, and Luanne Pfeifer for the photographs and memorabilia they so generously donated to the California Ski Library. Thank you to the Huntington Library, the Bancroft Library at the University of California, Berkeley, and the Western Skisport Museum for their assistance in securing images from their collections. My utmost gratitude to John K. Adams, Elmar Baxter, Glen Dawson, Karen Wullich Herbst, Ann Dormer Johnson, Gina Merz McGloskey, Claudia Benedikter Pedersen, and Chris Schwarzenbach for so generously sharing their personal photographs. Thanks to Barb Van Houten for gathering photographs of the Steinmann years at Holiday Hill. Thank you to Arcadia editor Debbie Seracini for advice and encouragement along the way. Thank you to Cheryl Nassar for reading and editing the manuscript. And thanks to Doug Pfeiffer for his ever-present encouragement, advice, and humor.

Unless otherwise noted, all photographs are from the California Ski Library located in Norco, California.

INTRODUCTION

In 1941, *The Mountaineer,* Big Bear Lake's weekly newspaper, gave this account of early-20th-century skiing: "Skis used in Big Bear valley thirty-five years ago had no swank. They had no trade mark or shimmering gloss. But they did work. They were made of one-by-fours with a tin can nailed on the end in such a manner that the wearers, three in number, might make the distance from Victorville, over 18 inches of snow, without being catapulted. The three men were John Long, Ed Knickerbocker, and Frank Miller who were bound for Big Bear from Goldfield, Nevada. The year was 1907 and the month was December, and the trip was made in 16 hours, the tin cans doing their valiant duty and the men arriving safely."

At the beginning of the 20th century, Southern Californians viewed snow as a hindrance rather than as a source of enjoyment. With the first hint of snowfall, those who worked and lived in Southern California's mountains in the non-winter months would make a hasty retreat to the lowlands until the roads were passable the following spring. By the 1920s, some Southlanders were beginning to discover that snow was more than just an obstacle to be overcome, and they began to travel to the higher elevations for "coasting" and snow play. Mountain travel was still limited by primitive snow removal techniques, and a trip to the mountains consisted of driving as far as one could until snow blocked the road to further travel.

By the 1930s, Lake Arrowhead had become the place to go for fun in the snow. It hosted hugely popular winter carnivals, which had begun there in 1927. Big Bear Lake became Southern California's winter sports capital, getting its first lift (a sling lift) in 1938 and its first chairlift in 1949. Big Pines became nationally known for its world-class ski jump, attracting ski jumpers from all over the world. Sierra Club Ski Mountaineers were some of the first to explore and make winter ascents of local mountains. They also began hosting annual races on Mount Baldy and San Gorgonio, and they built the San Antonio and Keller Peak Ski Huts that still exist today. Los Angeles had its first ski shop, Van Degrift's Ski Hut, by 1936, which provided much-needed equipment to the burgeoning number of winter sports enthusiasts. Ethel Severson (later Van Degrift) became one of the Southland's first ski column writers, spreading the fun and excitement of skiing to the masses.

The Scandinavians who headlined the ski jumping extravaganzas of the 1920s and 1930s proved that citizens of the sun-drenched Southland also had high peaks and ample snow to provide plenty of winter sports enjoyment. So popular were the Scandinavians and their daring-do that the state was at one time dubbed "Scandifornia." But the French, Austrians, and Germans who arrived on the scene—serving as instructors, alpine guides, and skilled practitioners of the sport—pioneered what had become Southern California's fastest-growing sport. They raced, taught, lectured, explored, built tows and lifts, designed ski equipment, wrote ski books and articles, made ski movies, founded and managed ski resorts, and, in some cases, provided the capital needed to develop and improve local resorts, most of which still exist today.

Eventually, there were enough skiers that those who met on a regular basis decided to form a club. After the birth of the California Ski Association in 1930 (it was renamed the Far West Ski Association in 1949), clubs had an organizing body and a voice—one that emphasized safety, promoted area development, and provided ski club programs.

In 1942, Mount Waterman became the home of Southern California's first chairlift. Thoughts and plans for ski area development came to a virtual standstill during World War II, but once life returned to normal after the war, those plans resumed with fervor. Frank Springer and Tom Triol installed Southern California's second chairlift at Blue Ridge in 1947. In 1949, the Lynn Lift was completed in Big Bear Lake, and Snow Valley's first chairlift opened for business. In the early 1950s, Holiday Hill, Mount Baldy, and Snow Summit constructed their first chairlifts. Most of these areas, developed with a passion for the sport and plenty of backbreaking work, are still in existence today.

When Mother Nature was stingy with her winter gifts, skiers would seek out distant areas with higher elevations and colder temperatures. Rope tows dotted the map along Highway 395, from Tom's Place to McGee Creek and north to Conway Summit. Skiers began to make the long trek to the Eastern Sierra once word spread (with the help of Hans Georg and Dave McCoy) of the abundant snow and variety of slopes to please all manner of skiers, from beginners to alpine ski mountaineers. From its humble beginnings with a rope tow here or there, Mammoth Mountain was born.

The selection of photographs that follows provides visual documentation of the wide spectrum of Southern California skiing: the first winter ascents of mountain peaks, the winter carnivals, the ski extravaganzas on department store roofs, the Hollywood hills, the outdoor arenas, the formation of ski clubs, the birth and development of ski areas, the areas that never grew beyond the drawing board, and the people who made it all happen.

One

Leading the Way

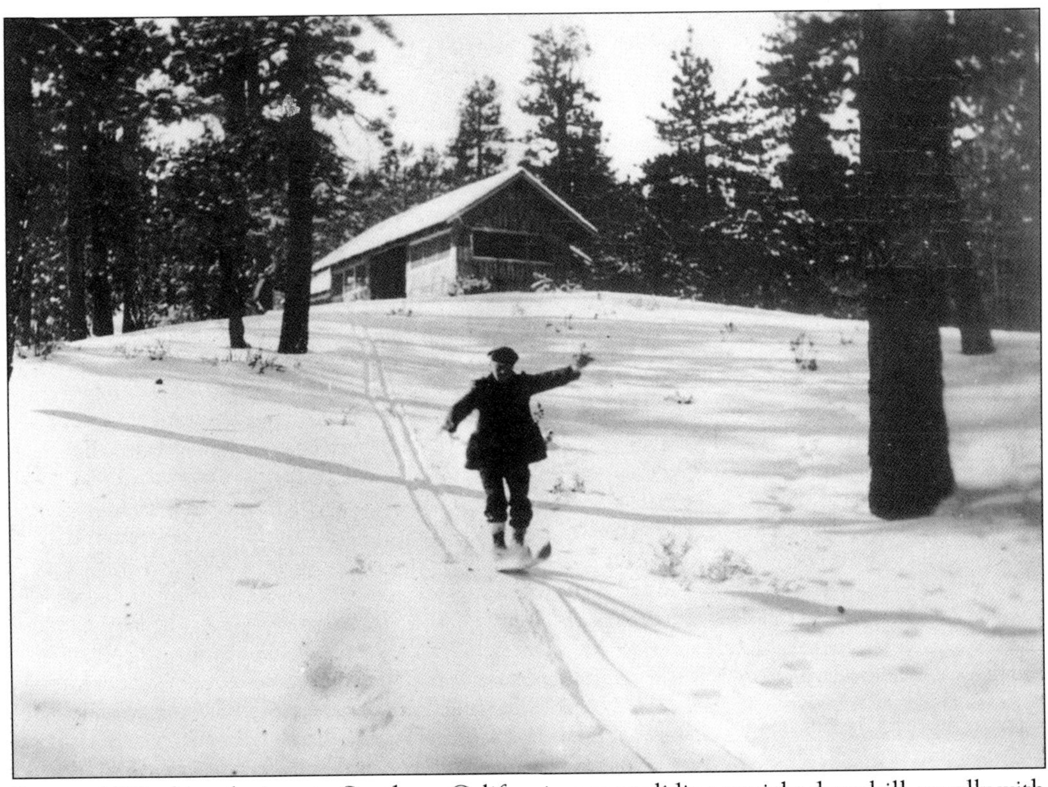

Prior to 1930, ski technique in Southern California meant gliding straight downhill, usually with no attempts at making a turn. The skier was happy if he or she made it to the bottom without a fall. The arrival of Europeans who had ski experience in the Alps brought ski technique and instruction to those eager to learn.

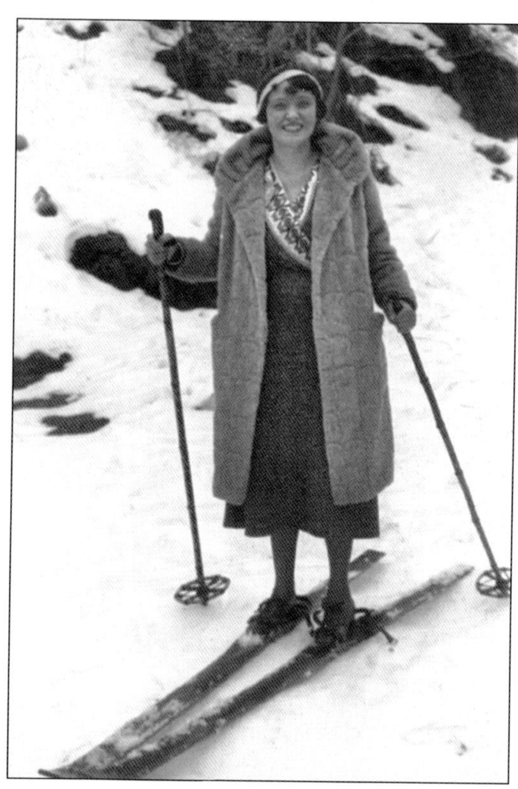

Skiwear in the early days consisted of whatever people could find in their closets. The dress and long coat did not seem to hinder the fun of this happy skier at Crystal Lake in the San Gabriel Mountains.

A beginner receives some "hands-on" instruction at Big Pines near Wrightwood. Before the arrival of ski instructors, skiers would often learn by watching better skiers and by lots of trial and error. (Courtesy The Huntington Library.)

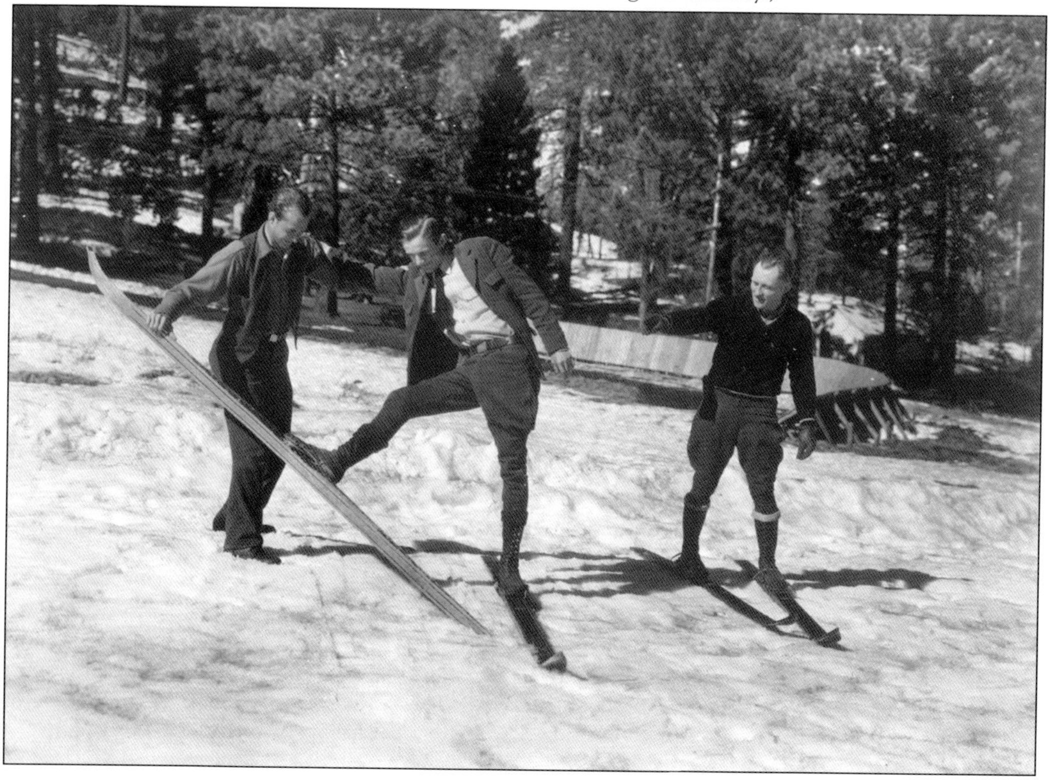

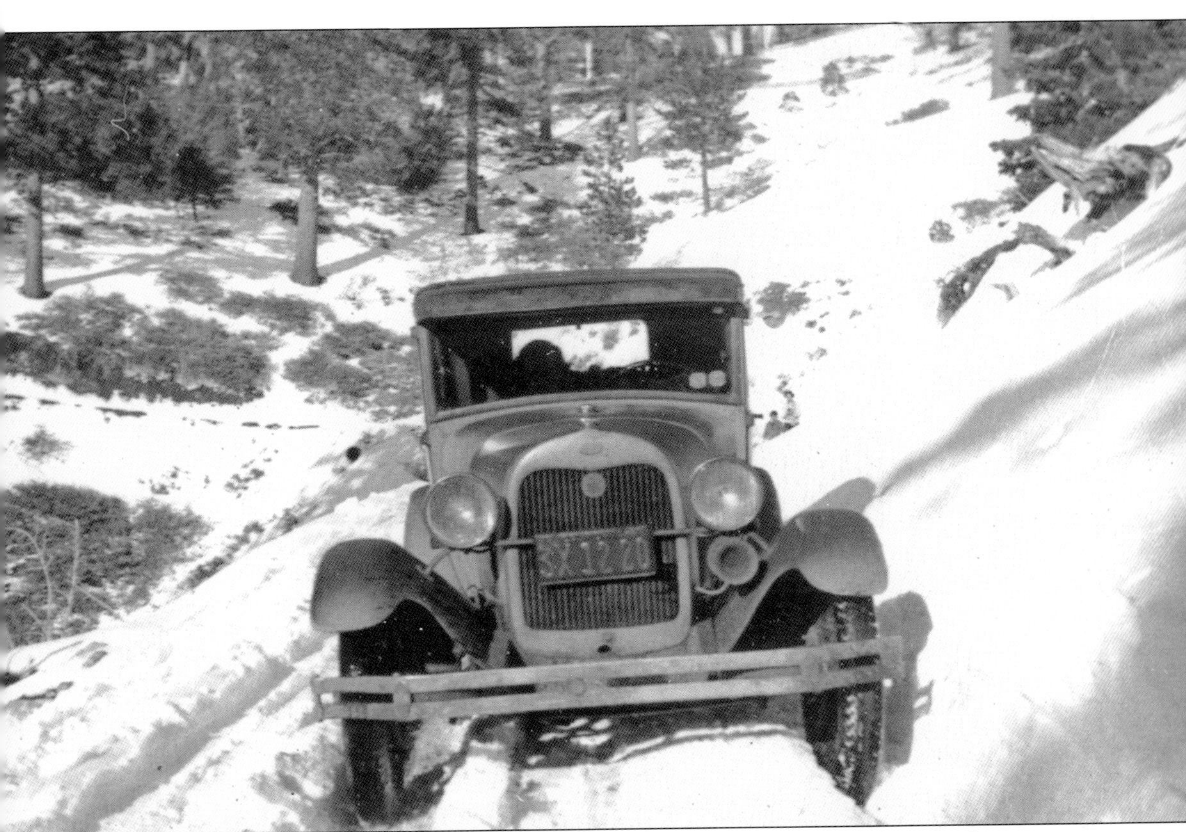

Snow-covered roads often prevented winter sports devotees from reaching their destinations. Prior to the development of more effective methods of snow removal, winter travel was difficult for those who wanted to spend their weekends partaking in snow-induced fun. This traveler, on his way to Big Pines in March 1935, probably did not make it much farther. Once the roads could be reliably cleared, winter resorts were born. They were able to guarantee that participants and spectators alike could reach ski-jump meets and winter carnivals.

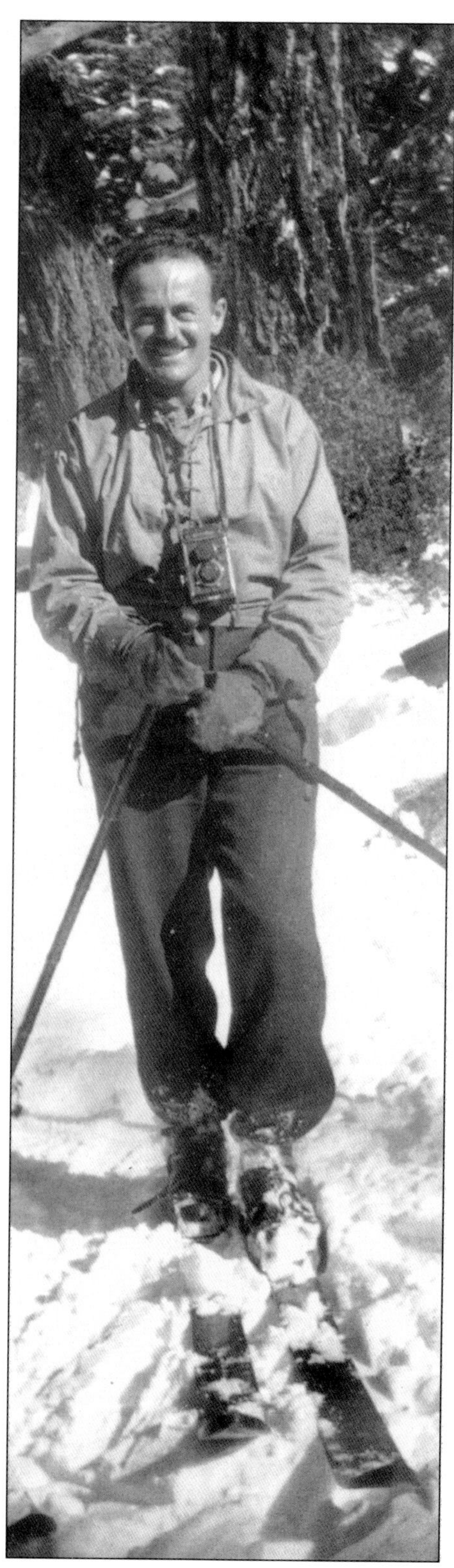

Walter Mosauer, shown here at Big Bear Lake in the late 1930s, is considered the father of skiing in Southern California. He was one of the inaugural members of the Sierra Club Ski Mountaineers and served as their first president. He wrote numerous ski articles for a variety of newspapers and magazines, and he wrote the first ski book published in Southern California. He was also one of the first ski instructors in the area. A zoology professor at the University of California, Los Angeles, he made groundbreaking studies of the locomotion of snakes. Sadly, Mosauer passed away at the young age of 32. He became ill and died on August 10, 1937, while on a reptile-hunting expedition in Mexico.

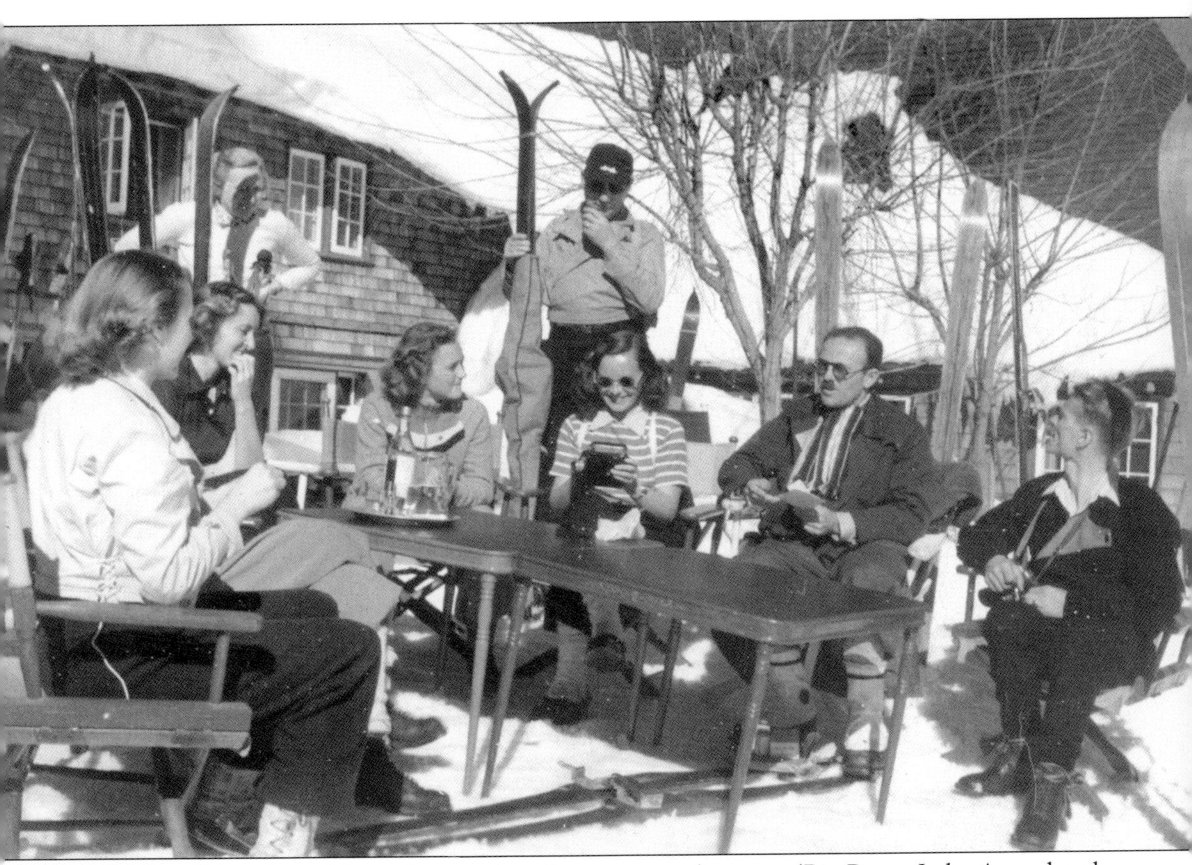

With a small number of skiers frequenting the most popular areas (Big Pines, Lake Arrowhead, and Big Bear Lake), ski clubs were born, and ski experts and instructors became well known. Walter Mosauer (in sunglasses), shown here holding court at Lake Arrowhead in January 1937, was the most enthusiastic and charismatic of the early ski instructors. Claudette Colbert (sitting at Mosauer's right) and Tyler Van Degrift (standing with skis) were two of many prominent skiers who frequented the slopes of Lake Arrowhead.

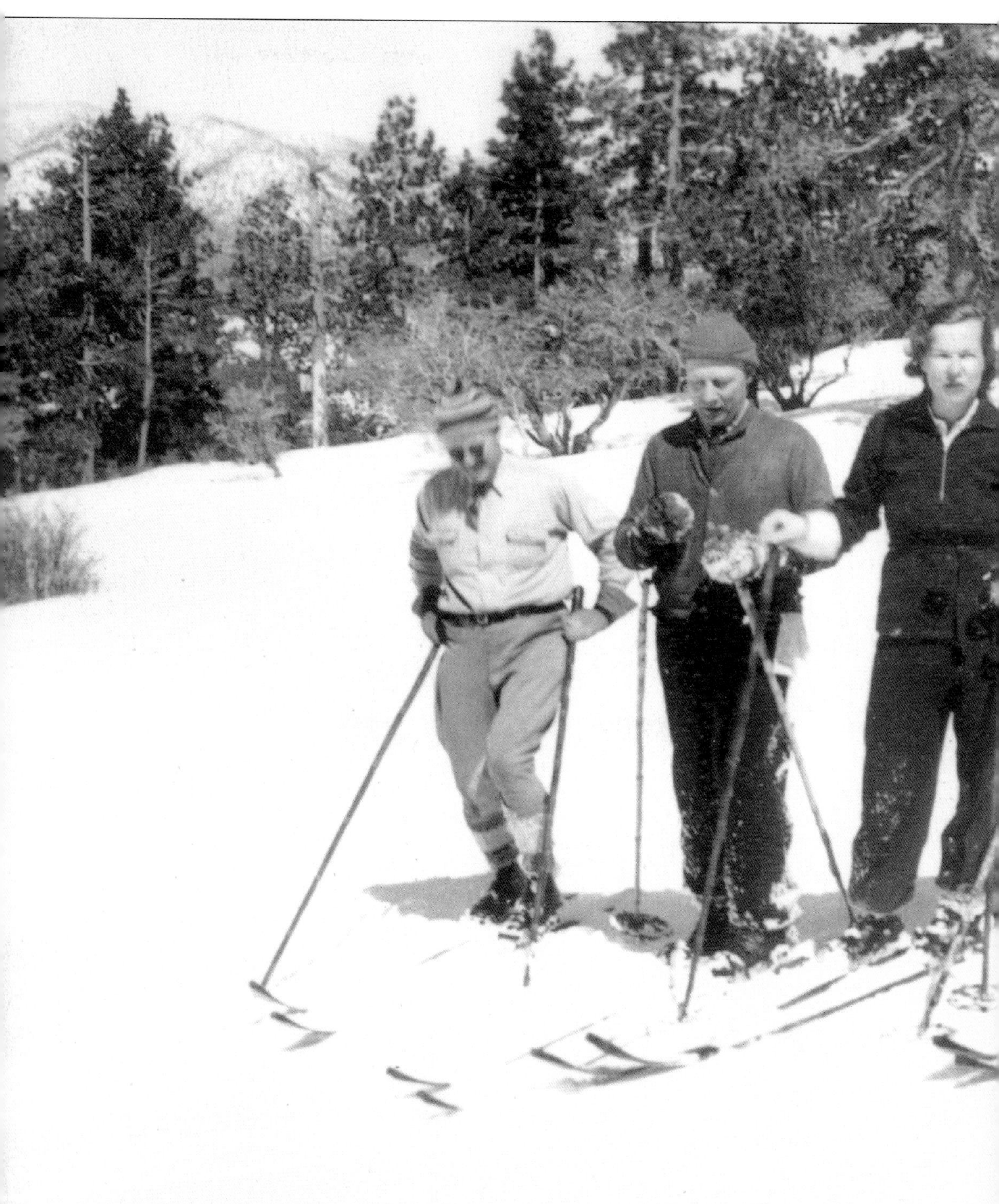

This Sierra Club group, taking a break during a 1935 ski trip to Big Bear Lake, includes three of Southern California's most ardent ski promoters of the 1930s and 1940s. Beginning second from left are Tyler Van Degrift, Ethel Severson Van Degrift, and Lester LaVelle. The other skier's identities are unknown. All three were longtime Sierra Club members and worked tirelessly to

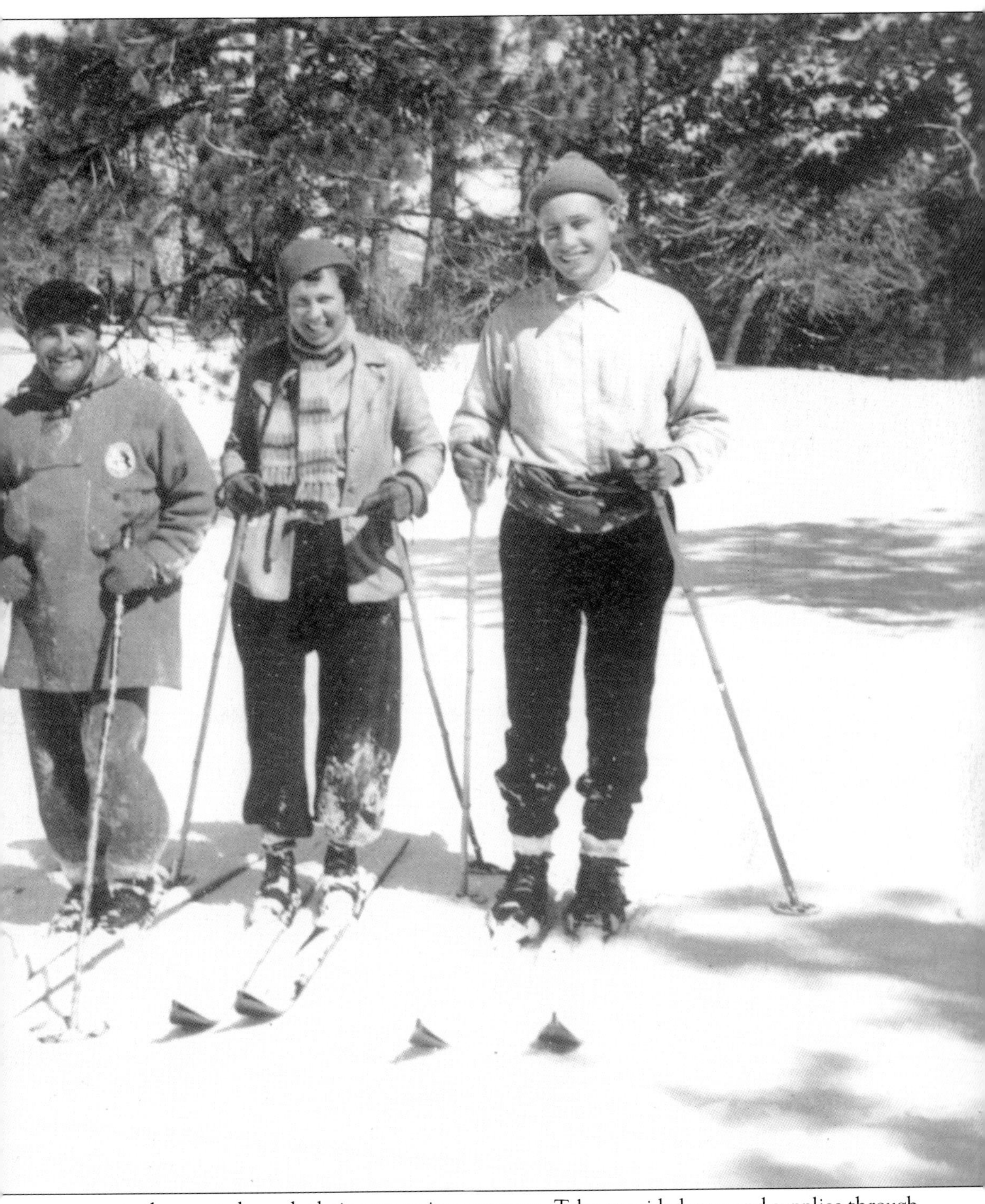

promote the sport through their own unique avenues. Tyler provided gear and supplies through Van Degrift's Ski Hut, Ethel was a longtime ski columnist for the Los Angeles Times, and Lester was a well respected and most effective ski teacher to thousands of newcomers to the sport.

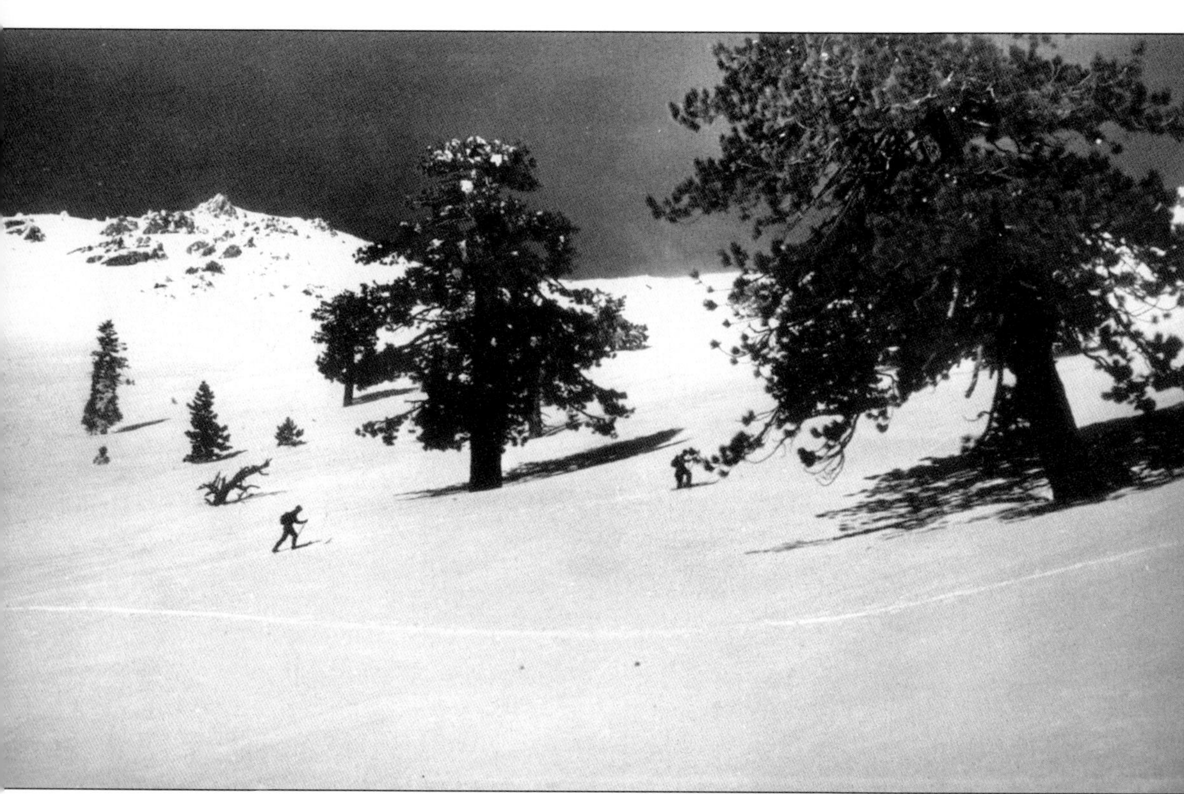

Murray Kirkwood and Walter Mosauer zigzag toward the saddle between Little Baldy and the summit. A student at Pomona College, Kirkwood frequented the slopes of Mount Baldy, located a short drive from the Claremont campus. Kirkwood, fellow Pomona College students Bill Cover and George Gibbs, and Claremont photographer Loyd Cooper made the first ski ascent of the 11,502-foot San Gorgonio on February 3, 1931. According to Cover, the group had limited previous experience, having only skied approximately a dozen times prior to this landmark trip. (Courtesy of The Bancroft Library, University of California, Berkeley.)

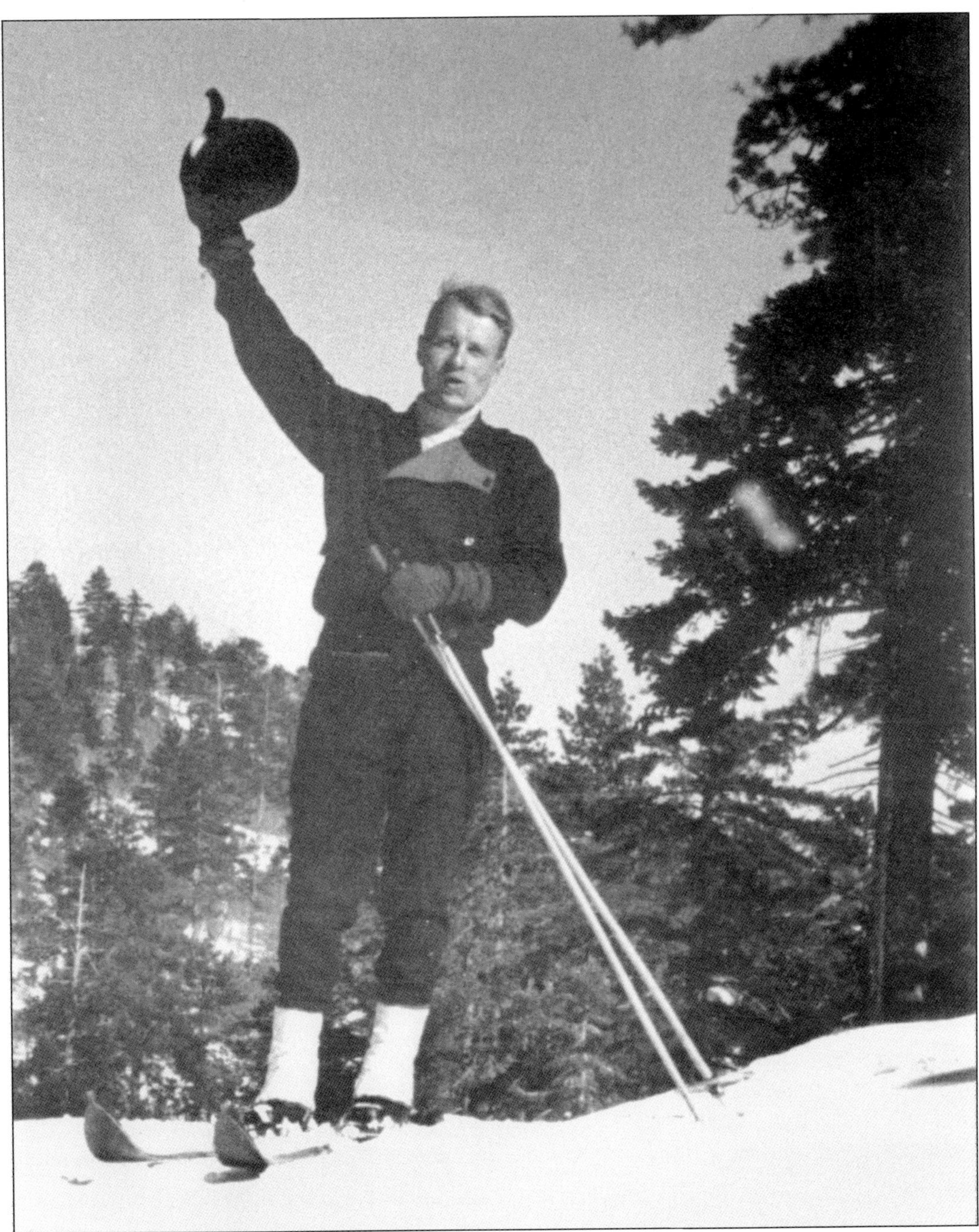

Egon Merz, enjoying a good snow day at Lake Arrowhead, was one of the founding members of one of Southern California's oldest ski clubs, Southern Skis. The club held their first organizational meeting on November 13, 1939, and filed Articles of Incorporation on December 27, 1939. The inaugural directors were Egon Merz, Dorothy Cooper, Paulette Goddard, John P. Lordan, Stan Mullin, Wallace Neff, Lucy Payne, Joel Pressman, Otto Steiner, and William Neff. Though Merz is probably better known for his horsemanship (he taught Elizabeth Taylor how to ride for National Velvet), he was an enthusiastic and enduring Southern California skier. (Courtesy Gina Merz McGloskey.)

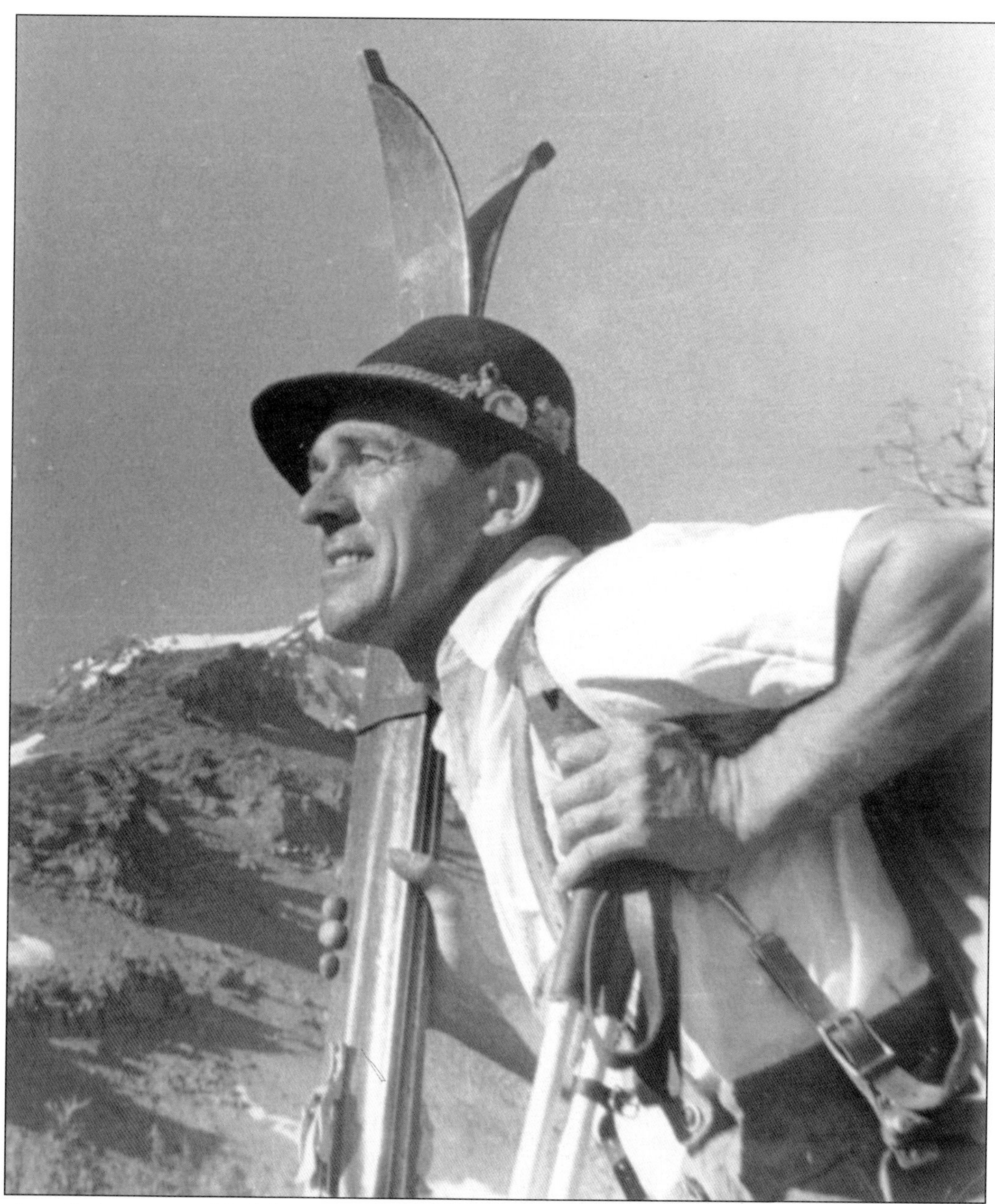

Otto Steiner, one of California's premier ski mountaineers, arrived in the United States from Germany in the late 1920s. He made a solo ski traverse of the Sierra during the winter of 1934–1935, becoming the first to discover the prime ski terrain in the Mineral King area. During the winter of 1935–1936, he became the first person to reach the summit of 14,161-foot Mount Shasta on skis. He was one of a handful of Southern California skiers who was proficient in all of the ski disciplines. This wide-ranging expertise led him to become well known in California locales. In 1937, he became coach of the UCLA ski team. That same year, he also became head of the winter sports program at Lake Arrowhead and mentor to the Lake Arrowhead Ski Club. In 1947, he became the first president of the California Ski Instructors' Association and was instrumental in standardizing instruction in California.

Sepp Benedikter, born on June 4, 1911, in Badgastein, Austria, began skiing at the age of two. When he was 16, he became an apprentice ski instructor and received an Austrian Ski Teacher's Certificate in 1929. In the summer of 1936, Averell Harriman, chairman of Union Pacific Railroad, recruited Benedikter to come to the United States to teach skiing at Sun Valley. Later that same year, when Sun Valley opened its chairlift—the first in the world—Benedikter was the first person to ride it. (Courtesy Claudia Benedikter Pedersen.)

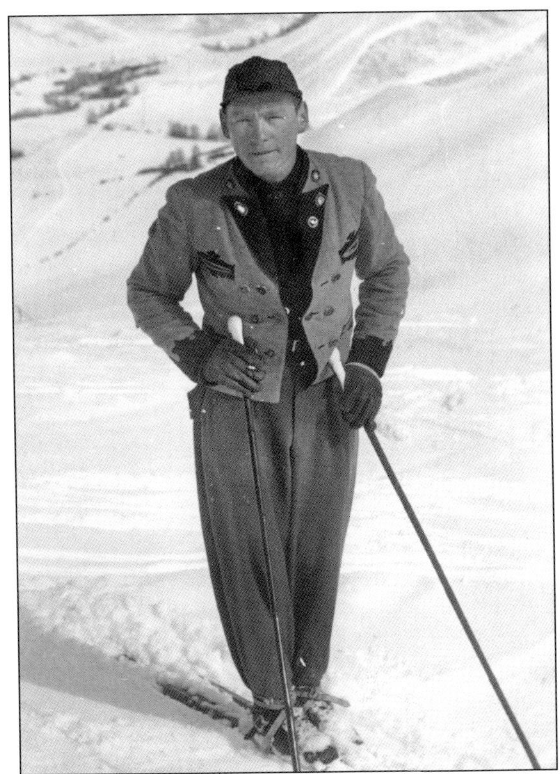

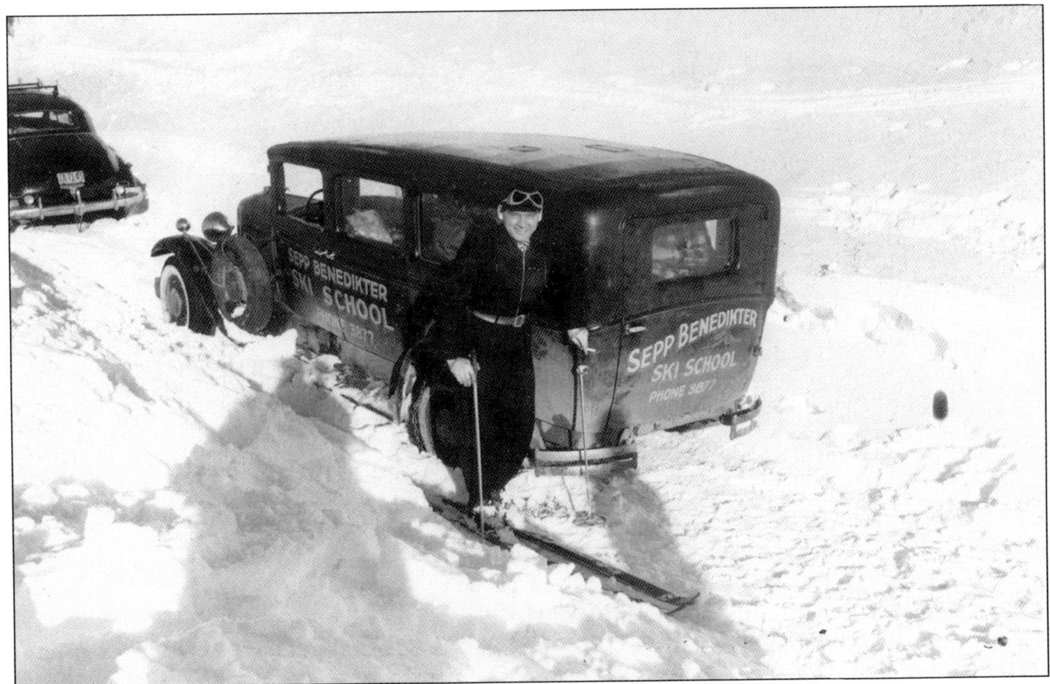

Benedikter poses with his "ski bus," a converted funeral coach. He drove this to California from Bogus Basin, Idaho, a ski area he started and developed during World War II. (Courtesy Claudia Benedikter Pedersen.)

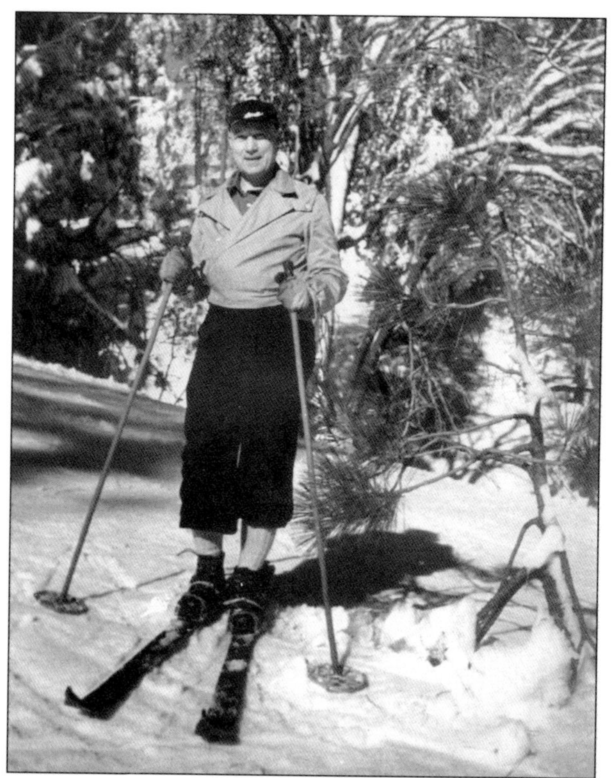

Tyler Van Degrift was a lifelong promoter and supporter of skiing. Born in Birmingham, Alabama, in 1891, he came to California with his parents in 1901. That same year, his father, A. F. Van Degrift, opened a shoe store called Van Degrift's in downtown Los Angeles. Tyler took over the operation in 1927, and in 1931, it became the first store in Los Angeles to sell ski equipment. He opened a complete ski department in the store in 1936. He passed away in 1957 at the age of 66.

Van Degrift's Ski Hut was extremely popular with Southern California skiers for more than 20 years. A full house attended the 20th anniversary celebration in October 1955.

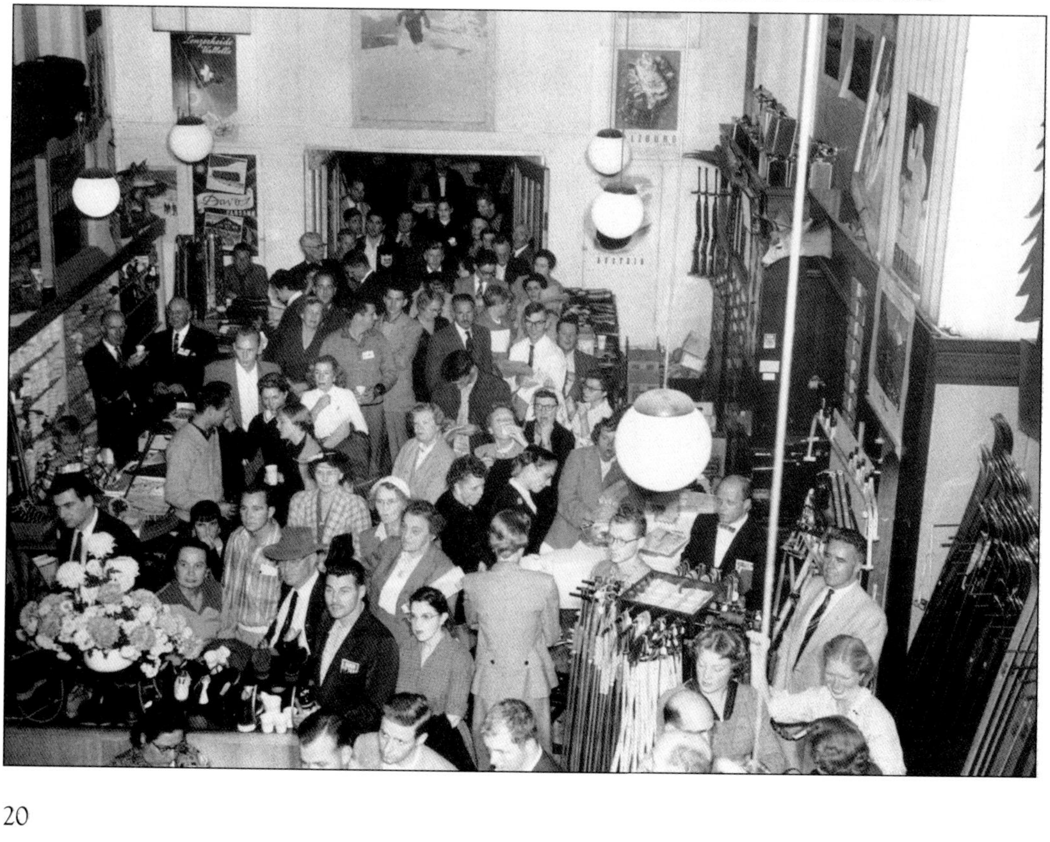

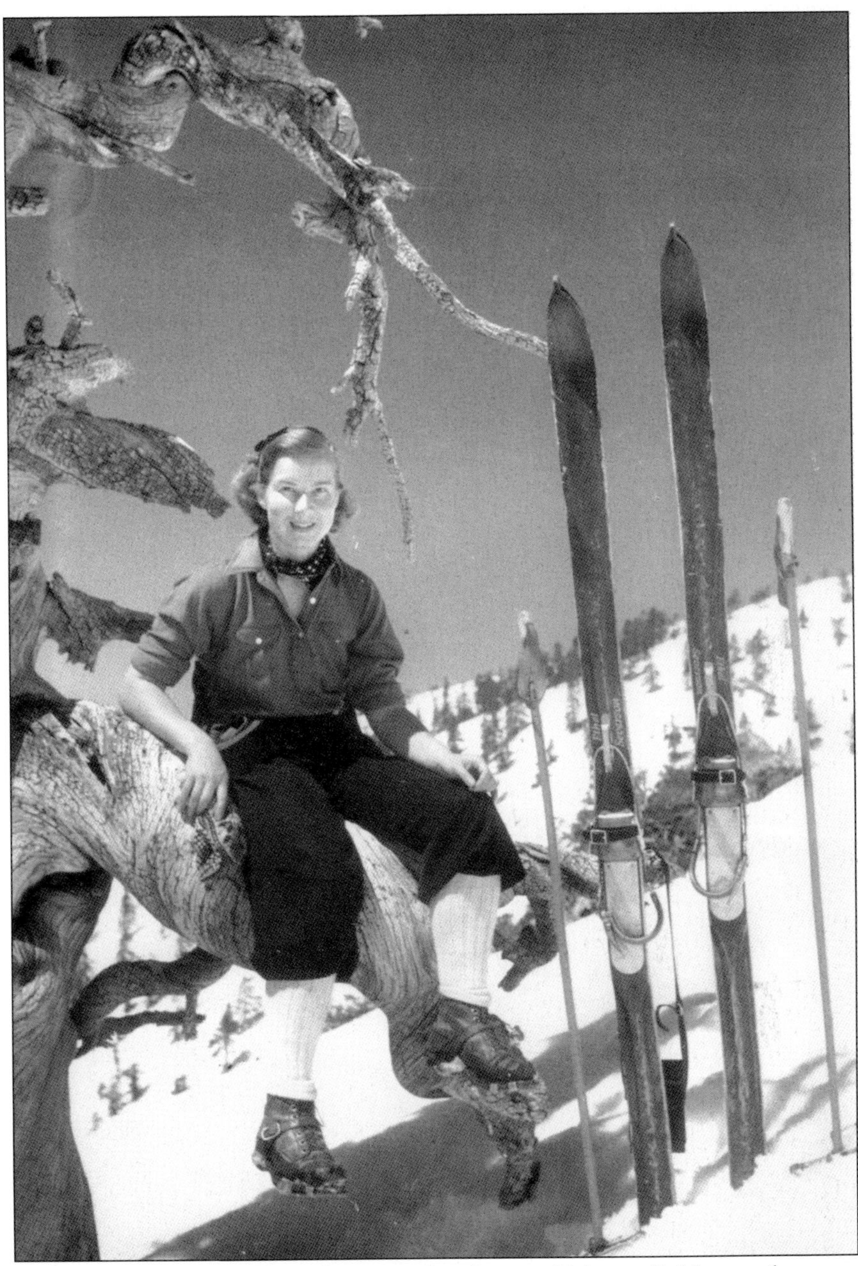

Ethel Severson Van Degrift, shown here on the slopes of Mount Baldy, was born on June 15, 1907, in Soldier, Iowa. She moved to Minneapolis, Minnesota, at the age of seven, and she came to California in 1932. It did not take her long to become acquainted with California's mountains. Between November 1933 and November 1934, she climbed nine peaks; their total elevation was 101,099 feet. She took up skiing in December 1933, an experience that launched a lifelong passion for the sport that would also become her profession. Severson wrote the column "Ski Slants" for the *Los Angeles Times* from November 28, 1939, to April 13, 1954, except for a three-year hiatus during the war. In 1938, she became the associate editor for *Ski Illustrated.* She wrote a regular column, "Winter Sports Parade," for the magazine from 1940 through 1948. She passed away on November 17, 1993.

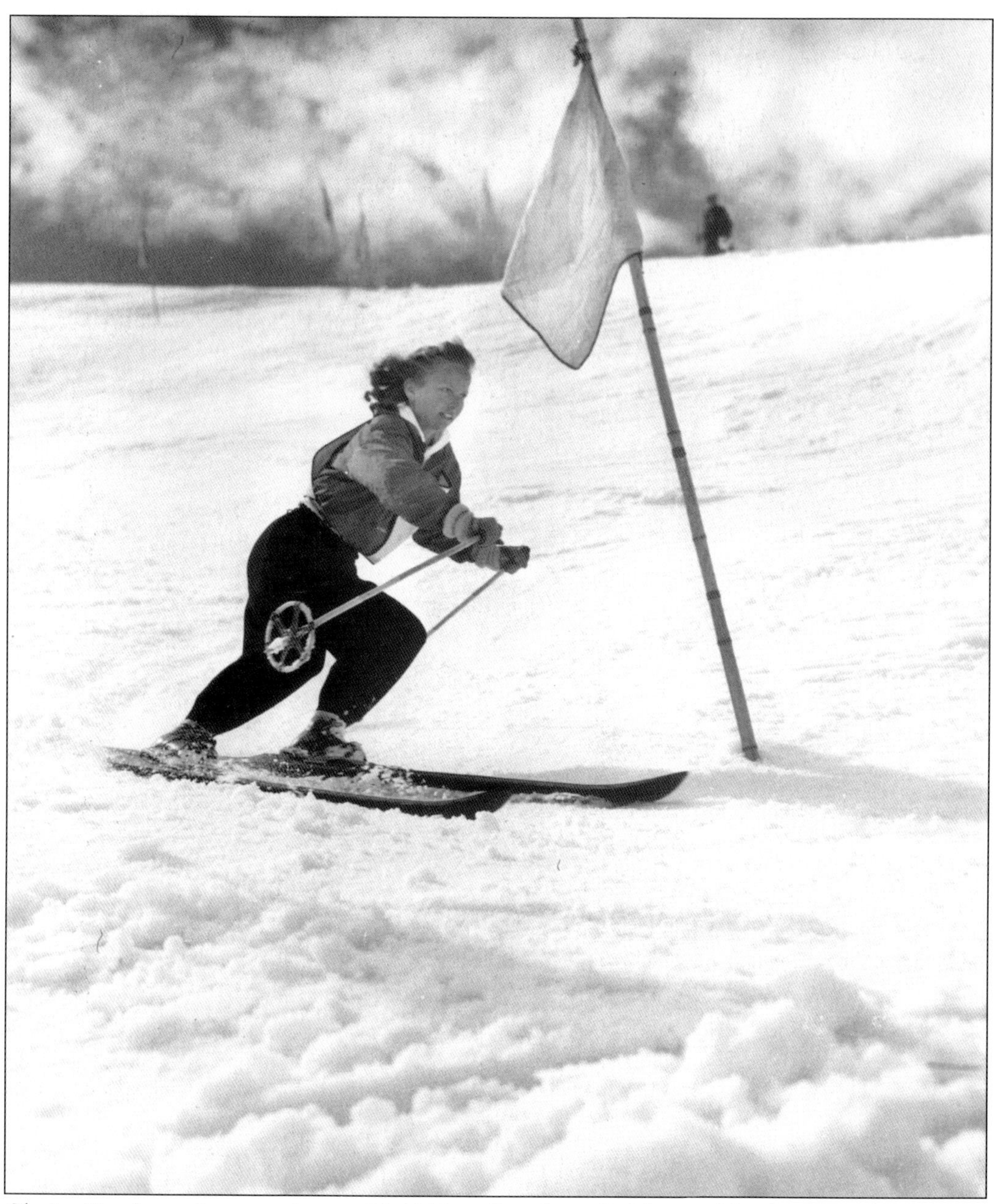

Clarita Heath was born on August 27, 1916, in Pasadena, California. Heath, shown here racing at Sun Valley, Idaho, was considered one of the 10 best women skiers in the world in the 1940s. She shocked the Europeans by improving in one year from a beginner to a first-class racer. Heath became a member of the United States' first women's Olympic ski team in the 1936 Winter Olympics. By 1939, she had beaten every outstanding skier in the world except for Germany's Cristl Cranz. Heath entered the treacherous Flying Skis Invitational, a four-mile-long downhill race from the top of Carson Peak in the Eastern Sierra. She and Nan Zischank were the only two women to enter the race. Heath beat out Zischank and placed fourth or fifth among the men. She was inducted into the United States Ski Hall of Fame in 1968. Heath passed away in October 2003.

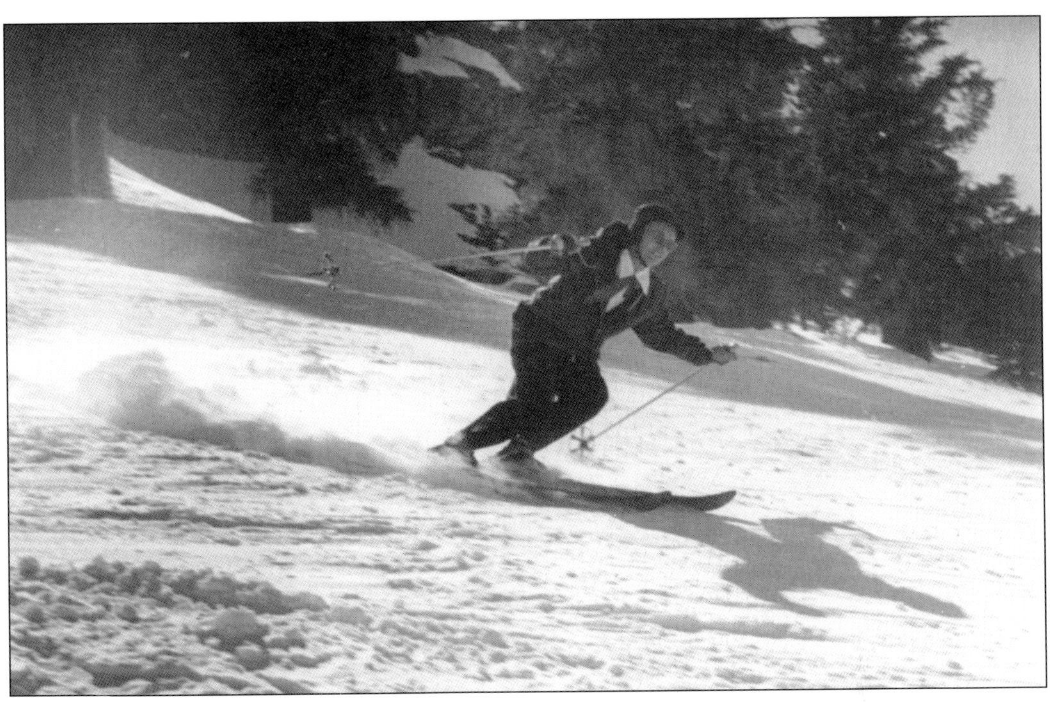

On January 12, 1942, after only three winters on skis, Dorothy McClung Wullich was named the National Ski Patrol's first woman member. She demonstrated her proficiency when she and five fellow members of the San Diego Ski Club carried 150 pounds of food to stranded rangers on Cuyamaca Peak in San Diego County. Wullich, in addition to being an accomplished patrolwoman, was a formidable racer, often finishing among the top three. (Courtesy Karen Wullich Herbst.)

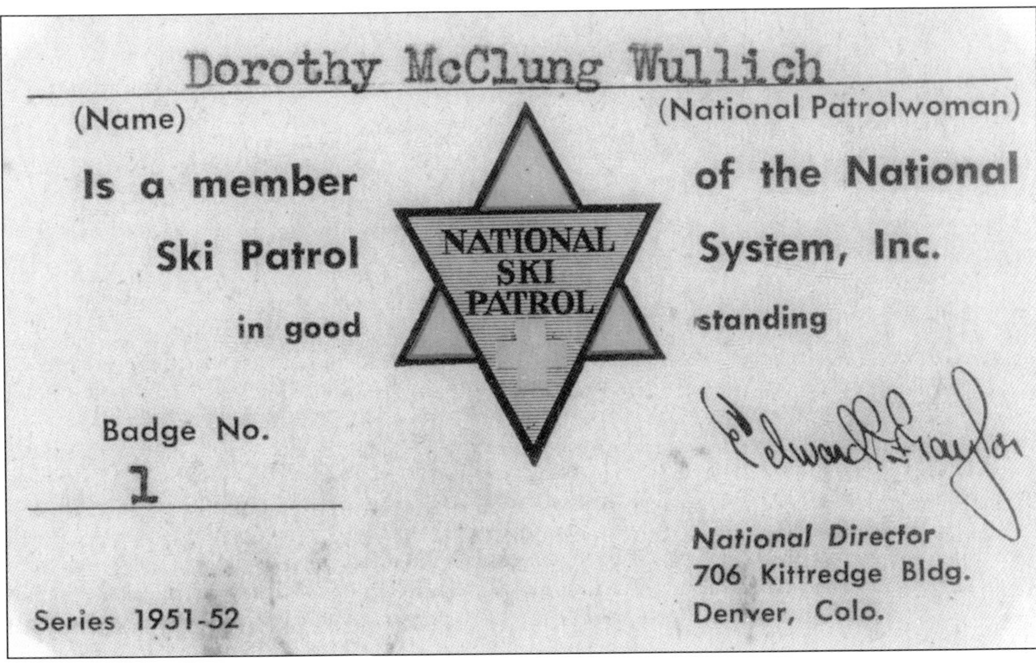

Dorothy McClung Wullich

(Name) (National Patrolwoman)

Is a member of the National Ski Patrol System, Inc. in good standing

Badge No.
1

Edward F. Taylor

National Director
706 Kittredge Bldg.
Denver, Colo.

Series 1951-52

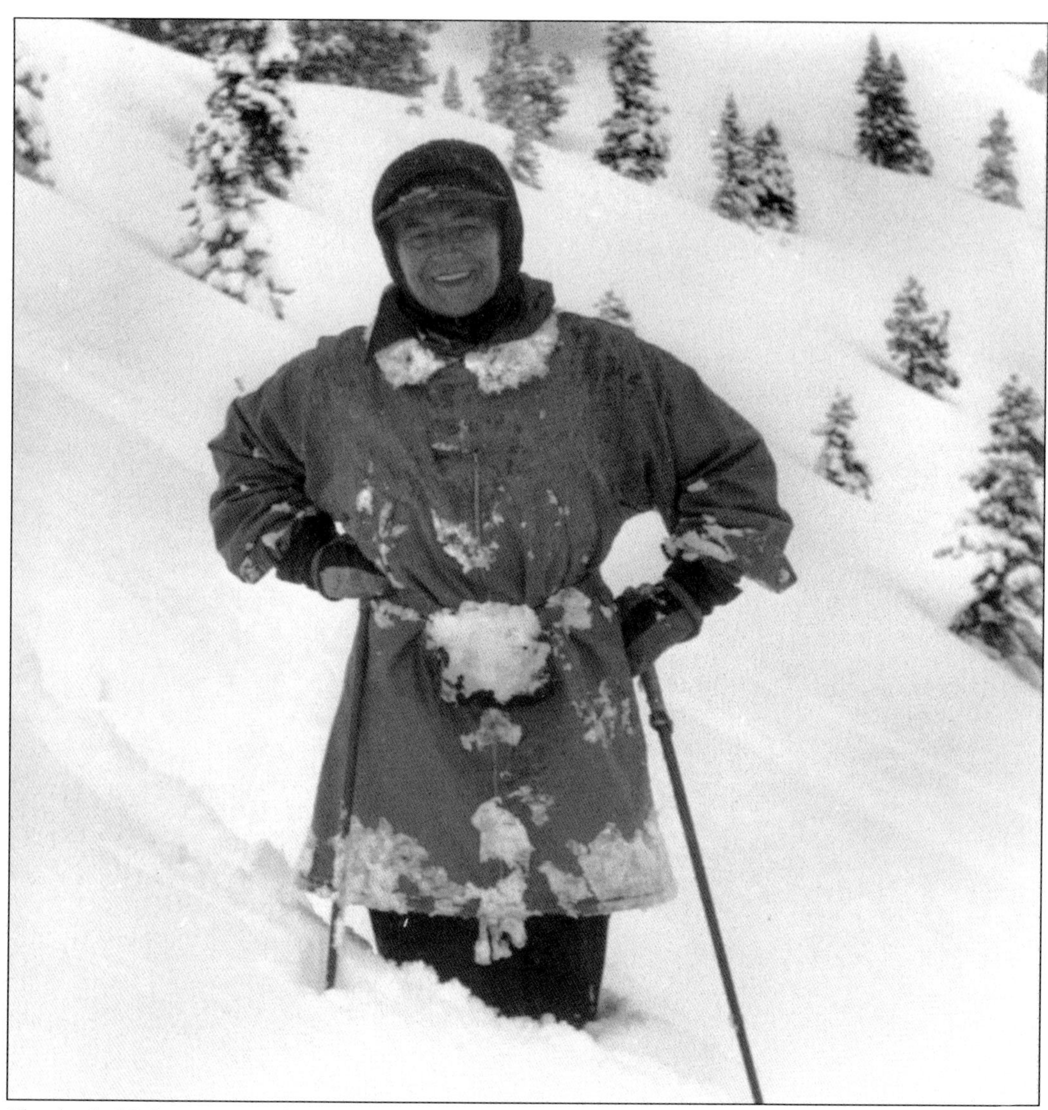

Elizabeth "Schatzi" Wood was one of the Southland's best all-around skiers in the 1920s and 1930s. On April 19, 1939, Schatzi, along with husband Ernest Wood, Perley Bennett of Lone Pine, and Hans Georg, attempted to tackle Mount Whitney on skis. None in the group reached the summit, but only strong, skilled skiers could even contemplate skiing the terrain on Whitney. Schatzi later became the 16th woman to be named to the National Ski Patrol.

Two

SIERRA CLUB SKIING

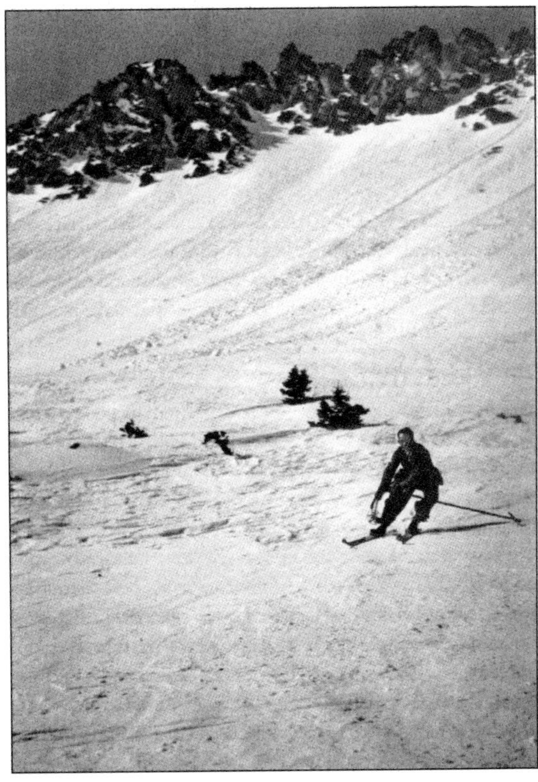

In this photograph, taken by Loyd Cooper, Walter Mosauer holds a tight turn on an open slope on Mount Baldy. Mosauer was one of the founding members of the Sierra Club Ski Mountaineers. The first meeting of the group took place at his home on November 7, 1934. Mosauer had learned to ski in his home country, Austria, when he was 10 years old. Prior to coming to California in 1932, he skied extensively in the Austrian Alps, Oregon, and Washington. His experience and enthusiasm for skiing made him an ideal choice for the Ski Mountaineers' first president. (Courtesy of The Bancroft Library, University of California, Berkeley.)

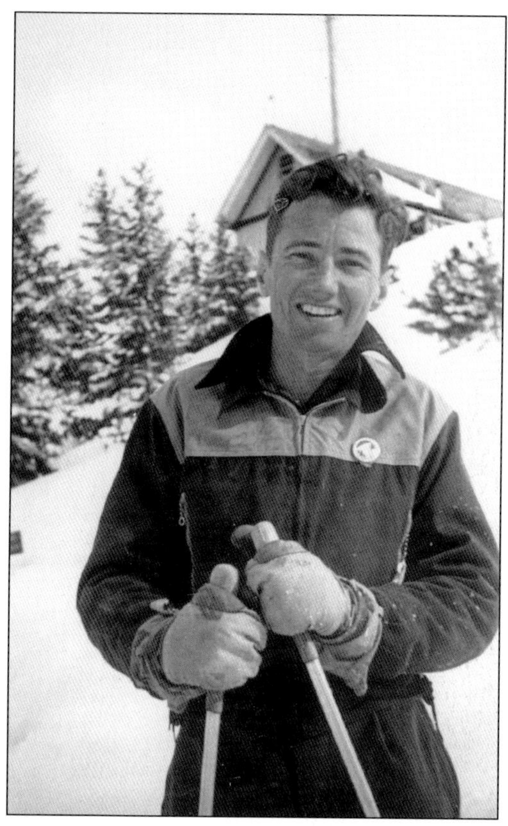

Glen Dawson was another inaugural member of the Ski Mountaineers. His name is synonymous with the early days of skiing in Southern California. Dawson was one of the top skiers on the ski team at the University of California, Los Angeles, in the 1930s. He competed in the first intercollegiate ski race at Yosemite in 1933. However, he was more interested in ski mountaineering than ski racing, making early ski ascents of Mammoth Mountain and Alta Peak. With their proficiency on skis and their knowledge of first aid and survival skills, talented Ski Mountaineers could earn certificates for the Sierra Club Winter Mountaineering Course. These much-needed skills made many of the Ski Mountaineers ideal candidates for the army's 10th Mountain Division. (Courtesy Glen Dawson.)

CERTIFICATE OF COMPLETION

WINTER MOUNTAINEERING COURSE

Conducted by

ROCK CLIMBING AND SKI MOUNTAINEERS SECTION

SOUTHERN CALIFORNIA CHAPTER OF THE SIERRA CLUB

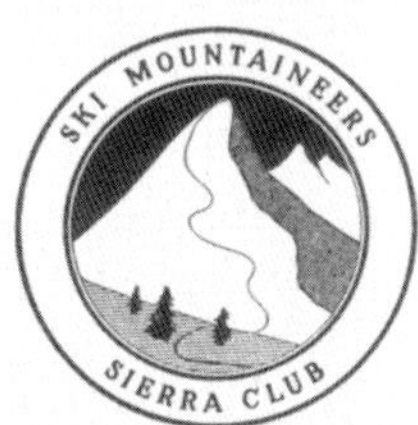

Los Angeles, Cal.
February 25, 1942

This is to certify that GLEN DAWSON **has successfully completed a course of class room instruction in winter mountaineering which included ski safety and first aid, snow camping, topographic map and compass reading, snowcraft and avalanche, ice and snow technique and proper equipment, clothing, first aid kits and food for extended mountaineering trips.**

Added seal in the lower left hand corner indicates that field trips have been attended correlating class room work with practical experience.

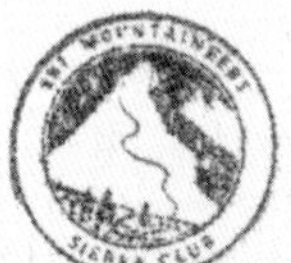

Chester L. Errett
Chairman, Rock Climbing Section.

Robert K. Brinton
Chairman, Ski Mountaineers Section.

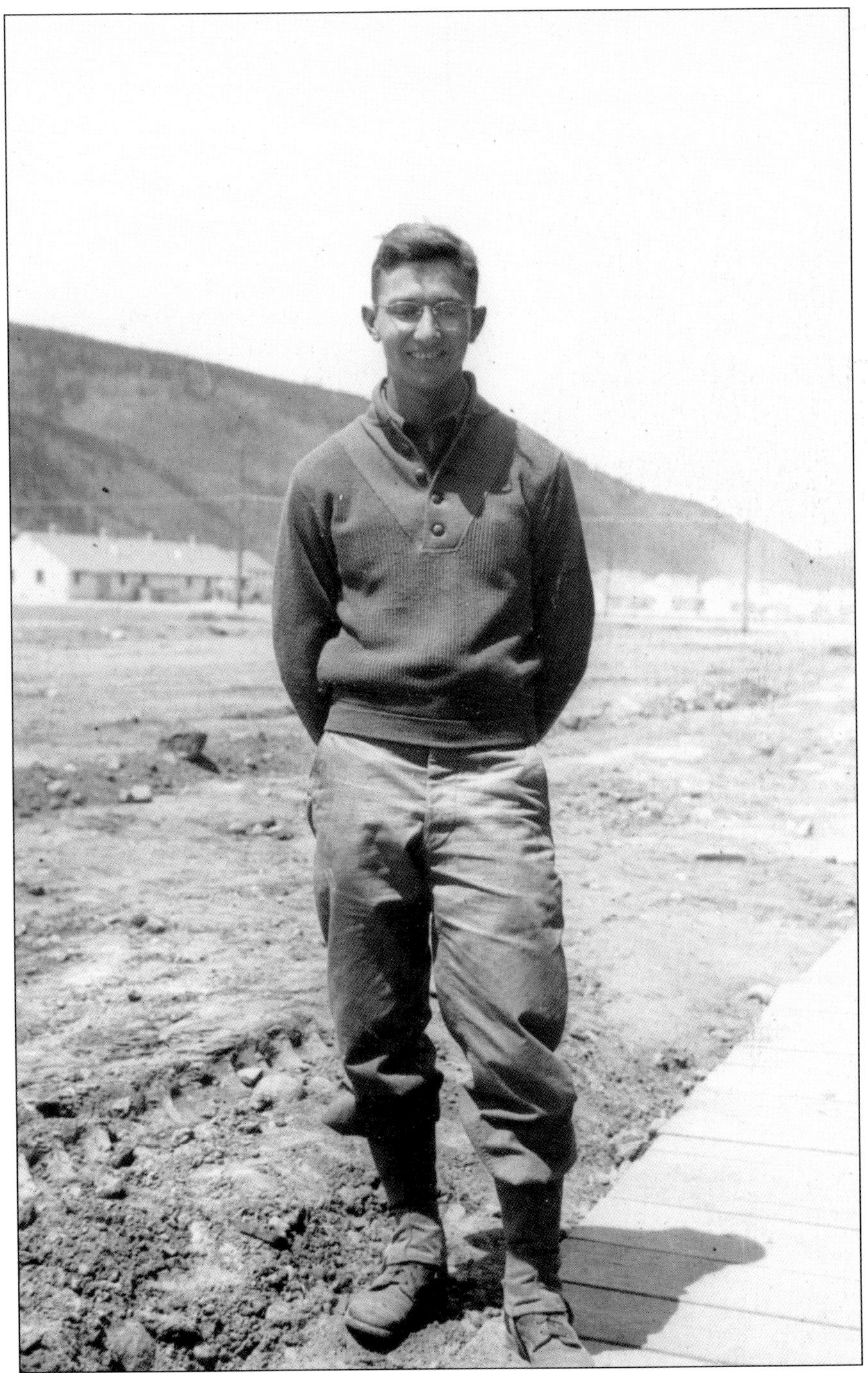

Muir Dawson, shown here at Camp Hale, Colorado, in 1943, learned to ski when he was 12 years old. His brother Glen was his instructor, and Muir often tagged along on ski trips. By the time he was 13, he had skied to the top of Mount Baldy from the falls. Muir was a skilled ski mountaineer and racer, repeatedly winning the annual San Gorgonio Downhill. He attributed his victories as much to his route-finding and mountaineering skills as to his ski expertise. He passed away on February 21, 2005. (Courtesy Glen Dawson.)

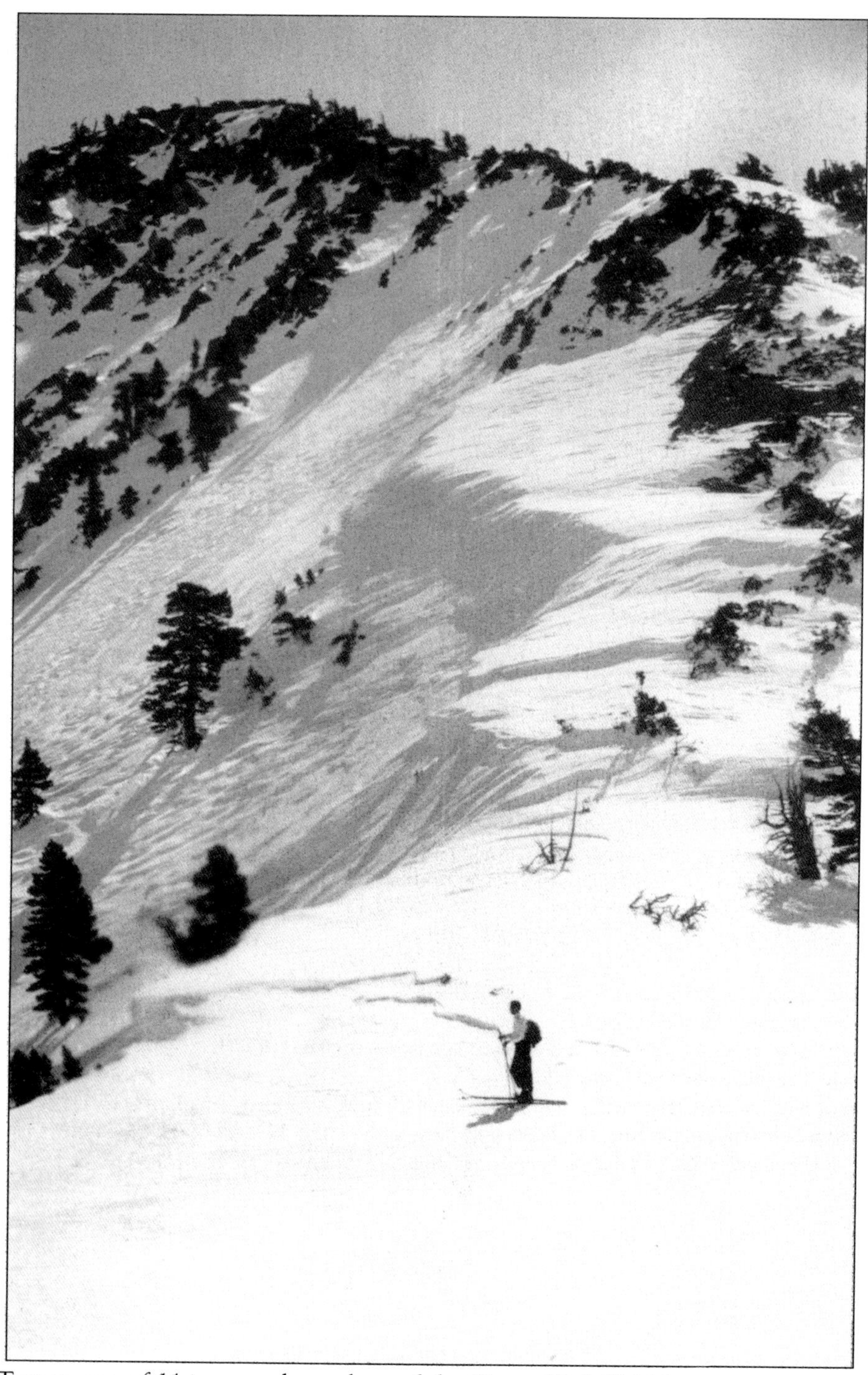

Louis Turner, one of 14 inaugural members of the Sierra Club Ski Mountaineers, surveys the winter landscape below the summit of Telegraph Peak in the San Gabriel Mountains. On February 22, 1933, Turner and Glen Dawson made ascents of Mount Harwood and Telegraph Peak using four-point crampons and skis. This may have been the first ascent of these peaks in winter. (Courtesy Glen Dawson.)

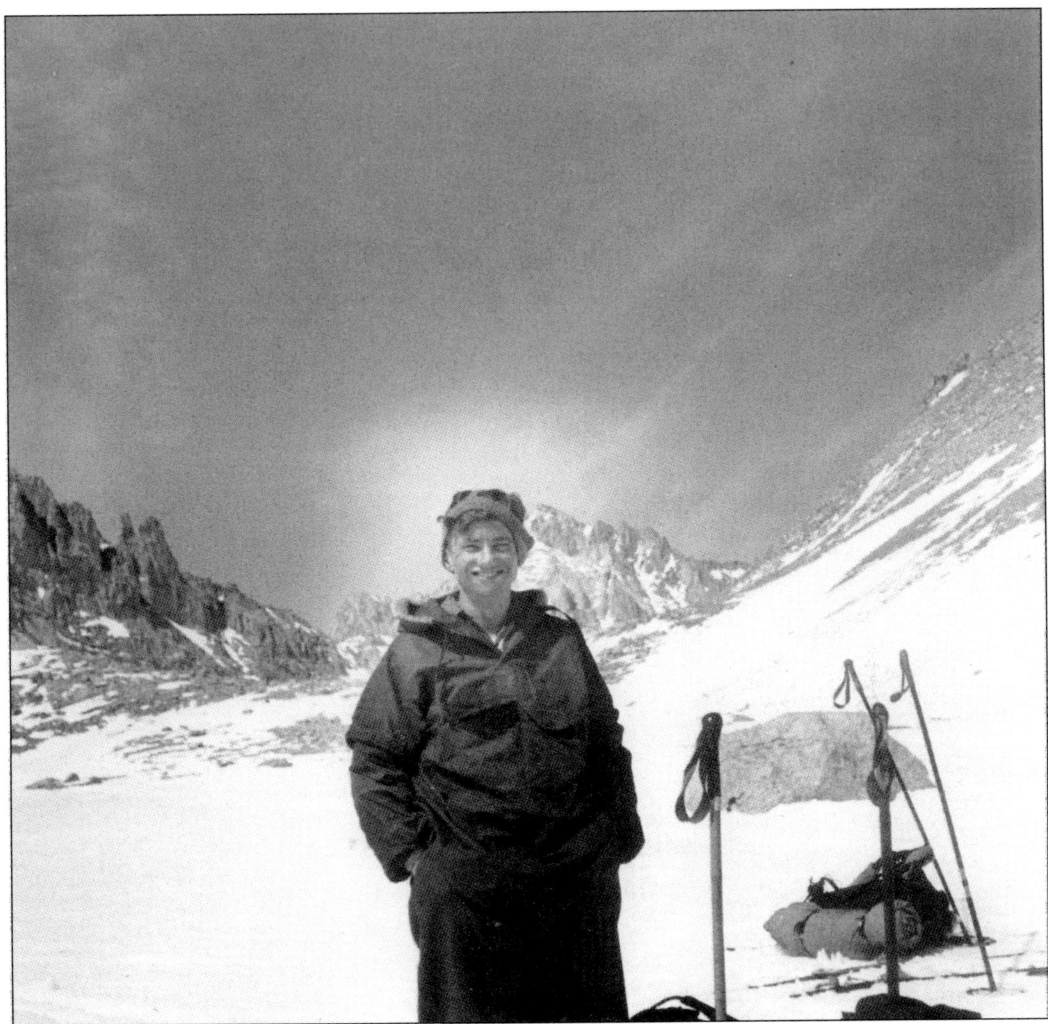

Glen Dawson pauses for a moment at Whitney Russell Pass in May 1938. Glen was a consummate ski mountaineer and carried out many ski mountaineering trips throughout California. His climbing accomplishments are legendary; perhaps the most well known is the first ascent of the East Face of Mount Whitney with Robert Underhill, Jules Eichorn, and Norman Clyde in 1931. His mountaineering and skiing skills served him well when he served in the 10th Mountain Division of the United States Army from 1943 to 1945. (Courtesy Glen Dawson.)

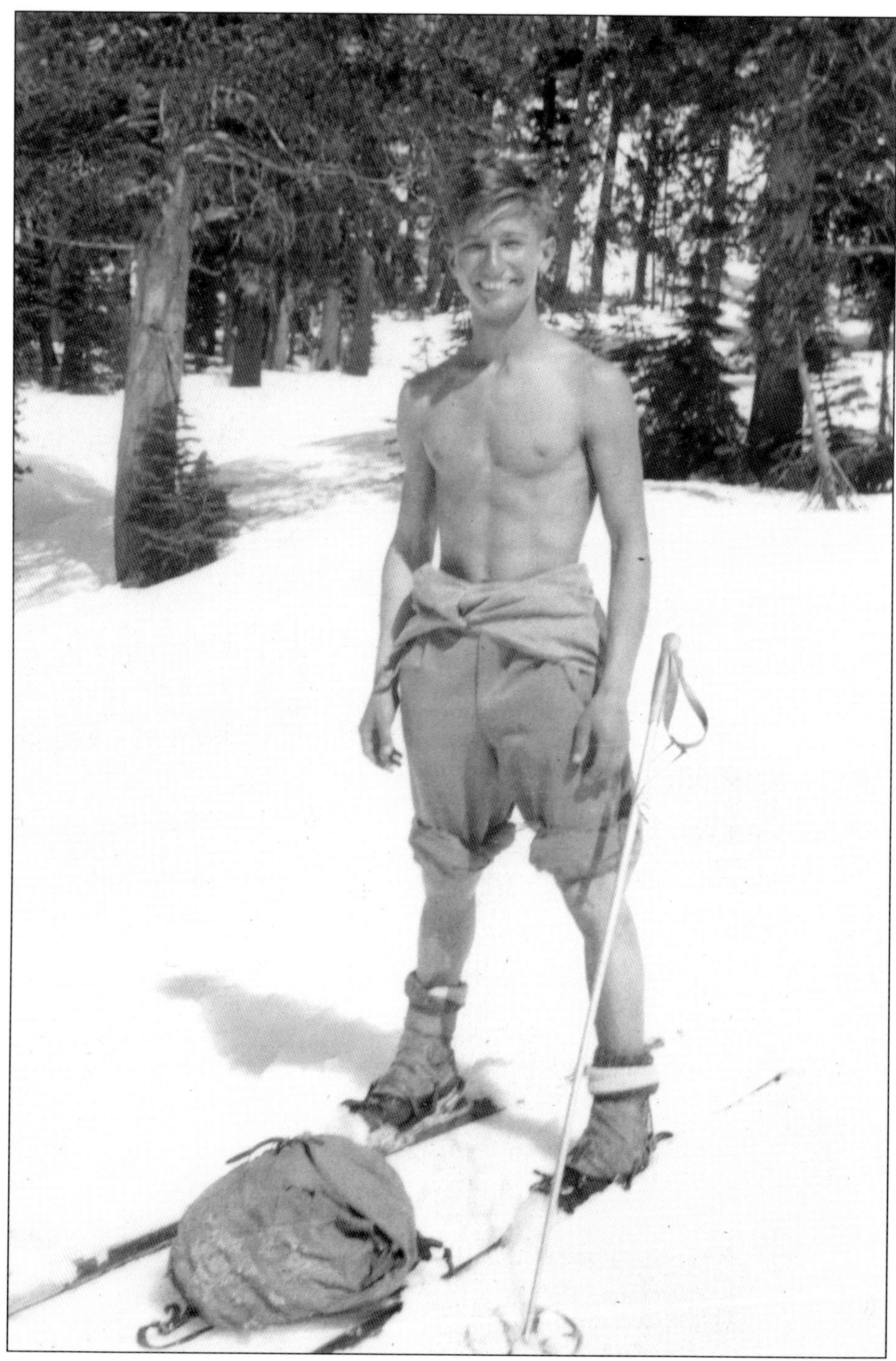

Muir Dawson, at Snow Valley in 1938, dons typical Southern California skier attire. As well as receiving plentiful snow at higher elevations, Southland mountains sometimes experience more balmy temperatures, especially later in the season. Muir attended Pomona College, the alma mater of many early Southern California skiers. He was in the class of 1944, but did not receive his degree in history until 1949 because of his service in World War II. (Courtesy Glen Dawson.)

Dick Jones, an inaugural and longtime member of the Ski Mountaineers, was an accomplished climber, accompanying Glen Dawson on many climbing trips. He was at Dawson's Book Shop when the first issue of the Ski Mountaineers newsletter, the *Mugelnoos,* rolled off the press on January 29, 1938. When the San Antonio Ski Hut was under construction, Jones put in more hours of work than any other member.

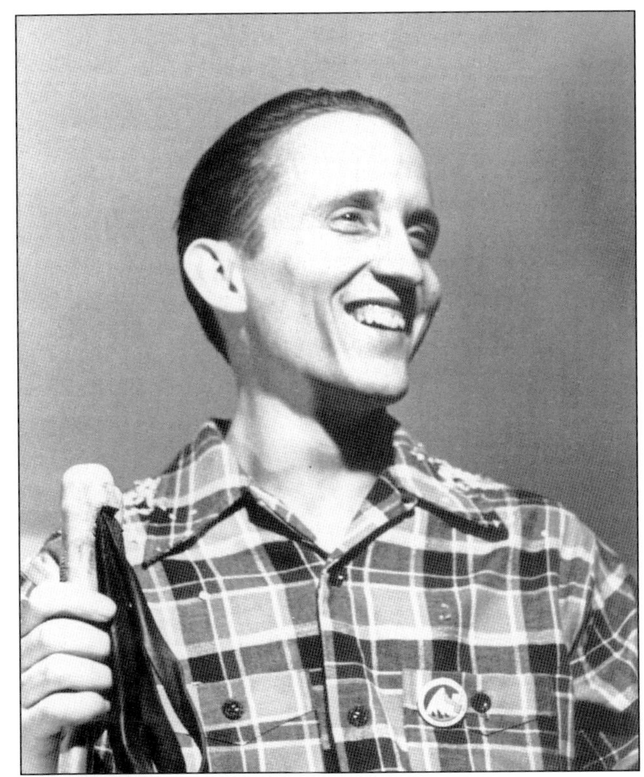

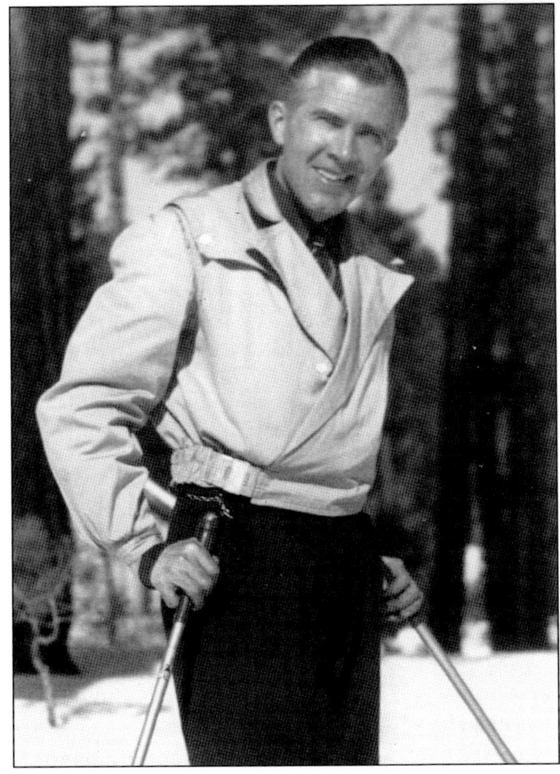

Leland Curtis, the Ski Mountaineers' first vice president, wrote the group's first constitution. Curtis, an accomplished artist who is well known for his paintings of the Sierra Nevada and Antarctica, designed the first Ski Mountaineers badge.

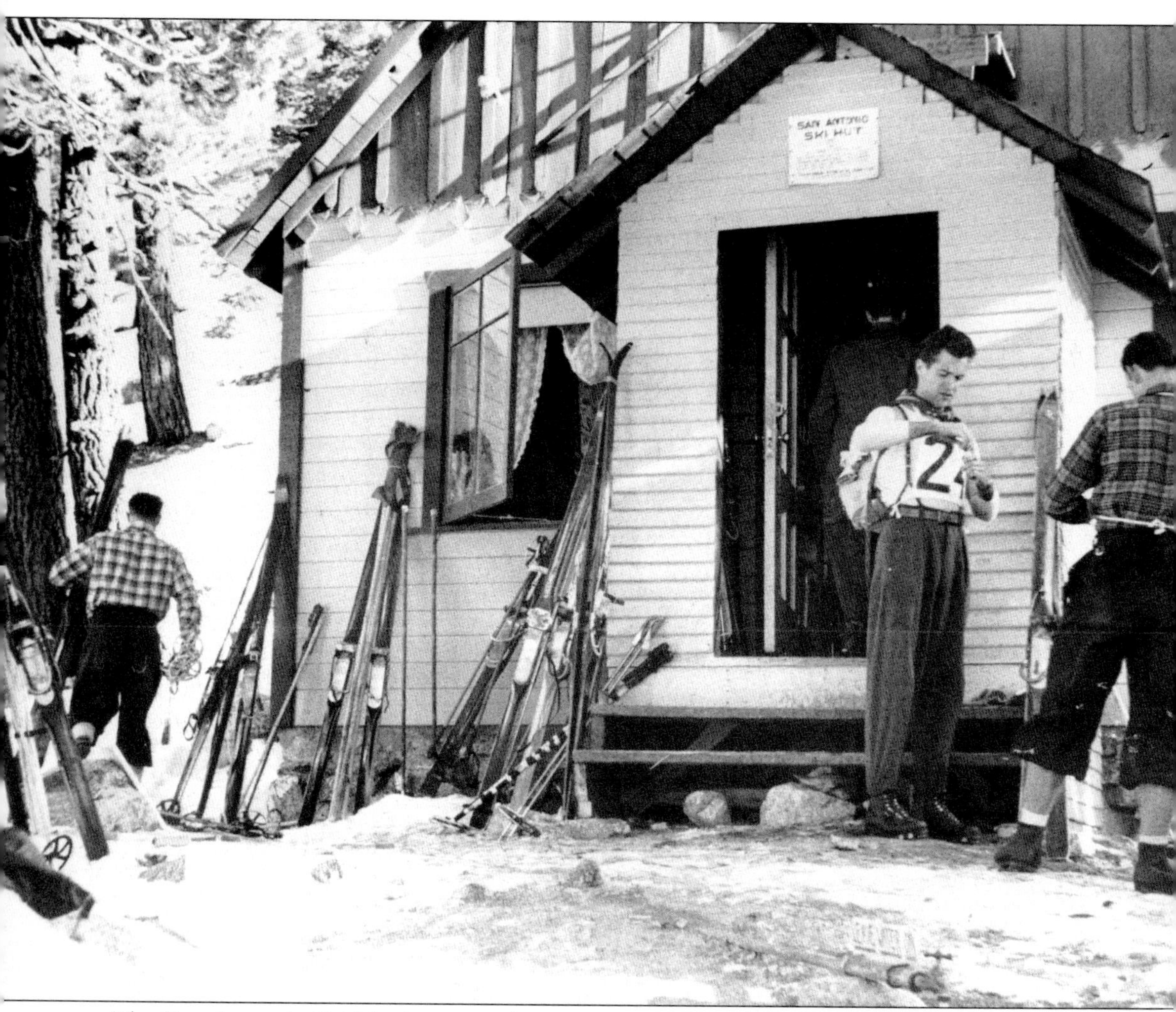

The San Antonio Ski Hut buzzes with activity on a San Antonio Downhill race day. The Ski Mountaineers built two ski huts in the Southern California mountains: the San Antonio Ski Hut on Mount Baldy and the Keller Peak Ski Hut near Snow Valley in the San Bernardinos. George Bauwens, who made the first ski ascent of Mount Baldy in 1922, became a member of the Ski Mountaineers in the spring of 1935. He was the visionary and driving force behind the Baldy hut. (Courtesy Karen Wullich Herbst.)

The San Antonio Ski Hut, shown under construction, was built by the backbreaking efforts of a number of Sierra Club members. Wolfgang Lert recalled that he never again engaged in such difficult physical labor. Some of the challenges of moving building materials and supplies to the construction site are evident at right. When all was said and done, club members had carried eight tons of building materials up two and a half miles of steep trail. The hut was finished in January 1936. Unfortunately, in September 1936, it was destroyed by fire. Not to be defeated by the setback, the Ski Mountaineers built a new hut, which was ready by the following winter. Thankfully, burros carried the heavy loads for the construction of the new hut.

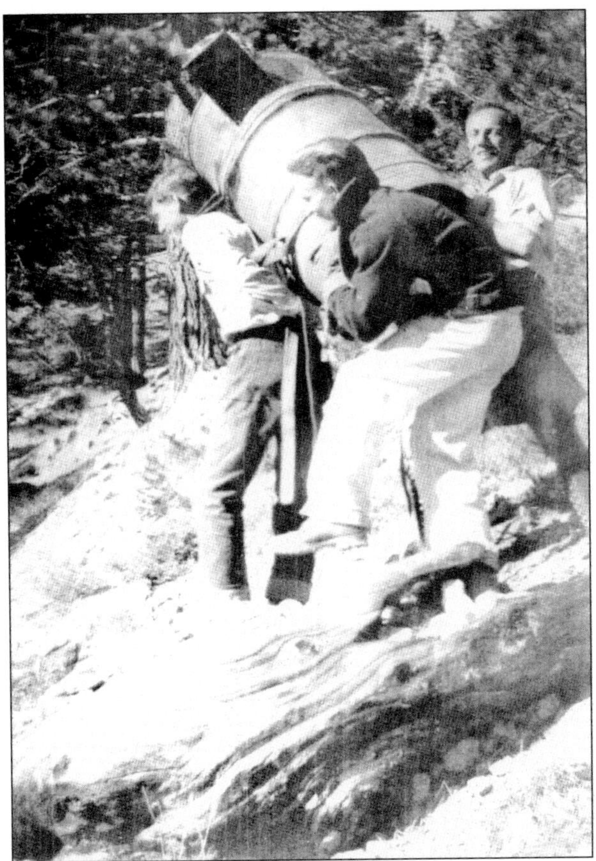

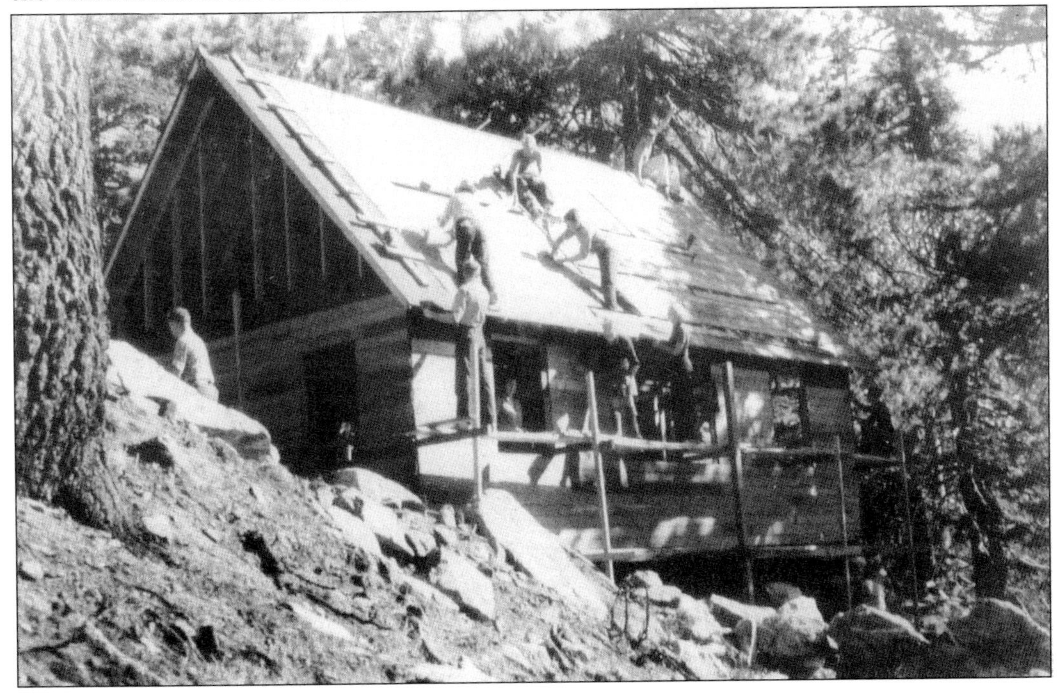

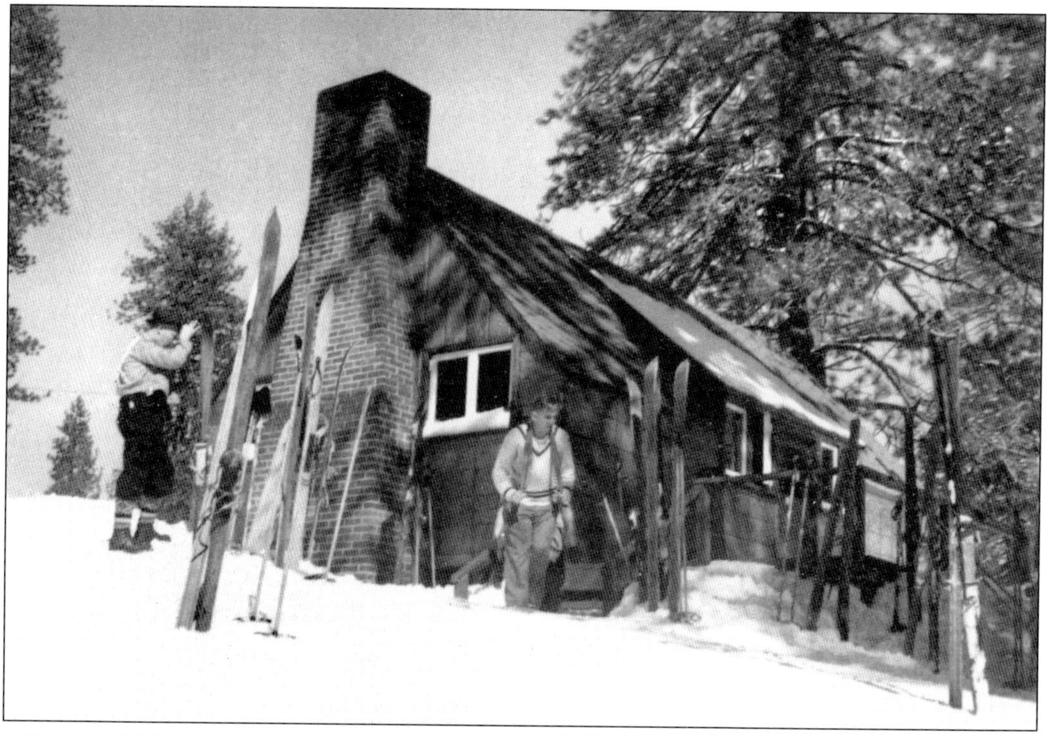

Following Walter Mosauer's death in 1937, the Ski Mountaineers launched a plan to build the Walter Mosauer Memorial Lodge on the slopes of San Gorgonio. After the Forest Service denied them permission to build there, club members constructed the Keller Peak Ski Hut near Snow Valley in 1938. It was immediately popular, and it is still a favorite weekend destination for Sierra Club members today.

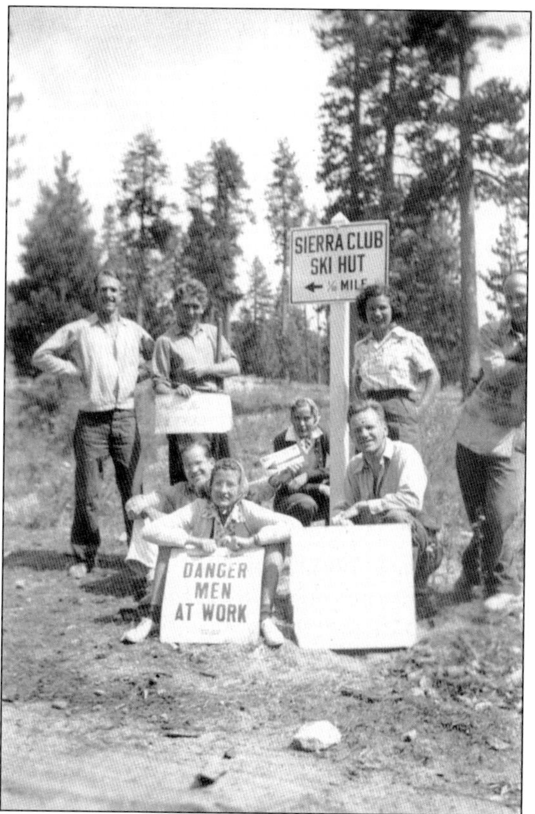

The Sierra Club ski huts resulted from many hours of work by club members. Members volunteered time, effort, and any special skills they possessed. Camaraderie developed among work parties like the one shown here. The work party tradition continues today, and any member who uses one of the huts is expected to contribute to its maintenance. (Courtesy Glen Dawson.)

Ethel Severson Van Degrift takes a moment to sign the summit register on Mount Baldy in 1936. Van Degrift was the only woman at the first meeting of the Sierra Club Ski Mountaineers, and in September 1936, she became the first woman member.

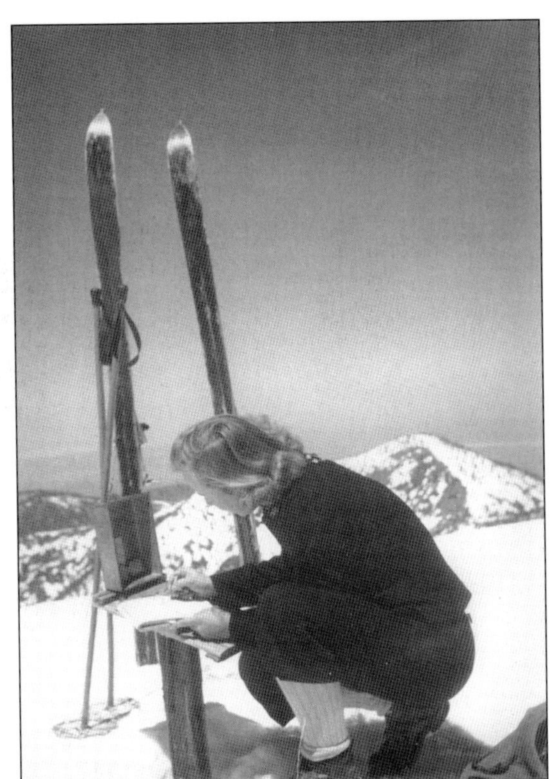

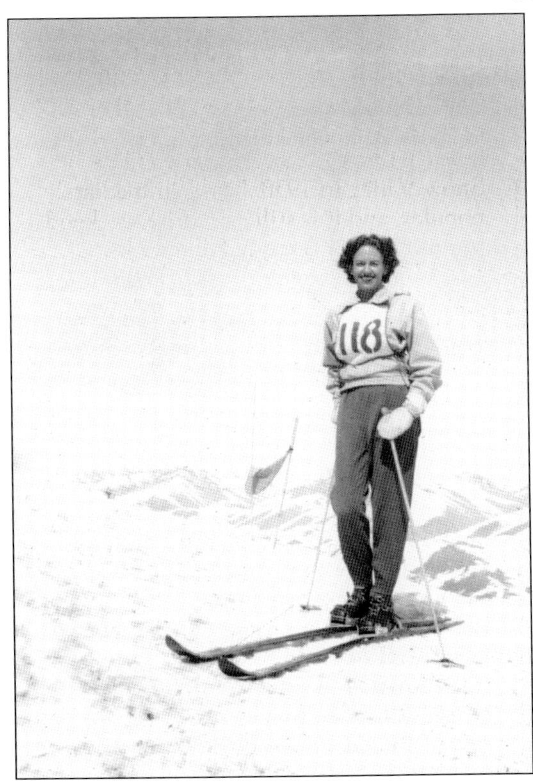

Mary Jane Edwards was probably the most talented skier among the early women Ski Mountaineers. She entered many of the local races and participated in ski mountaineering outings. Her numerous winter trips to San Gorgonio are documented by her entries in the Edelweiss Hut register. Her first stay at the hut was on March 29, 1936. (Courtesy Glen Dawson.)

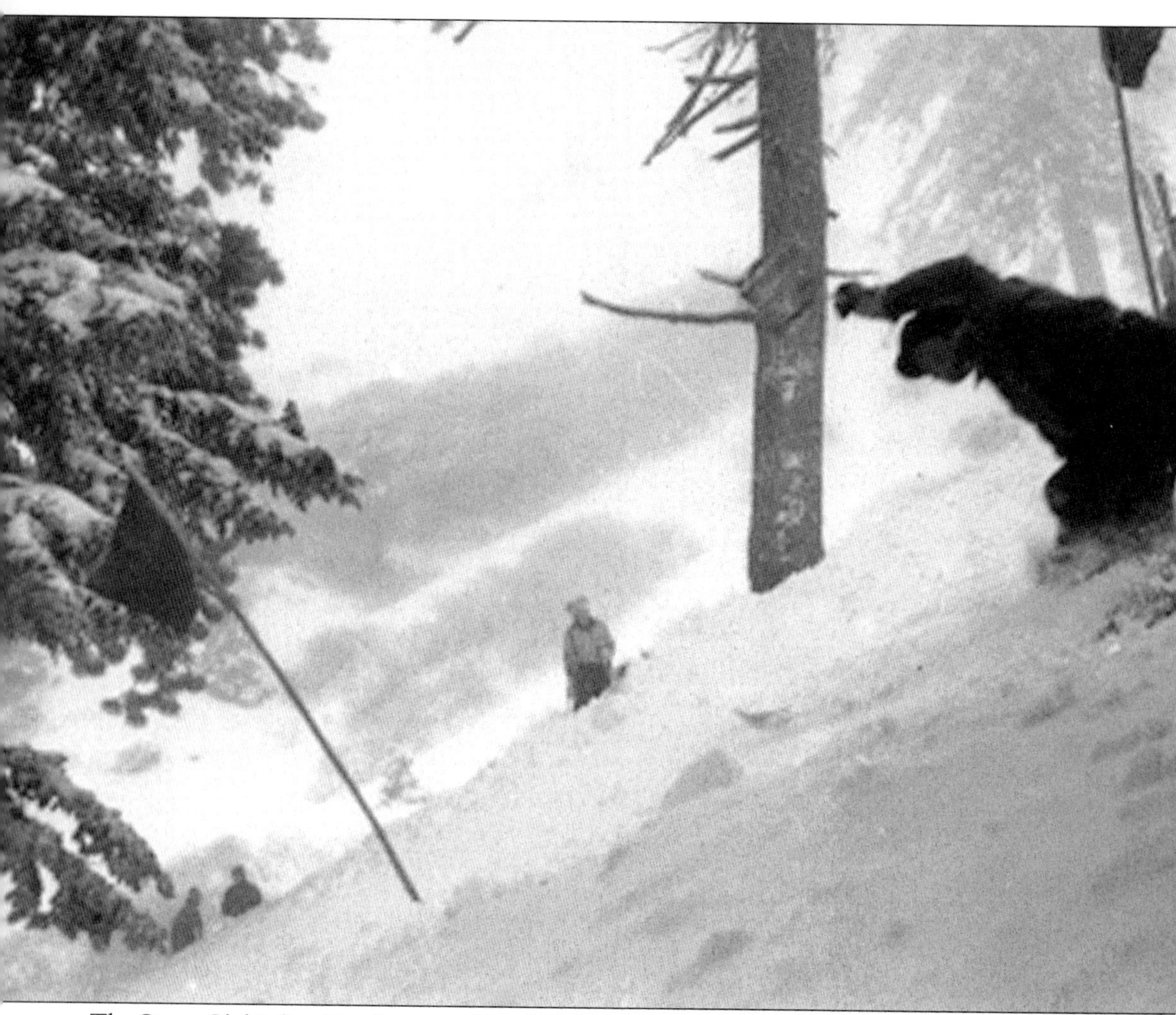

The Sierra Club's first San Antonio Downhill Race took place on March 16, 1935. The race began at the summit, at an elevation 10,080 feet, and finished near the Sierra Club hut, a 1,500-foot vertical drop below. The first San Antonio Slalom Race was held the following day. Wolfgang Lert won the downhill, and Otto Steiner won the slalom. Steiner was the originator of the race. This skier is making his way through some of the challenging ski conditions that could be encountered during the race.

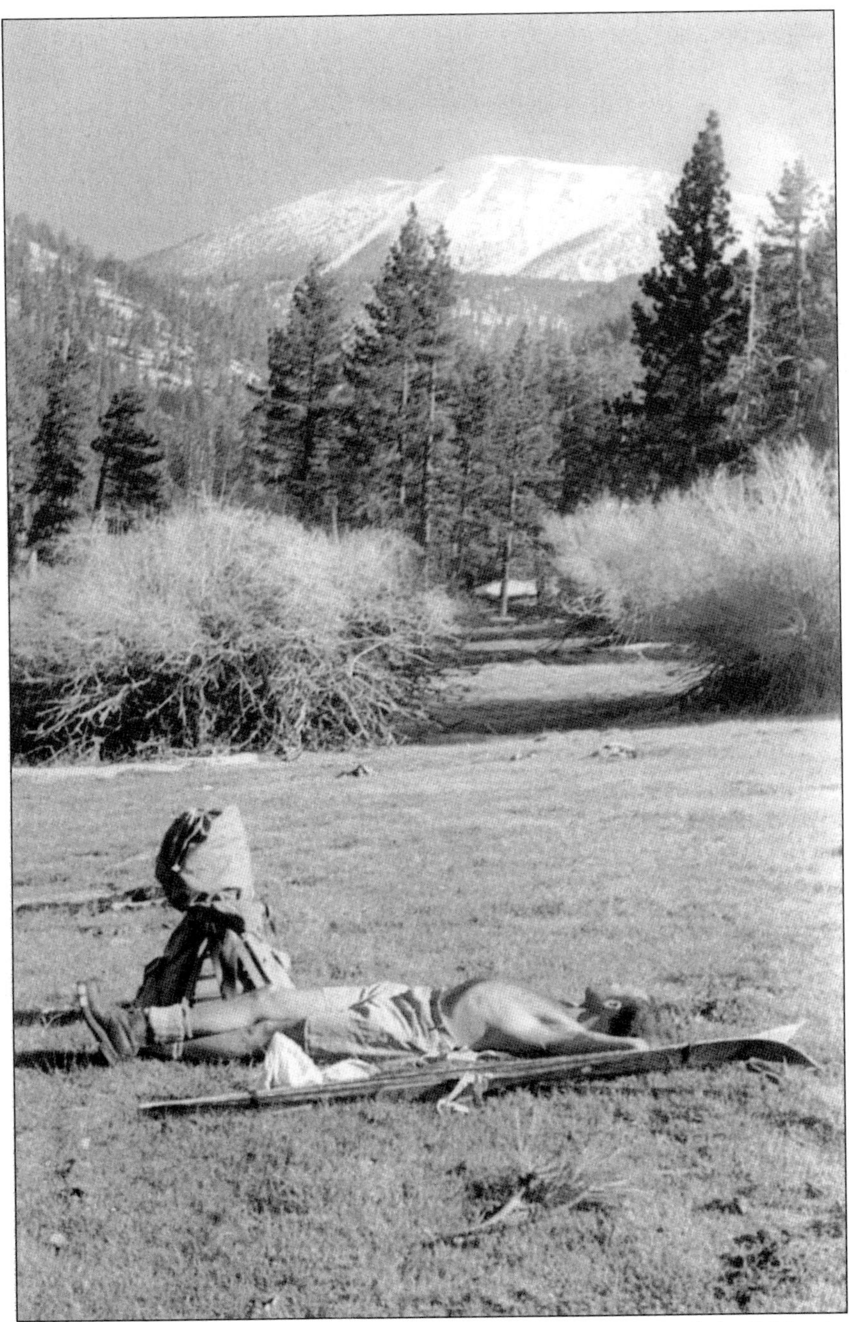

The first San Gorgonio Downhill, sponsored by the Ski Mountaineers and the Edelweiss Ski Club, was held in April 1940. Racers whizzed down 2,000 feet over the two-and-a-half-mile course. The race was not for the unfit: participants had to hike six miles from the end of the road to the top of the race course. If the hike did not do the racers in, sometimes the course could. In the 1947 race, 50 racers started, but only 35 finished; the rest either became lost on the course or crashed into trees. With San Gorgonio as his backdrop, Walter Mosauer rests after a long day of climbing and skiing. The clear upper slopes, as well as the timber-covered lower slopes that sometimes tripped up racers, are in clear view.

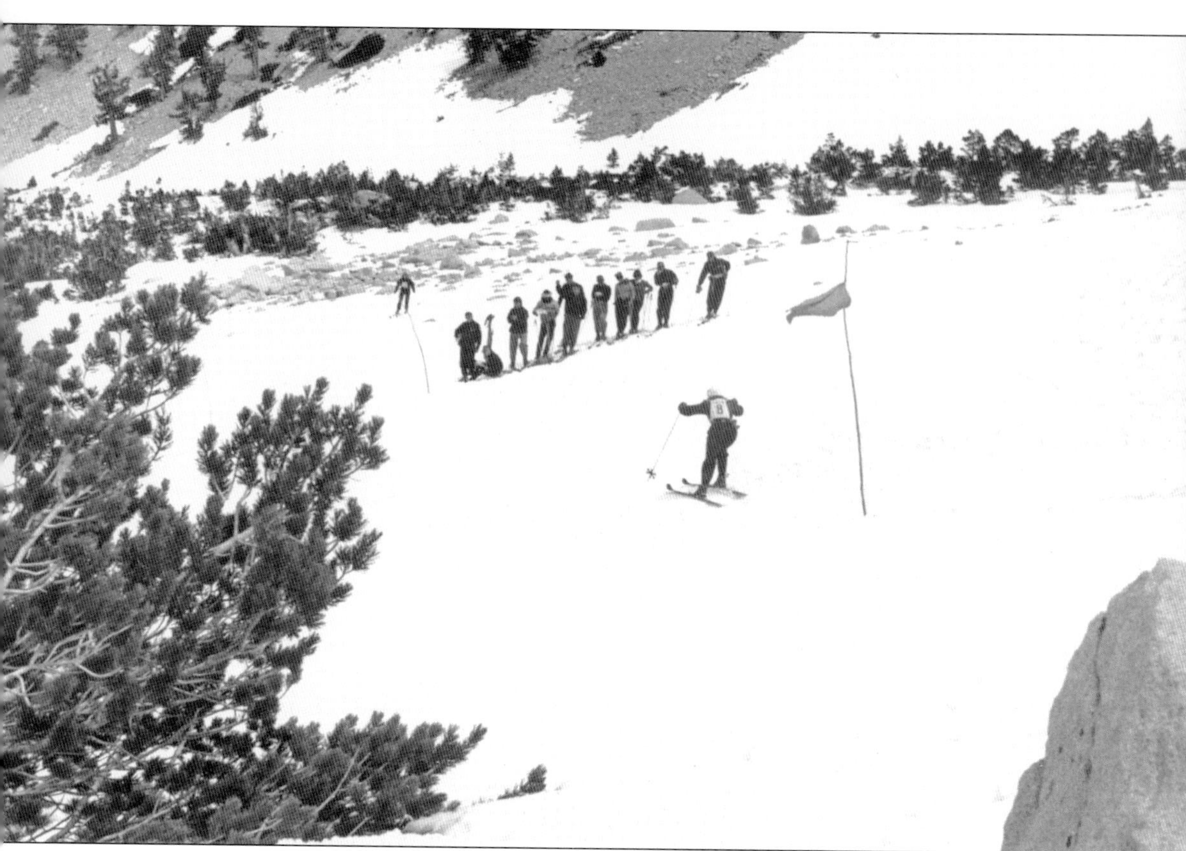

Ski Club Alpine took over the sponsorship of the San Gorgonio Downhill in 1949. It was probably the last of the "hike-up" races in the West. The race was also probably farther from transportation than any other race in the world. At the request of the Forest Service, the race became a giant slalom. The reason for the change, no doubt, was that the Forest Service thought there would be fewer accidents if the race was held only on open slopes, as shown here, rather than in forested areas that required skiers to weave their way through trees.

Three

Ski Jumping

THRILLS! REAL SNOW!

SKI JUMPING TOURNAMENT

HOLLYWOOD BOWL
1 DAY ONLY
Sunday, Jan. 20th
at 2:30 P. M.

Sponsored by
HOLLYWOOD SKI CLUB and
NORDIC CIVIC LEAGUE

World Champions in Spectacular and Daring Exhibitions of Skill on the Most Sensational Hill Ever Constructed.

General Admission 55c - Children 25c
Limited Number Seats at $1.10
ON SALE AT
Southern California Music Co. Ticket Office
737 So. Hill Street - TUcker 1144
KELLY MUSIC, 6367 Hollywood Blvd.

The newly formed Hollywood Ski Club hosted two ski jumping events at the Hollywood Bowl during the 1934–1935 ski season. Ski jumping ace John Elvrum directed both events. The first was held on December 29 and 30, 1934, and the second was a one-day affair held on January 20, 1935.

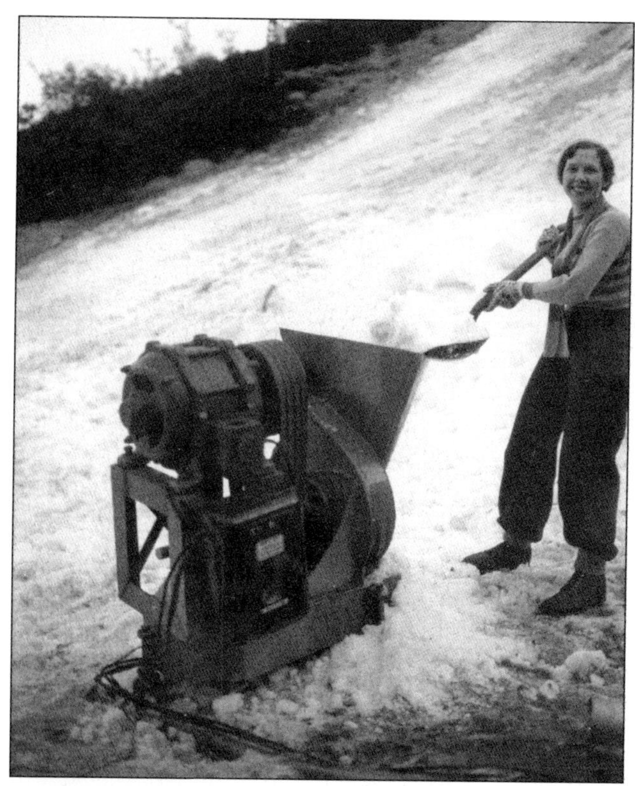

Using one of the hills behind the bowl as the runway, John Elvrum and his crew built the takeoff. Twenty-five tons of ice were hauled to the site and spread over the 600-foot course. The ski jumpers took off from the top of the hill and landed (hopefully upright) on a narrow, steep incline. This was the first ski jump meet ever held in metropolitan Los Angeles. The woman at left works with the ice-crushing machine, which was used to convert the ice into a suitable ski surface. The gallery below is positioned around the landing area of the jump in preparation for the eagerly awaited start of this novel event. (Courtesy The Huntington Library.)

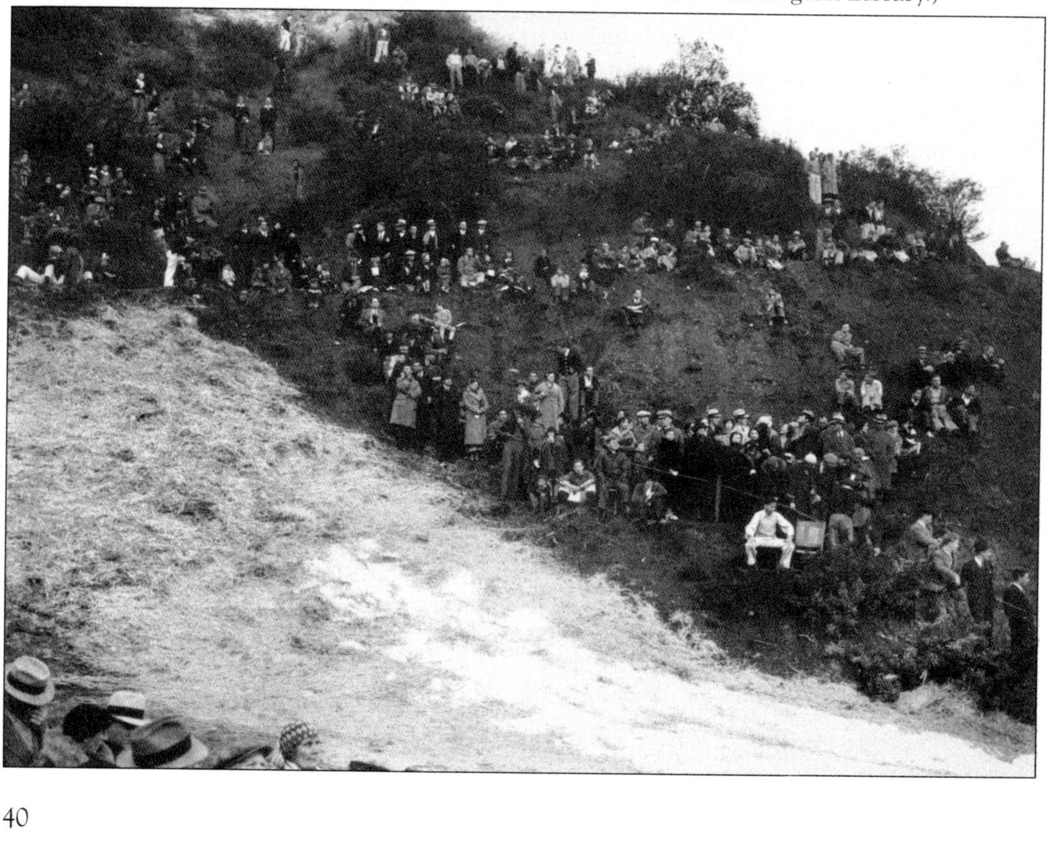

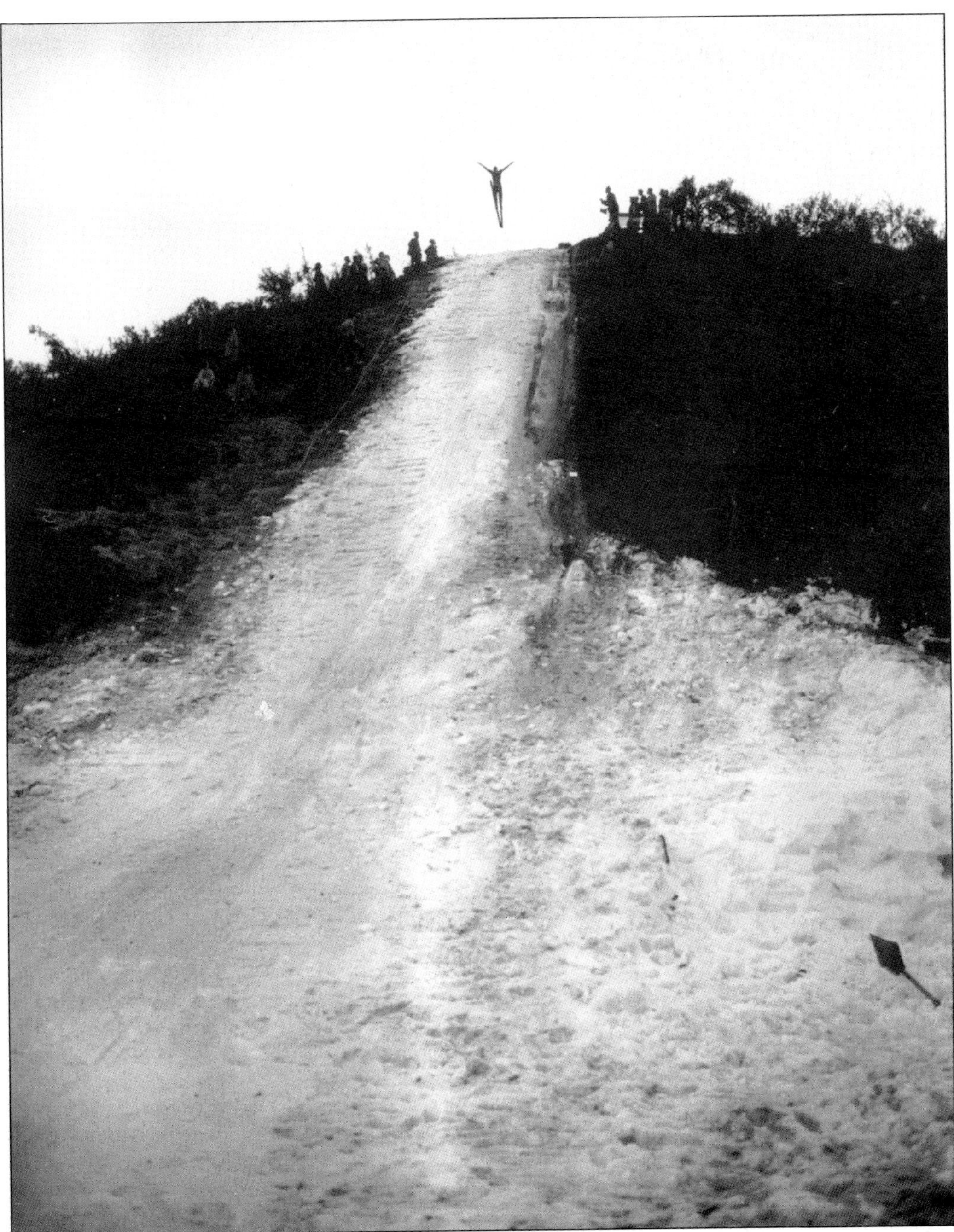

The Hollywood Bowl tournament attracted many skilled jumpers from local ski clubs. Among the competitors were Olaf Tellefsen of the Viking Ski Club; Jonas Hille, the former amateur champion of Minnesota and a member of the Hollywood Ski Club; Einer Eikenger; Arthur Ronstad, the former Midwestern junior champion; Ludwig Hasher; "Nip" Whitman; Fred Dorge; and Gil Gilberston. (Courtesy The Huntington Library.)

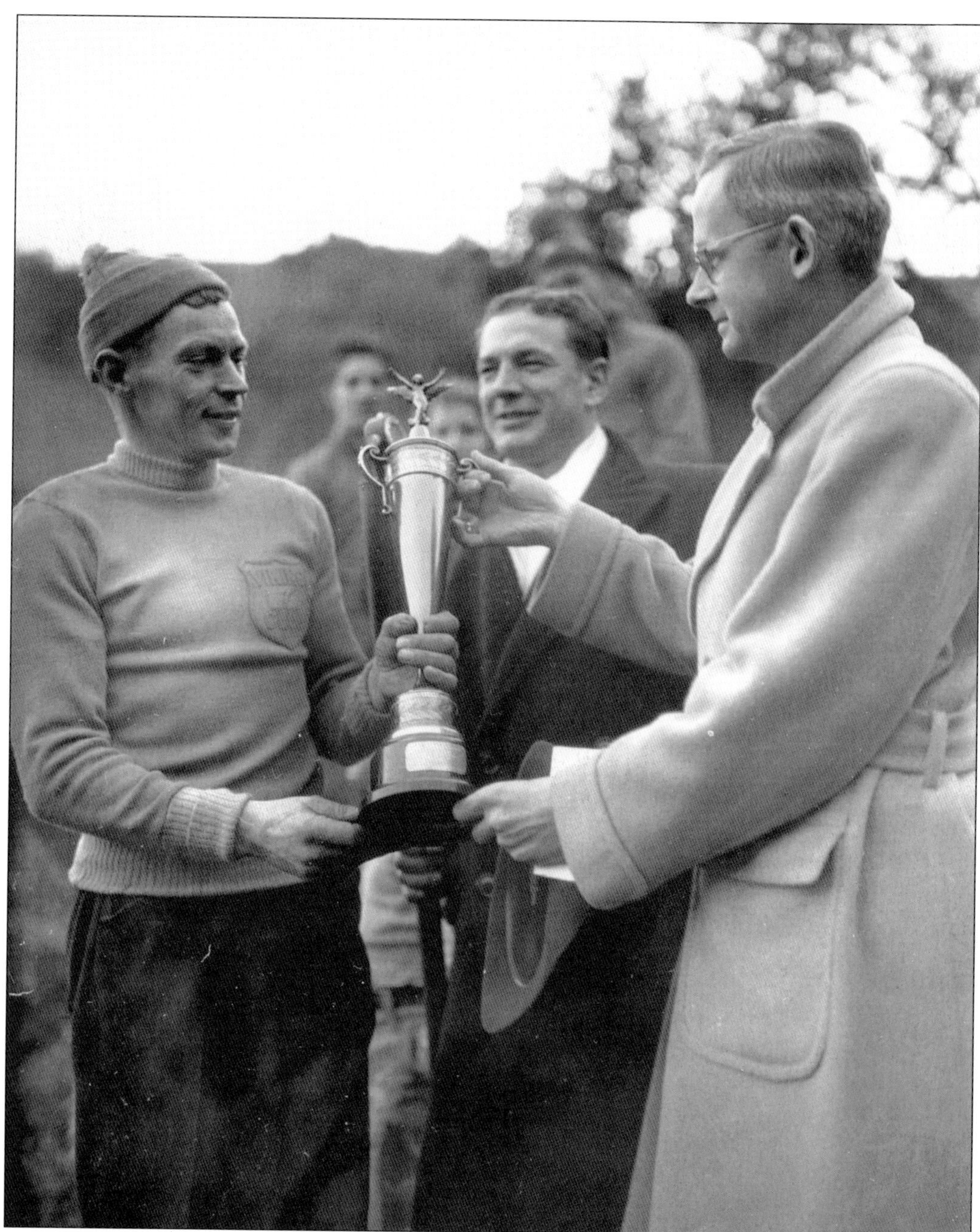

Olaf Tellefsen, the team captain of Los Angeles's Viking Ski Club, receives the winner's trophy for the 1934 Hollywood Bowl Ski Jumping Tournament. Tellefsen made the winning jump of 120 feet. John Elvrum was favored to win the event, but he fractured a rib in a fall on Saturday and was not able to compete on Sunday. Tellefsen won many of the early Southern California ski meets, becoming California's amateur ski jump champion in 1933. At that meet, held in Big Bear Lake on a hill that he built, he outjumped 15 other competitors with a leap of 148 feet. (Courtesy The Huntington Library.)

The Lake Arrowhead Ski Jump was built in 1932, with Halvor Halstad assisting in its design and construction. The jump was located 500 yards south of Lake Arrowhead Village. Given the name "Halstad Hill," it became the centerpiece for the popular winter carnivals held in the 1930s and 1940s. The hill was christened in December 1932 with exhibition jumping by Halstad, Lars Haugen, Einar Fredbo, and Steffen Trogstad. In 1933, the hill was enlarged and improved to accommodate jumps up to 250 feet. Lars Haugen, a champion ski jumper, redesigned the hill so that jumpers of all abilities could use it.

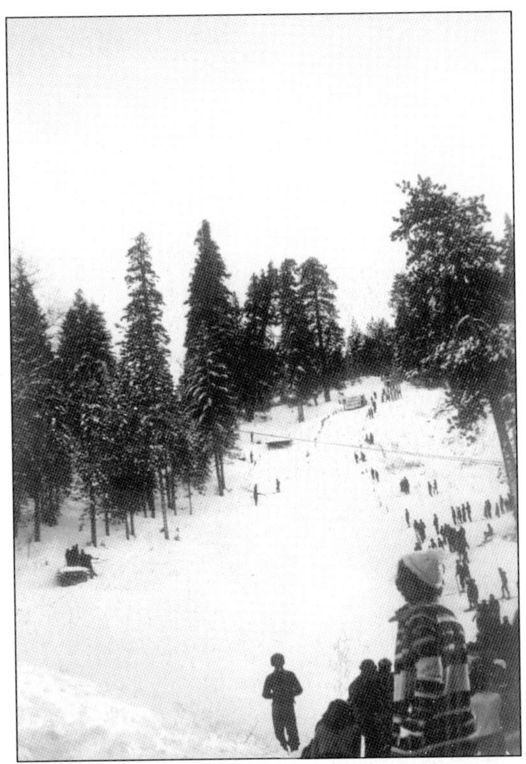

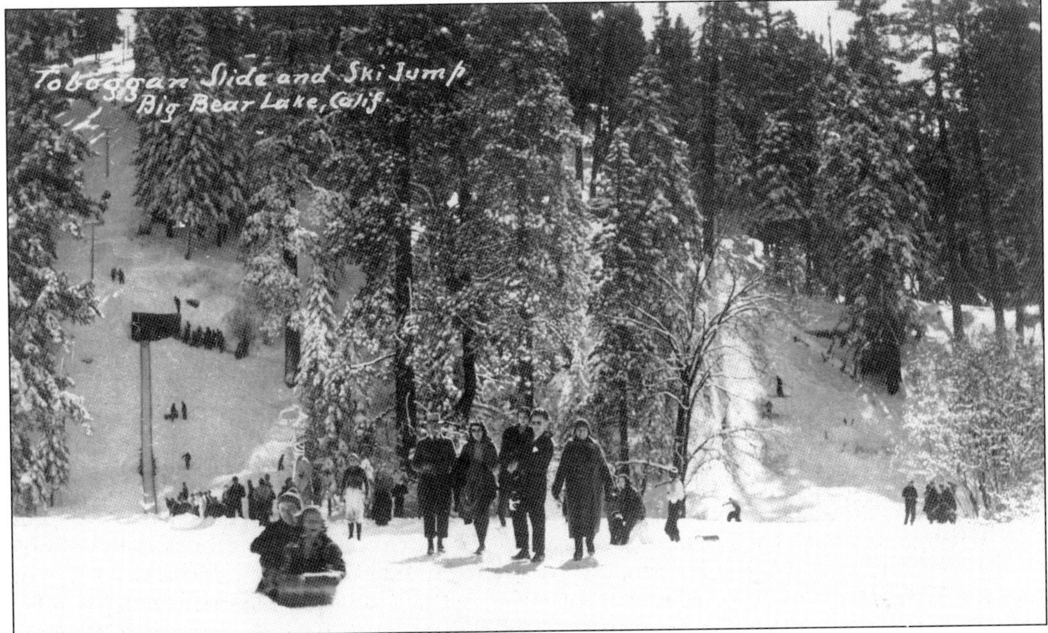

Once snow removal became more reliable, Big Bear Lake began providing first-class facilities to accommodate the influx of winter visitors. A ski jump was built at Pine Knot in 1932, and in February 1933, it became the home of the California State Ski Championships. The event was hosted by Los Angeles's Viking Ski Club and by Big Bear Lake, which was becoming the ski capital of the west.

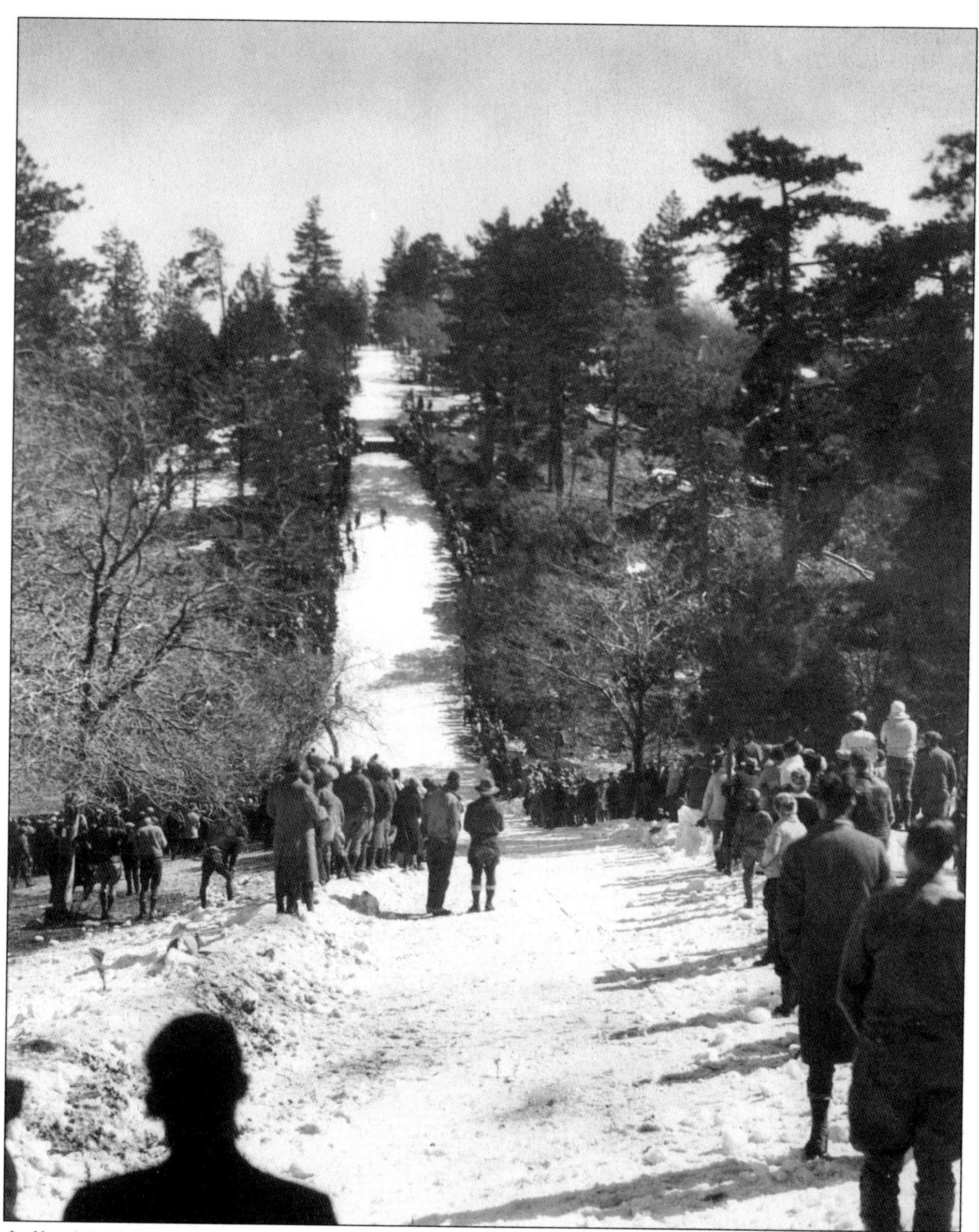

Of all of Southern California's jumping hills, Big Pines was the most well known, attracting national and international competitors. Big Pines Park opened on Labor Day in 1924 and hosted its first winter carnival in 1927. Because of the success and popularity of winter sports and the hope to secure the 1932 Winter Olympic Games, the Los Angeles County Department of Parks and Recreation and the Los Angeles Junior Chamber of Commerce began work in 1929 on a world-class ski jump. The 1,150-foot-long jump was finished in time for the Third Annual Big Pines Winter Carnival in 1929. The three-day event was a huge success, with over 19,000 people attending. In spite of the event's popularity, the Winter Olympics were awarded to Lake Placid, but Big Pines had secured its place as one of Southern California's best winter sports centers. (Courtesy The Huntington Library.)

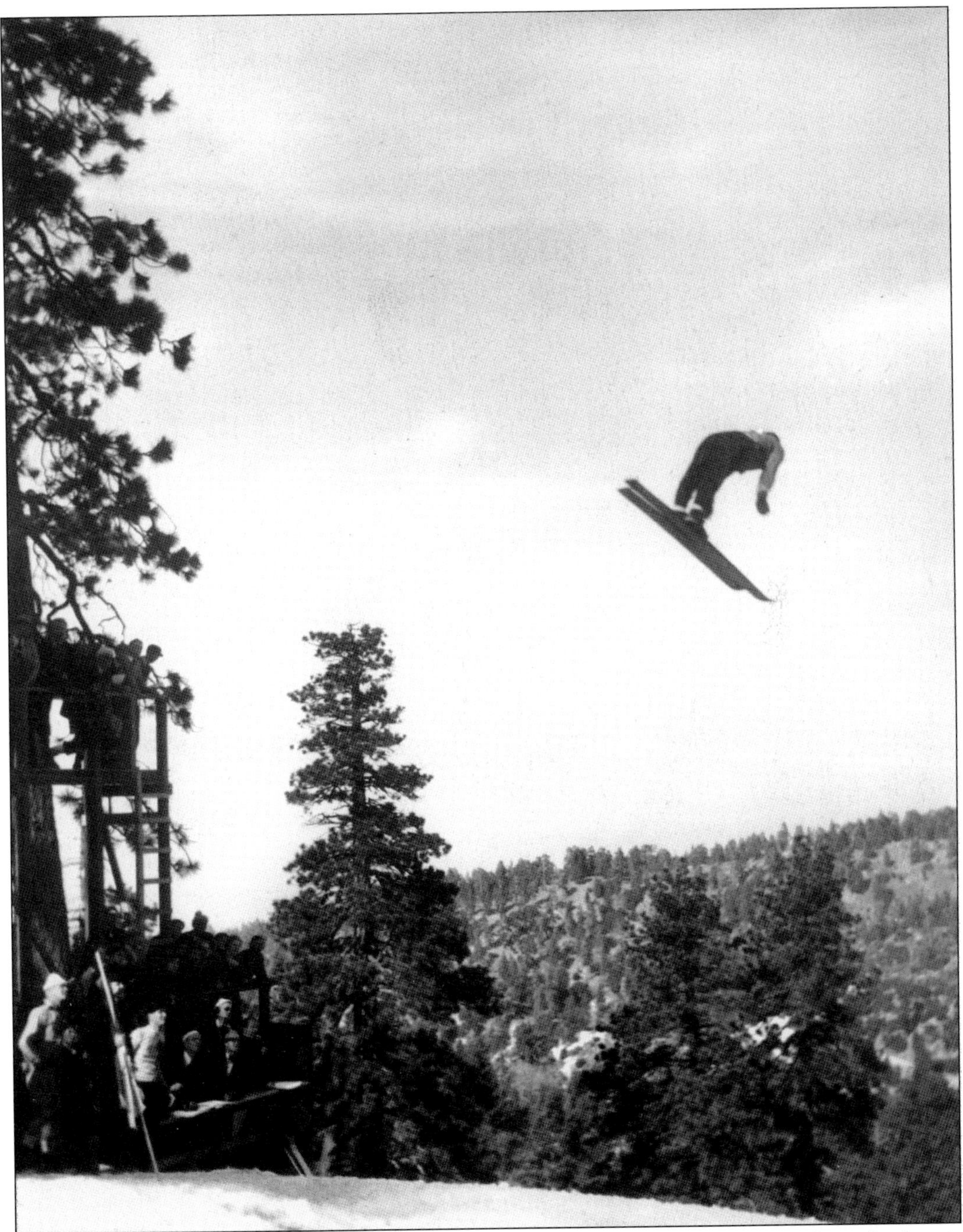

The size of the jumping hill and the inherent excitement of a skier soaring through the air following a rapid descent on a long inrun captured the attention of many in Southern California. Many winter sports fans made the trek to Big Pines just to see the ski jumpers. (Courtesy Ann Dormer Johnson.)

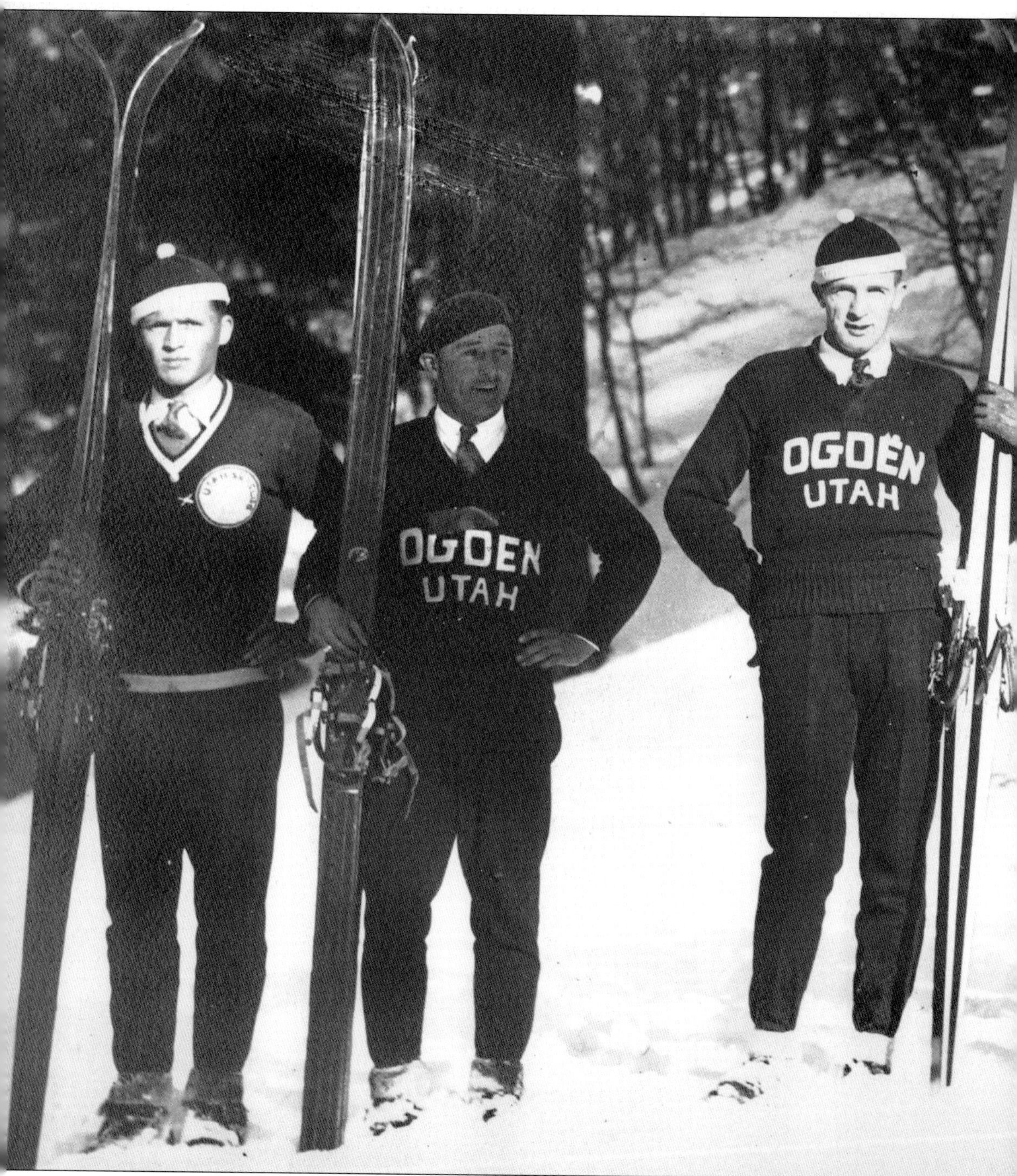

The first world-record ski jump made at Big Pines came in February 1930, when Halvor Bjorngaard soared 137.5 feet. But it soon became evident to competitors and officials that the hill would need to be enlarged if Big Pines were to continue to host major jumping meets. Lars Haugen, a national champion jumper and a noted ski jump designer, was enlisted for the job. The new jump was finished by 1931 and was claimed to be the world's longest. It was 1,516 feet from the start to the outer rim of the apron. On January 22, 1931, two weeks after the grand

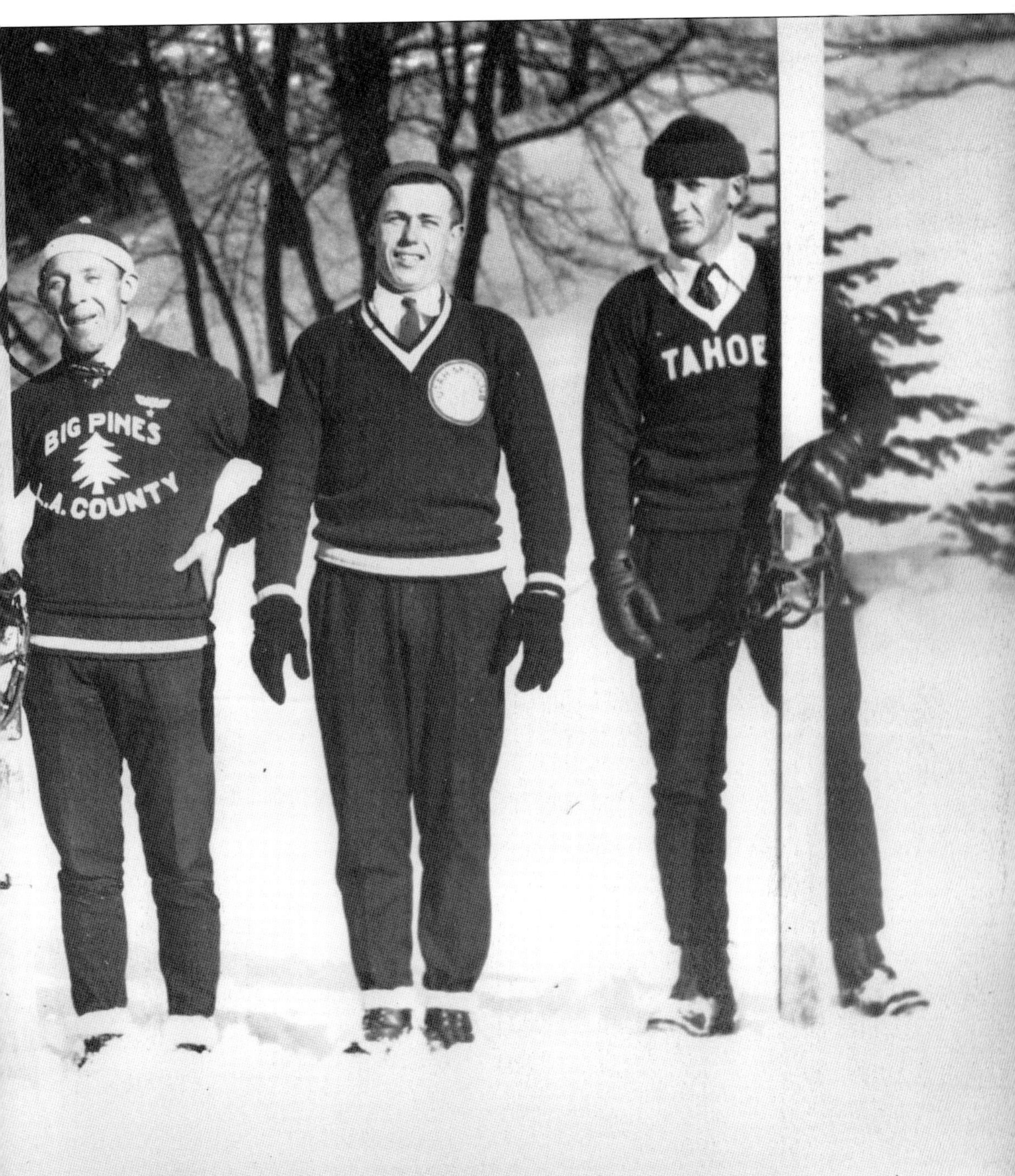

opening of the new hill, Halvor Halstad made an unofficial world-record jump of 250.05 feet. A series of record-breaking jumps followed quickly thereafter. On January 30, Alf Engen and Lars Haugen both jumped 231 feet. Then, on February 1, Engen bettered this mark, jumping 243 feet. This portrait captures some of the nation's best jumpers at Big Pines. Pictured from left to right are Sverre Engen, Ted Rex, Steffan Trogstad, Halvor Halstad, Einar Fredbo, and Lars Haugen. (Courtesy Ann Dormer Johnson.)

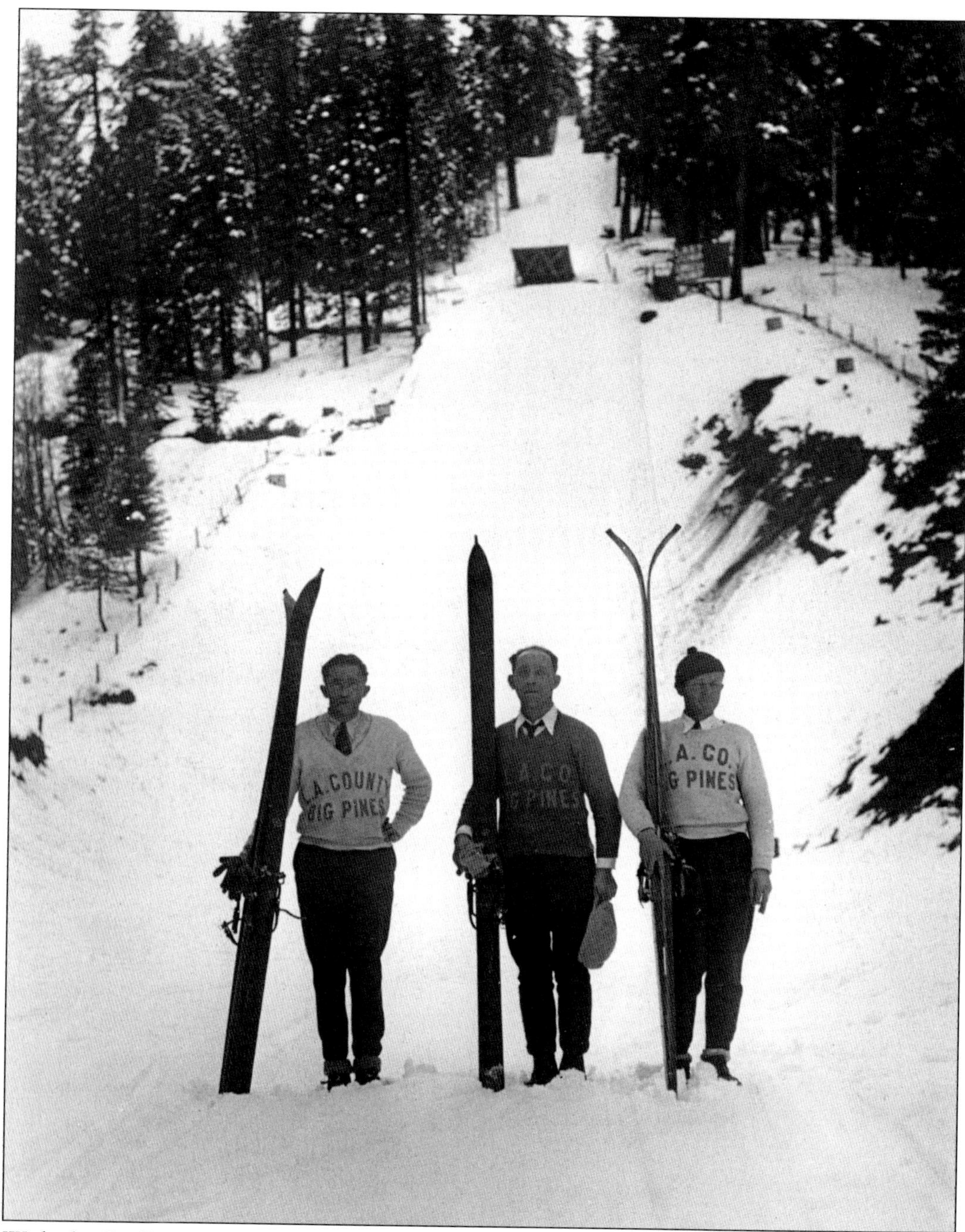

With the Big Pines jump as a backdrop, Halvor Halstad (center) poses with fellow ski jumpers sporting Big Pines sweaters. Halstad built many small jumps throughout California. He helped design and build the ski jump at Lake Arrowhead and managed the Big Pines jump. He earned the nickname "Dynamite" for some of the spectacular falls he made, and he was a well-known competitor in national jumping meets throughout the 1930s and 1940s. Halstad was inducted into the United States Ski Hall of Fame in 1977. (Courtesy The Huntington Library.)

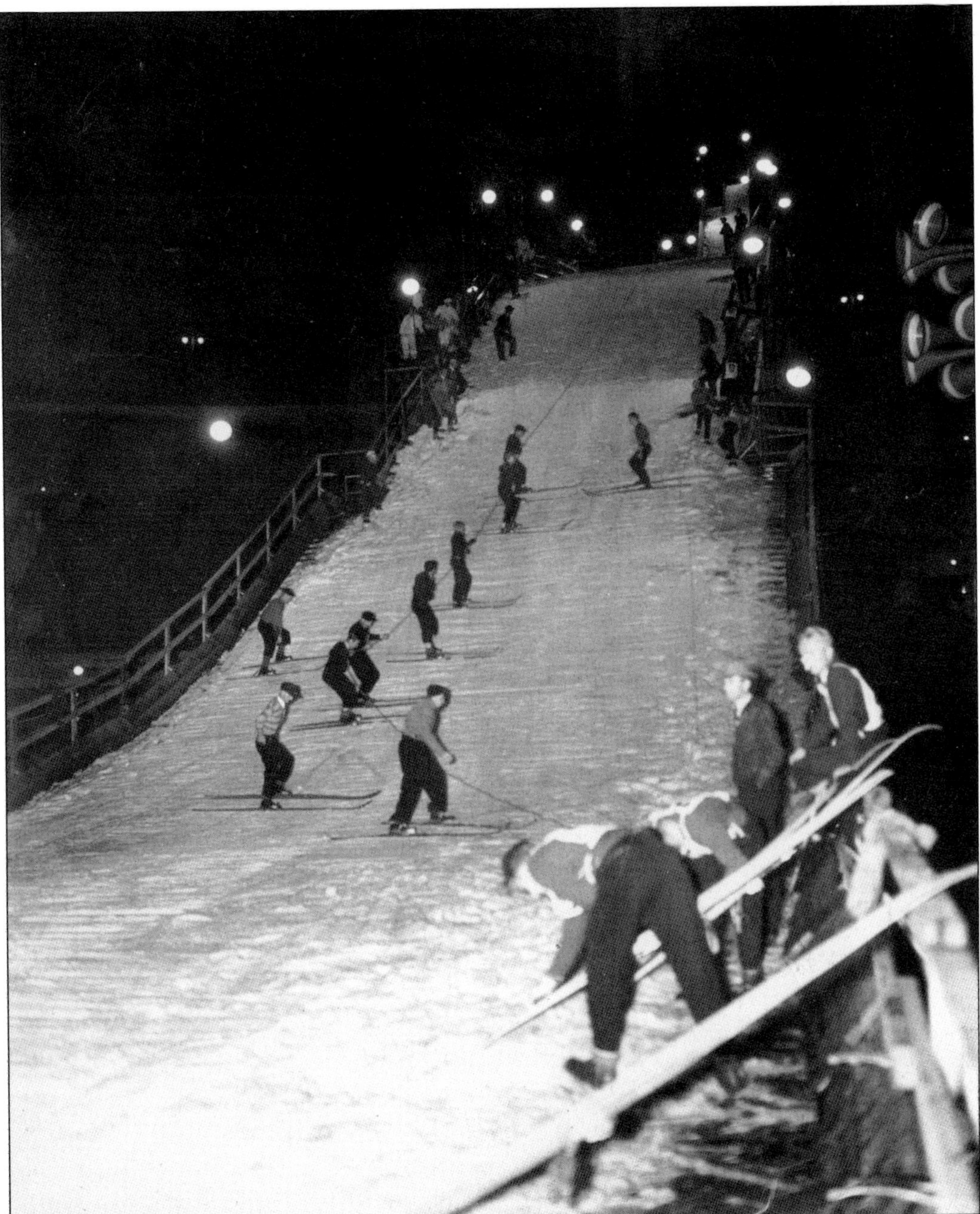

In 1938 and 1939, the Lake Arrowhead Ski Club held the First and Second Annual Southern California Open Ski Meets at the Los Angeles Coliseum. The events drew well-known ski jumpers from all over the United States and Scandinavia. Roy Mikkelsen, Sverre Engen, Sigmund and Birger Ruud, Hannes Schroll, Wayne Poulsen, John Elvrum, and Casper Oimoen were just some of the well-known jumpers who participated. Both tournaments were sanctioned by the California Ski Association and captured front-page coverage by local newspapers. (Courtesy The Huntington Library.)

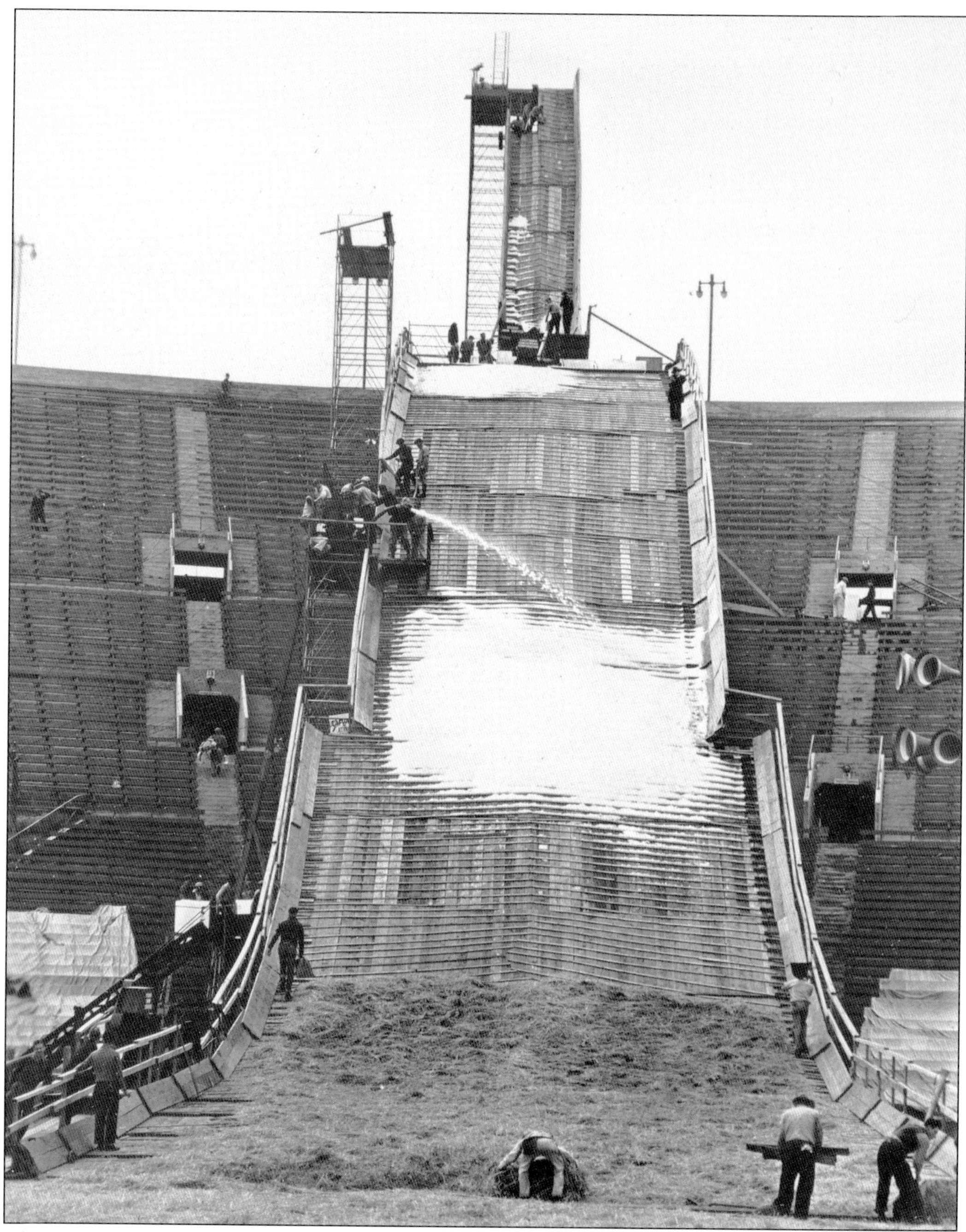

The imposing scaffold rose 60 feet above the rim of the coliseum, with a slope of 40 degrees. Similar jumps had been built at Madison Square Garden in New York and Soldier Field in Chicago, but this was a first for the Los Angeles Coliseum. (Courtesy The Huntington Library.)

The giant slide was covered with snow prepared by five snow machines, which ground large ice blocks and then blew snow onto the jump. The coverage varied from eight inches to five feet, with the greatest depth in the landing area. (Courtesy The Huntington Library.)

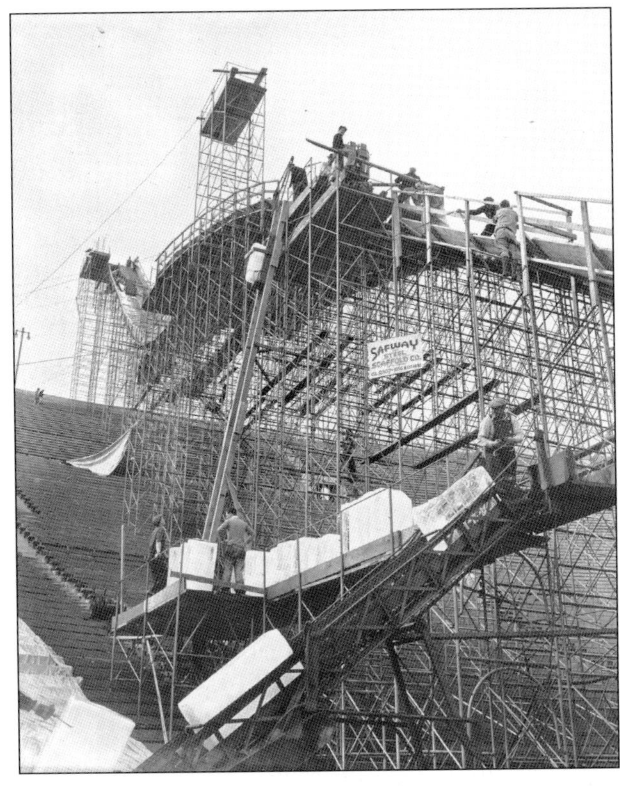

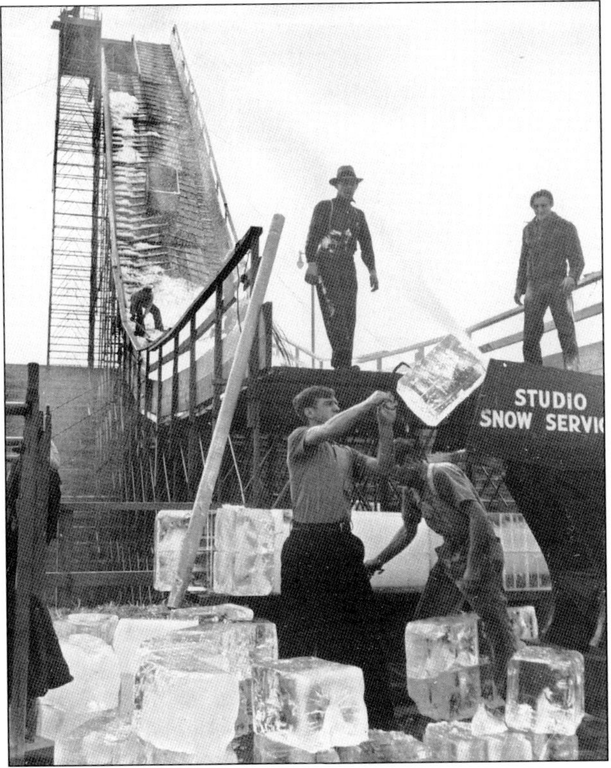

It took the snowmaking machines about 12 hours to grind enough ice to cover the jump and the landing area. Tom Gallery managed and promoted the meets, inspiring local reporters to dub the jump "Mount Gallery." Both meets were a success, even with the rescheduling of the 1938 meet due to rain. Birger Ruud won the 1938 meet with jumps of 131 and 136 feet. Reidar Anderson won the 1939 meet with jumps of 154 and 146 feet. (Courtesy The Huntington Library.)

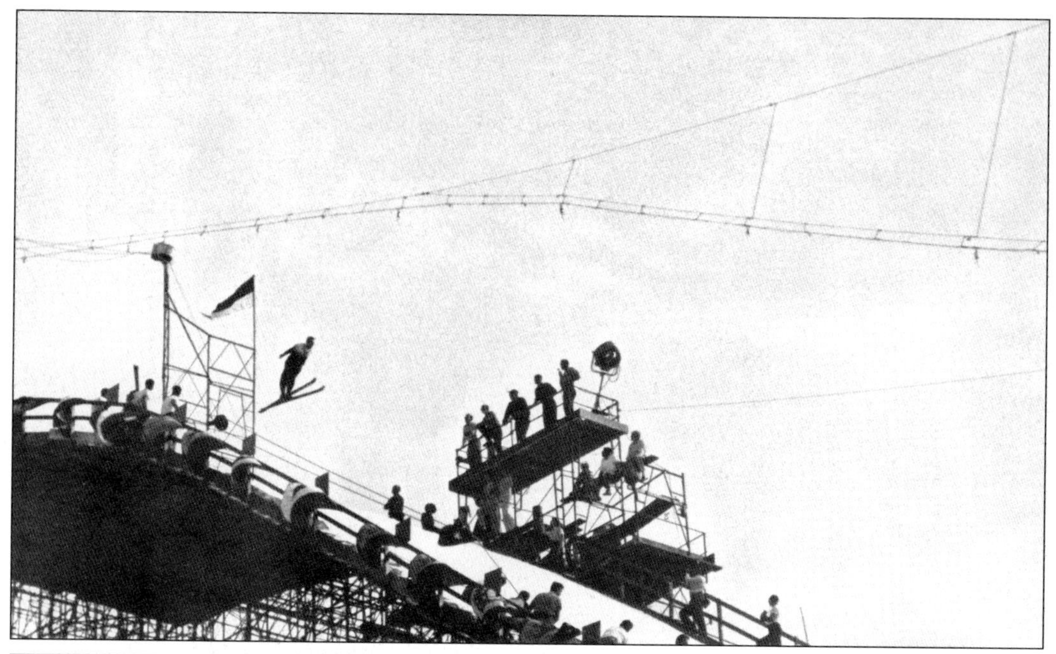

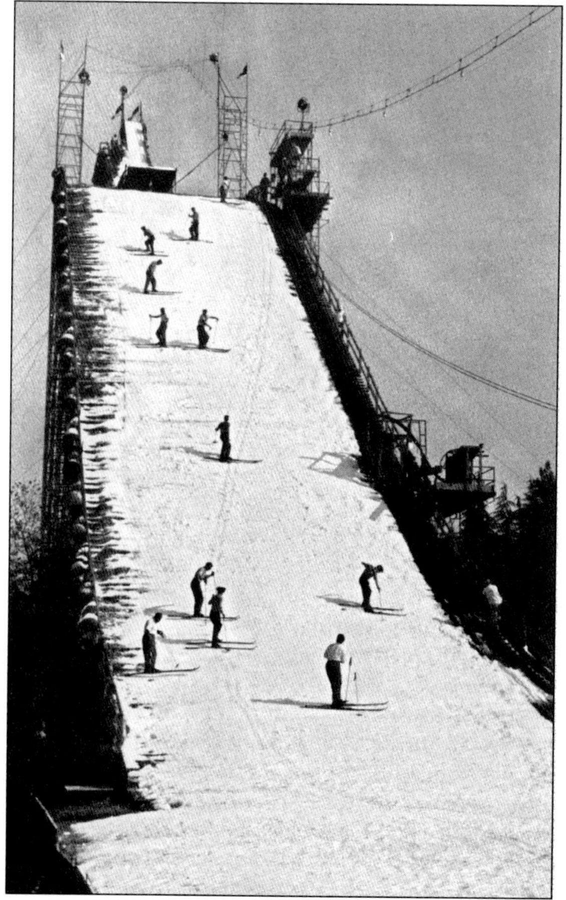

In 1951, a 60-meter ski jump was built at the Los Angeles County Fair in Pomona. Sepp Benedikter organized and directed the hugely popular event, which took place from September 14 to September 30. During the fair, a total of 800,000 people watched the ski jumpers at the Pacific Southwest Mid-Summer Ski Jumping Tournament. Sanctioned by the Far West Ski Association, the meet featured nine members of the 1952 Olympic ski jumping team. (Courtesy Elmar Baxter.)

Preparing the jump for daily competition was no easy feat. Shaved ice was applied to the jump and packed by volunteer skiers. Keeping the slide iced in the 100-degree temperatures that plagued the event was, according to Benedikter, like creating a snowy mountain in the desert and having to rebuild it every day. (Courtesy Elmar Baxter.)

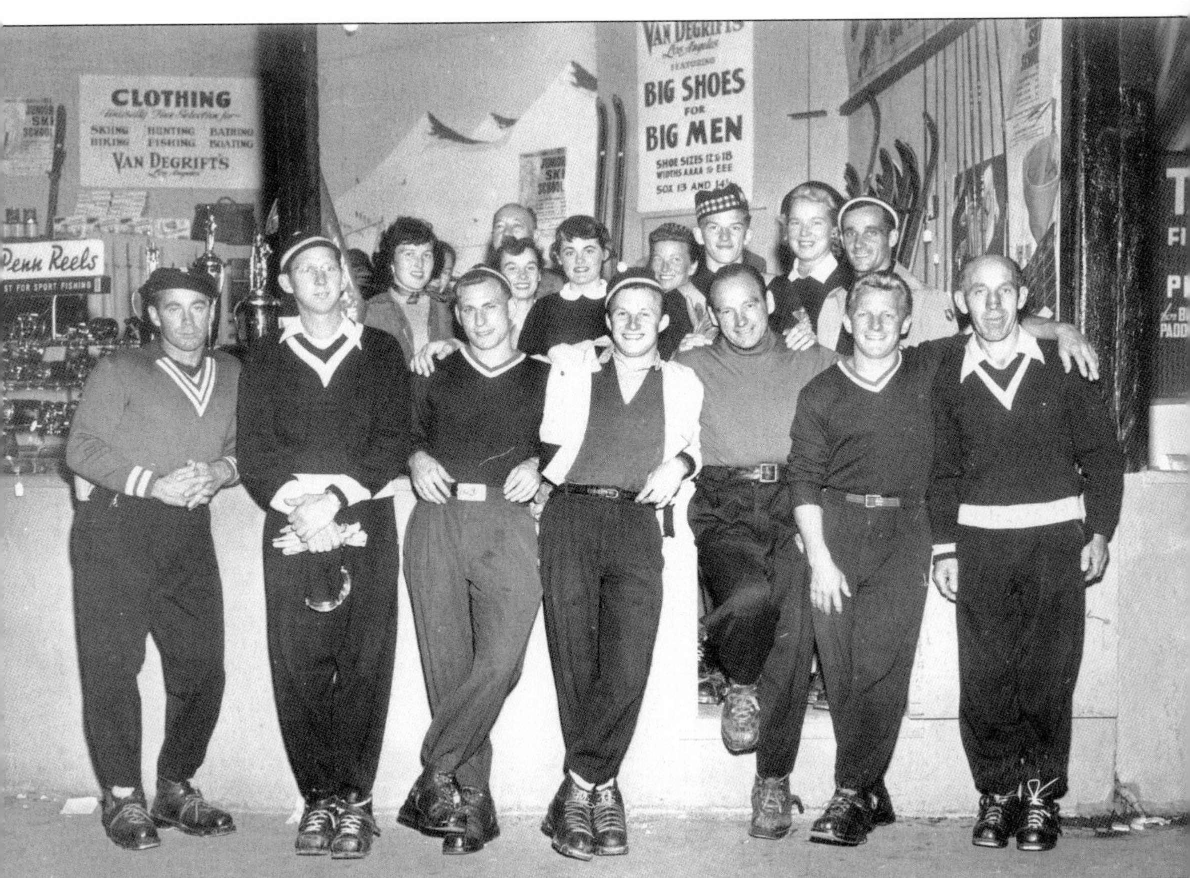

Members of the United States Olympic Ski Jumping Team take a break from the competition to visit the Van Degrift's Ski Hut booth at the fair. Pictured from left to right are the following: (first row) Stan Watters, Sverre Fossheim, Wilbert Rasmussen, Dave Freeman, Sepp Benedikter, Coy Hill, and Halvor Halstad; (second row) Joan Law, Tyler Van Degrift, Hildegard Spitz, Suzi Harmon, Clarita Heath, Joan Bednarz, Ethel Van Degrift, and Paul Perrault. Coy Hill won the tournament with a jump of 160 feet. Halstad, in his mid-40s, competed every evening and finished in third place. He was nicknamed "the Flying Grandfather". The women in this group were also competitors, participating in the slalom races that were a part of the event.

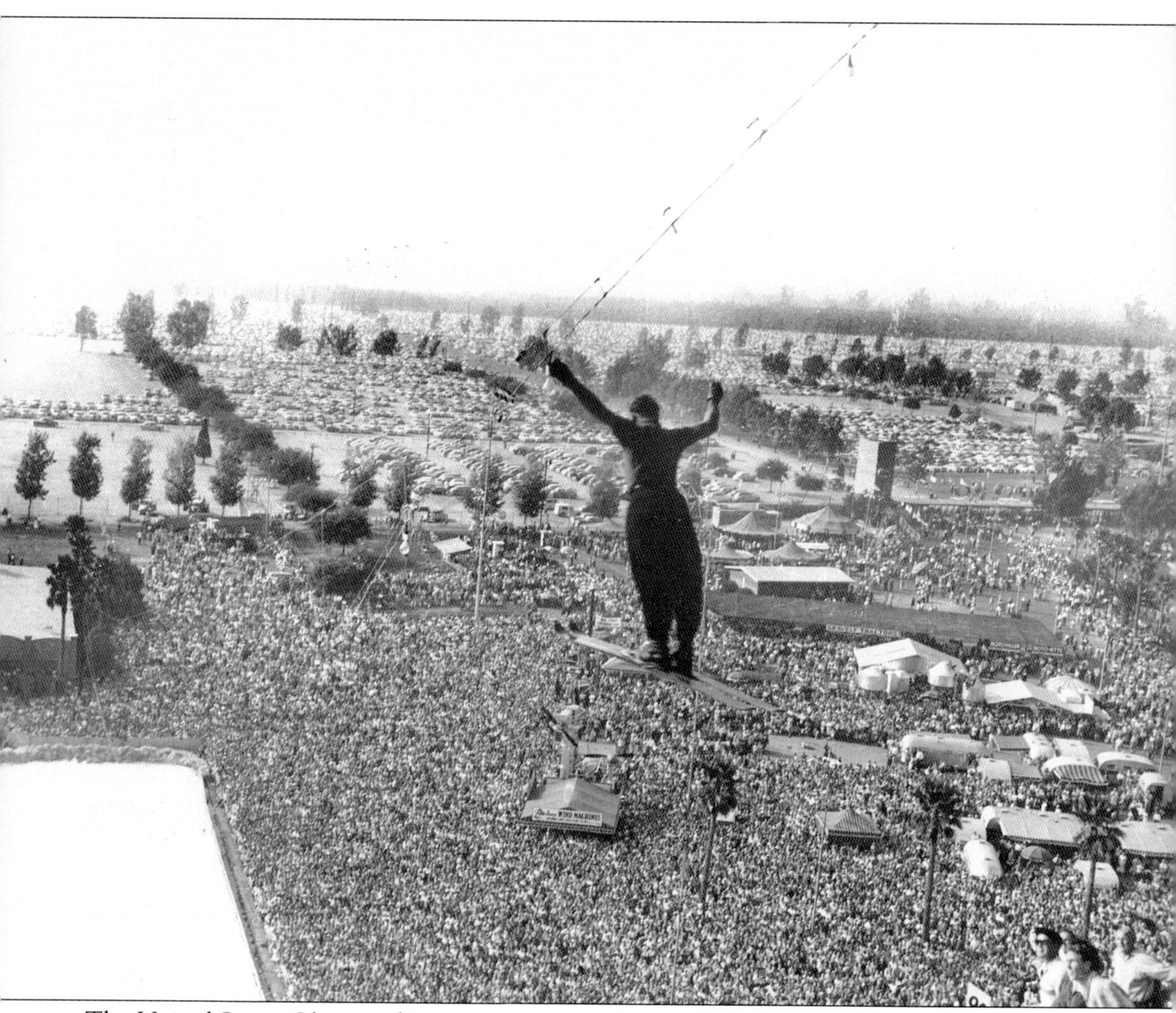

The United States Olympic ski jumpers competed twice daily, but many in the crowd were just as excited to see the mastermind of the jump in action. Benedikter soars through the air to the delight of the estimated 40,000 to 50,000 spectators that took in the event everyday. (Courtesy Claudia Benedikter Pedersen.)

Four

NO SNOW, NO PROBLEM

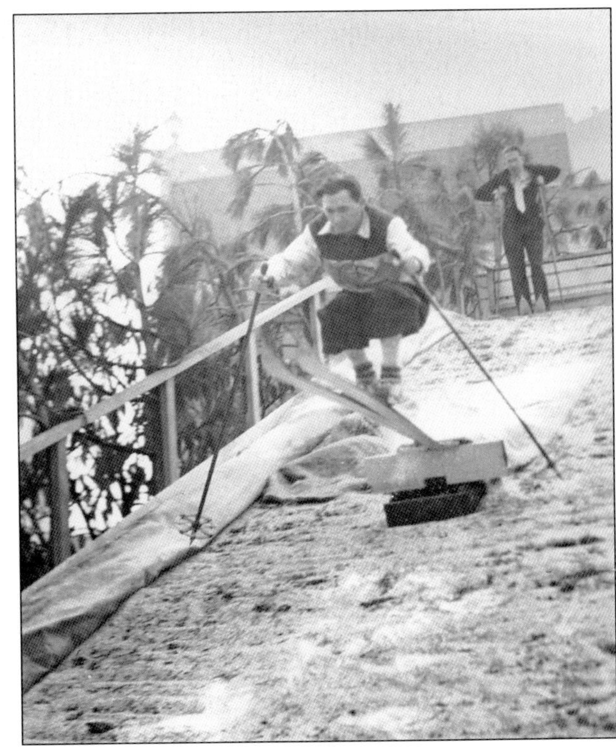

By the 1930s, the Southland seemed to have caught ski fever. To draw more attention to the sport and to provide dryland practice for those eagerly awaiting winter's first snowfall, a variety of unique "slopes" took shape. In October 1937, the May Company in Los Angeles announced the opening of the city's first ski slide, located on its roof. Hannes Schroll gave a daily exhibition, while Ludwig "Vic" Hasher, pictured here, served as ski instructor. (Courtesy Western Skisport Museum.)

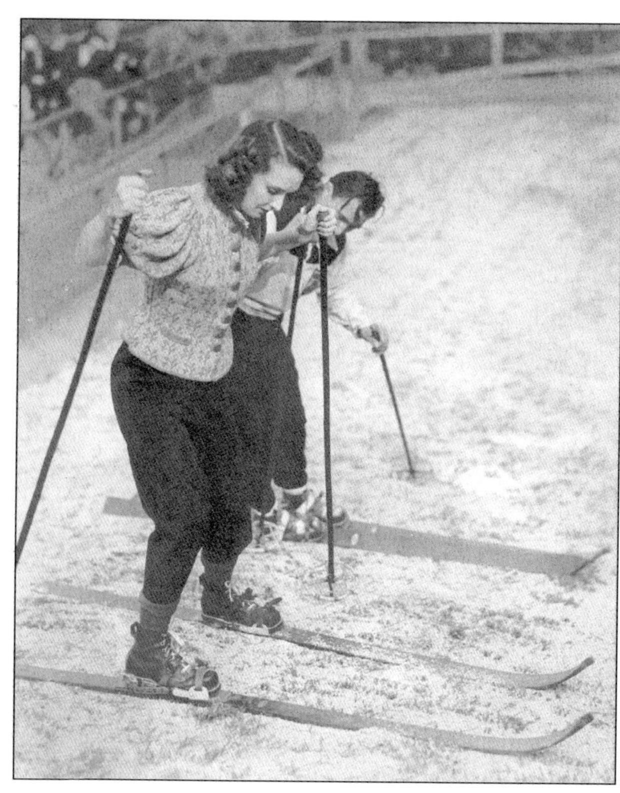

The May Company ski slide, at 16 feet high and 84 feet long, was not too steep or dangerous, but its borax-covered surface was slippery enough to simulate the feeling of a snow-covered hill. Left, Hasher instructs a fashionable novice. Below, she demonstrates the results of his instruction. (Courtesy Western Skisport Museum.)

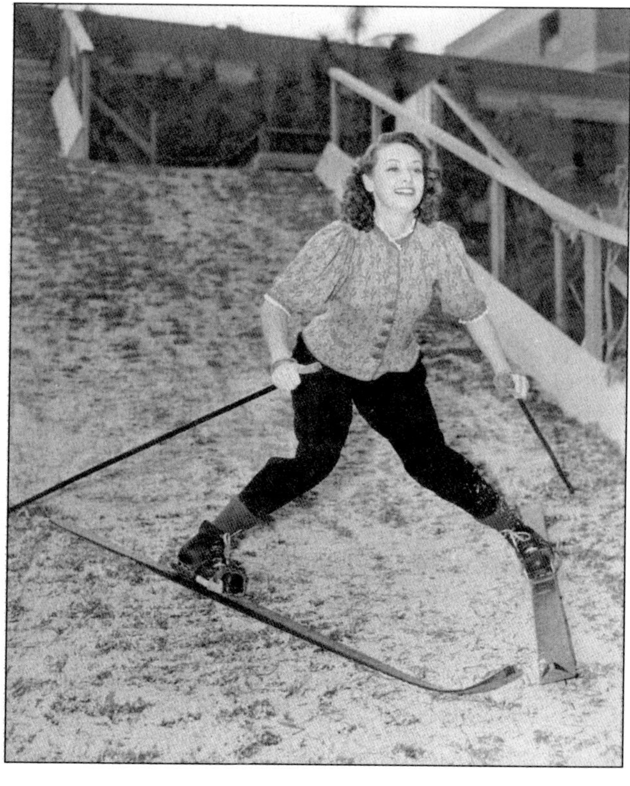

Ludwig "Vic" Hasher, a ski instructor, snow surveyor, and ski-equipment distributor, was eager to lead nonskiers to the sport. Not afraid to use unusual gimmicks or locations, he planned and hosted a cross-country ski race at Manhattan Beach in 1946. He is shown here demonstrating classic sand-skiing form. (Courtesy Western Skisport Museum.)

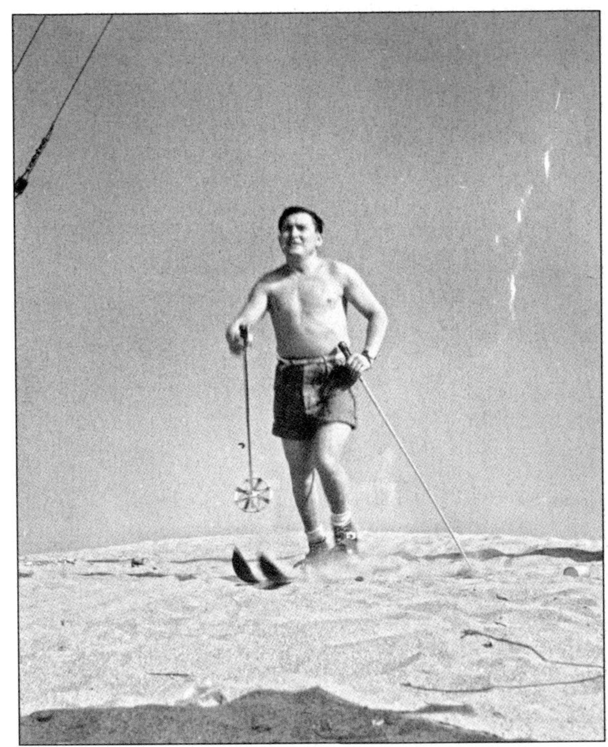

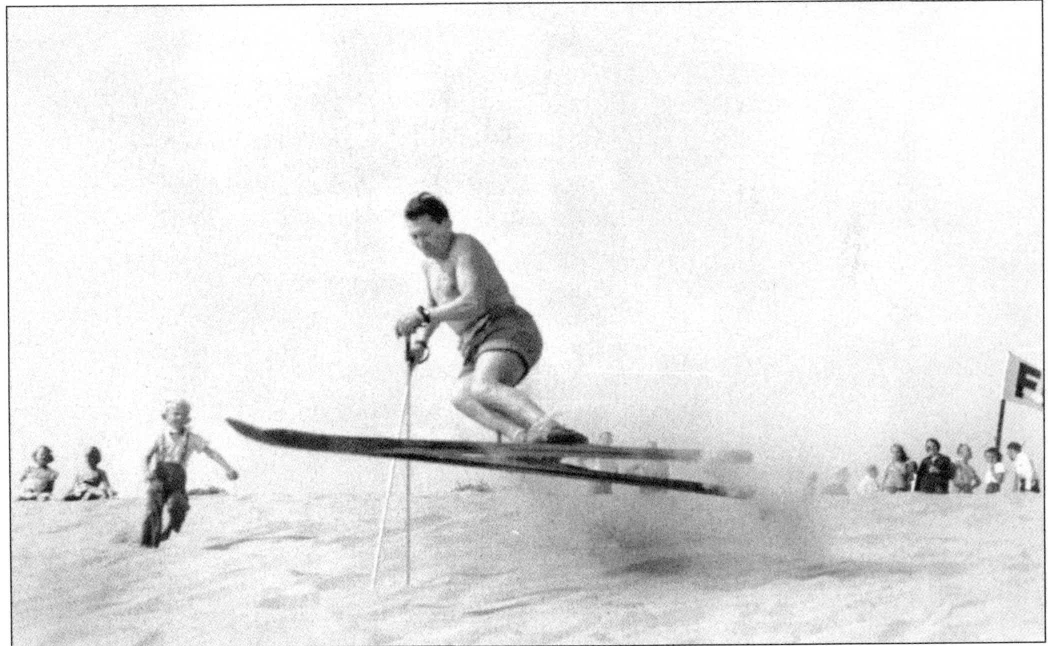

Hasher demonstrates a jump turn on the dunes of Manhattan Beach. His efforts on the May Company slide and the Manhattan Beach ski race drew recognition to the sport and encouraged people to learn to ski. In 1947, Hasher and his wife, Bea, began a two-year stint in Mineral King, working to collect data and evaluate the potential for ski-area development in the region. (Courtesy Western Skisport Museum.)

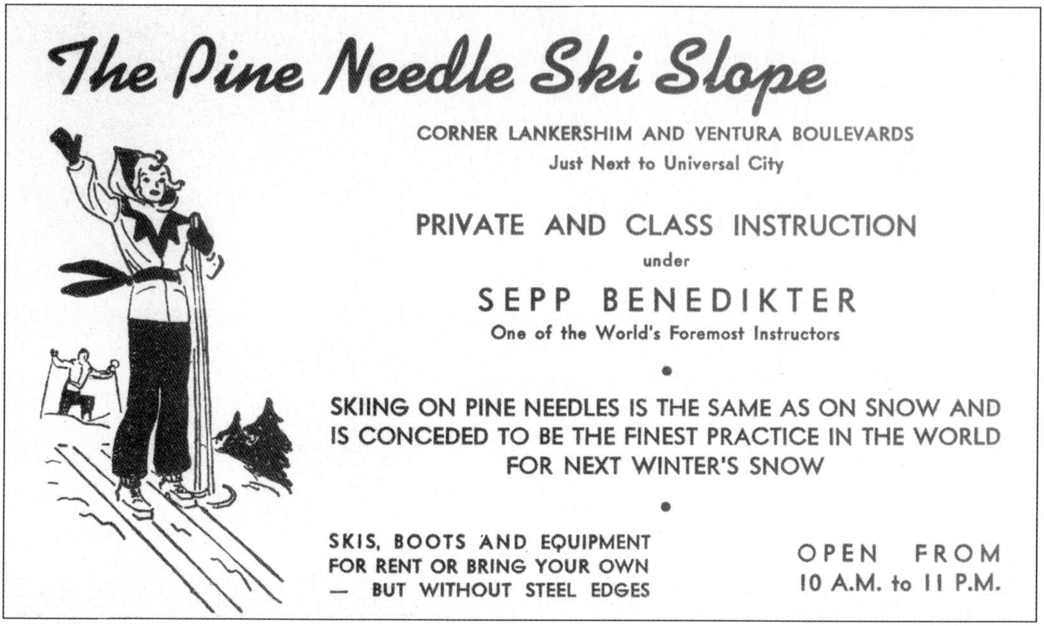

The Pine Needle Ski Slope

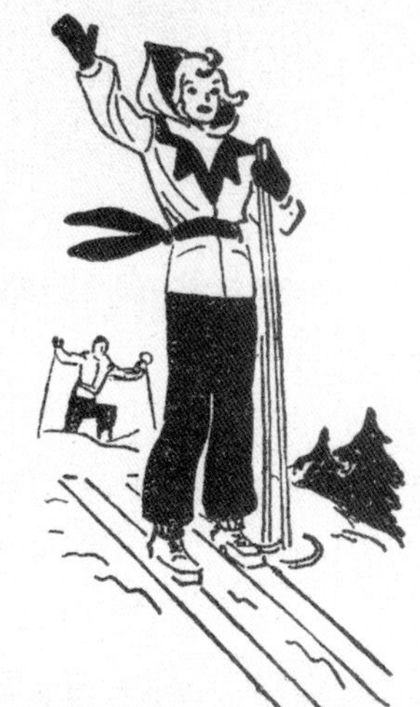

CORNER LANKERSHIM AND VENTURA BOULEVARDS
Just Next to Universal City

PRIVATE AND CLASS INSTRUCTION
under
SEPP BENEDIKTER
One of the World's Foremost Instructors

•

SKIING ON PINE NEEDLES IS THE SAME AS ON SNOW AND IS CONCEDED TO BE THE FINEST PRACTICE IN THE WORLD FOR NEXT WINTER'S SNOW

•

SKIS, BOOTS AND EQUIPMENT FOR RENT OR BRING YOUR OWN — BUT WITHOUT STEEL EDGES

OPEN FROM 10 A.M. to 11 P.M.

Sepp Benedikter, a name synonymous with skiing from the 1930s through the 1970s, opened a pine-needle ski slope in June 1939. Located at the corner of Lankesheim and Ventura Boulevards, the slope was covered with 3,000 sacks of pine needles gathered from the Sierra Nevada. The facility was outfitted with a ski-rental shop owned by Tyler Van Degrift, a ticket office, and dressing rooms.

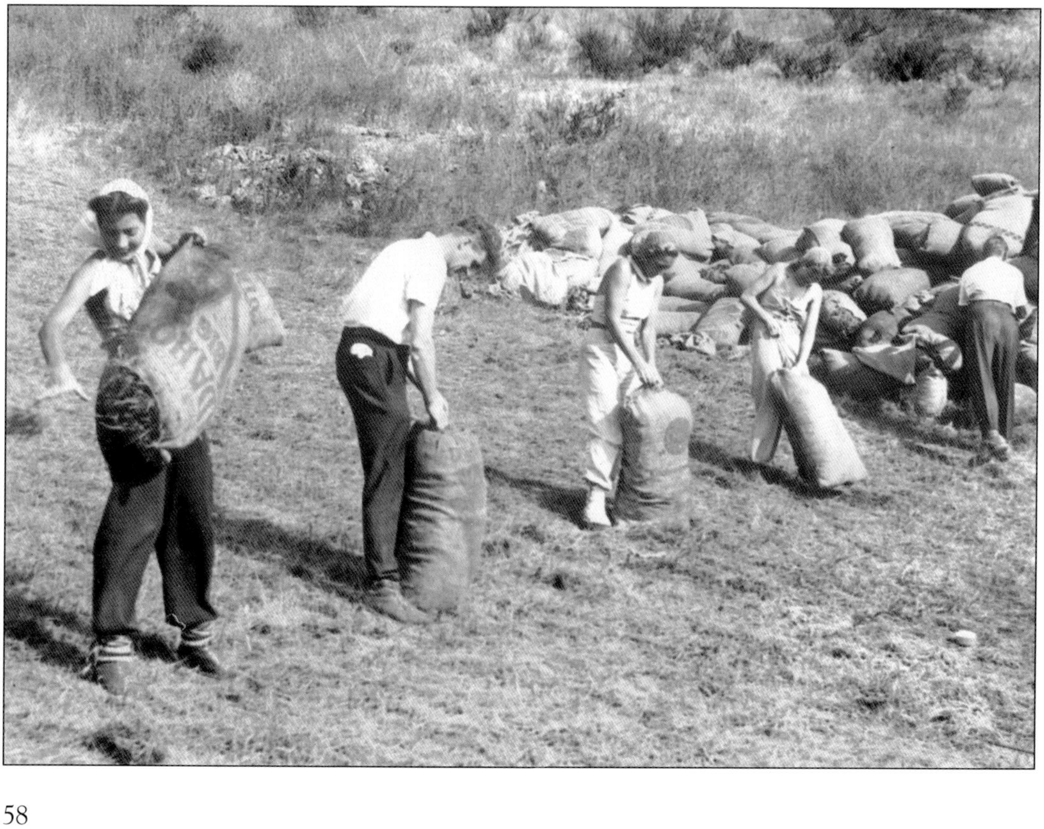

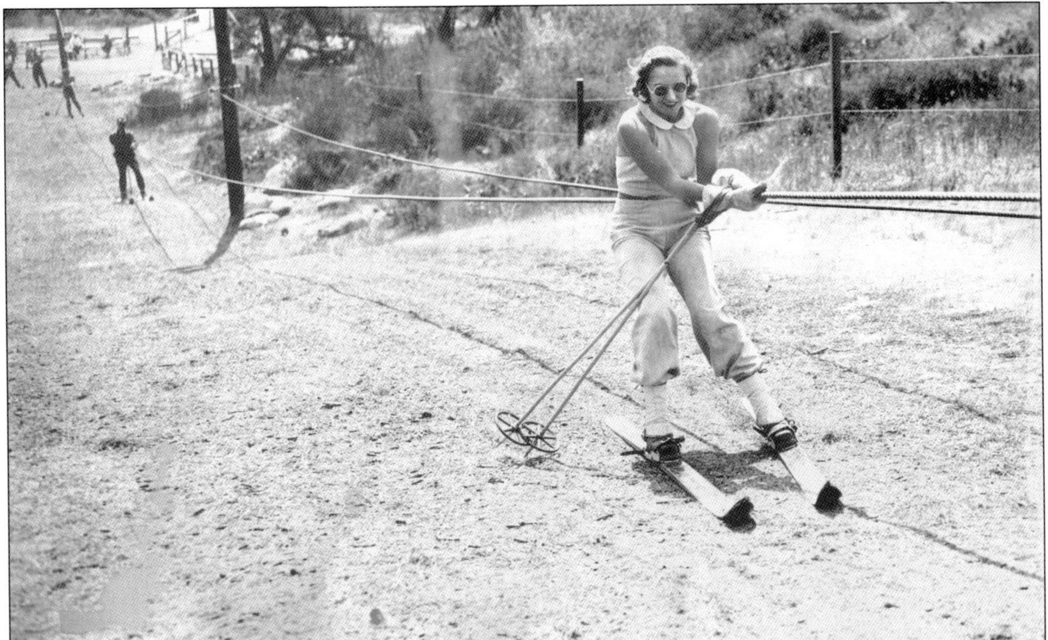

Benedikter installed two rope tows to whisk skiers to the top of the slope. Thanks to his reputation as a ski instructor and the proximity of the slope to Hollywood, opening night proved to be a gala affair. Numerous Hollywood personalities made it to the star-studded event, including Henry Fonda, Gary Cooper, Robert Taylor, Claudette Colbert, and James Cagney.

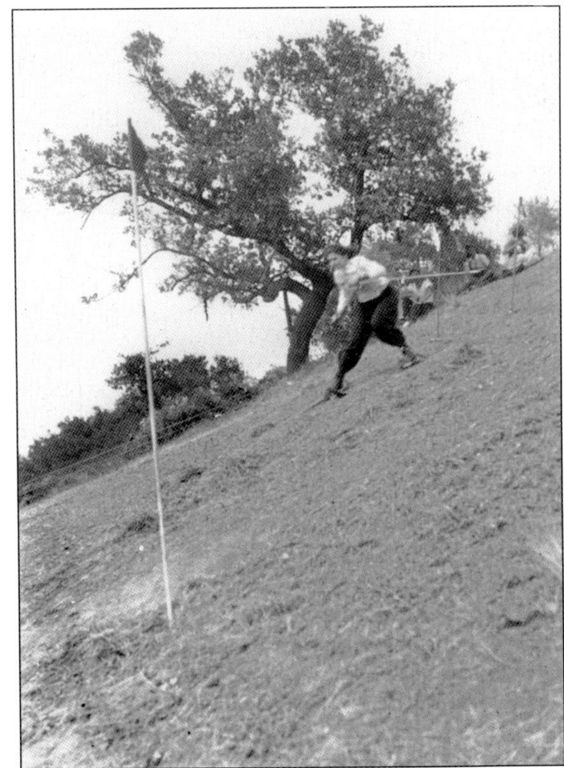

Benedikter planned and hosted a number of special events and races at the hill. Sigi Engl, Dave McCoy, Fred Iselin, Ethel Van Degrift, Clarita Heath, and many others participated in the pine-needle ski-slope races.

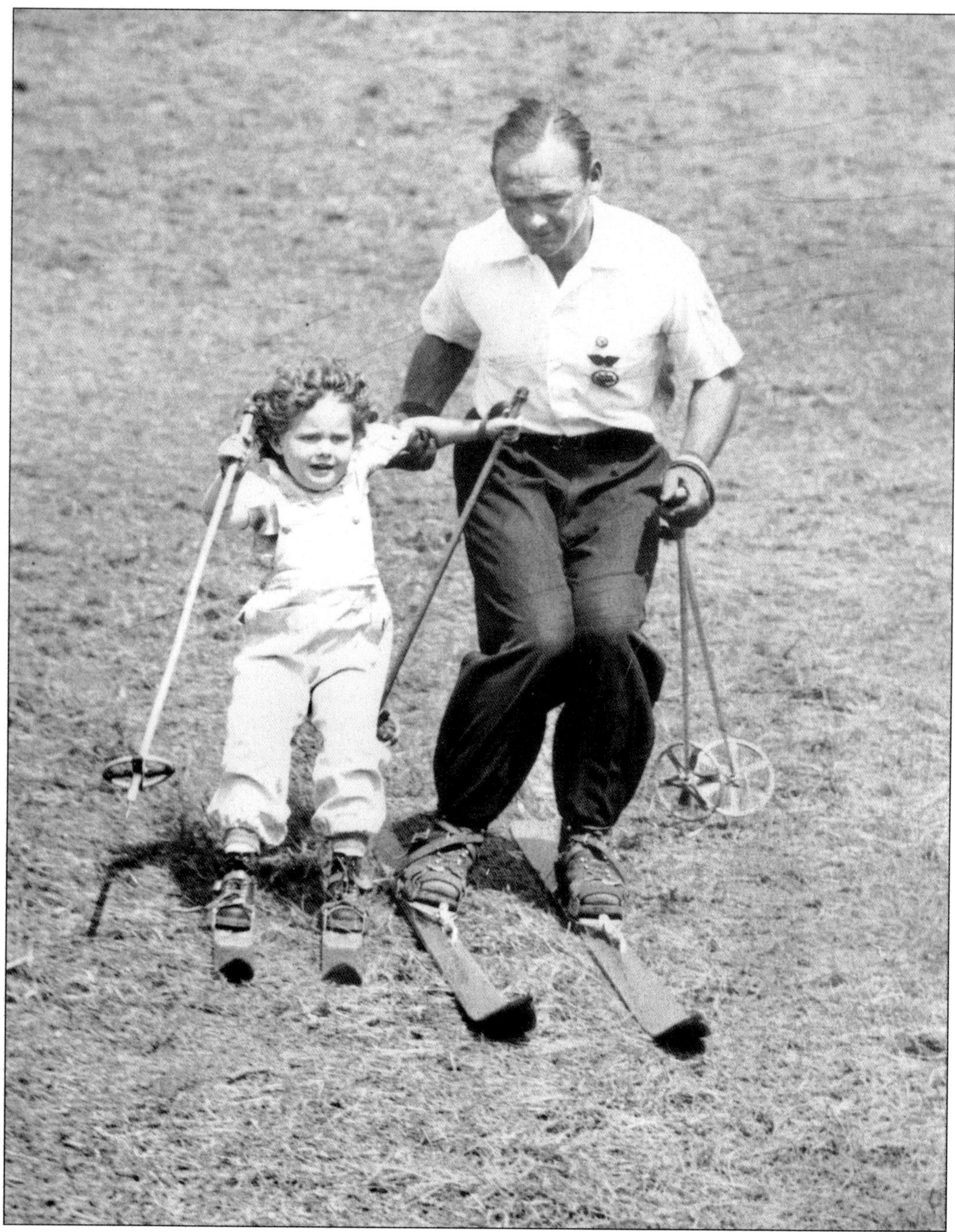

Benedikter teaches a youngster to master ski skills on his pine-needle ski slope, readying her for the real thing. He felt that many people in Southern California were afraid of snow and would not venture to the mountains to try skiing. By teaching people on the dry course in the summer, he hoped they would become interested and lose some of their aversion to the sport.

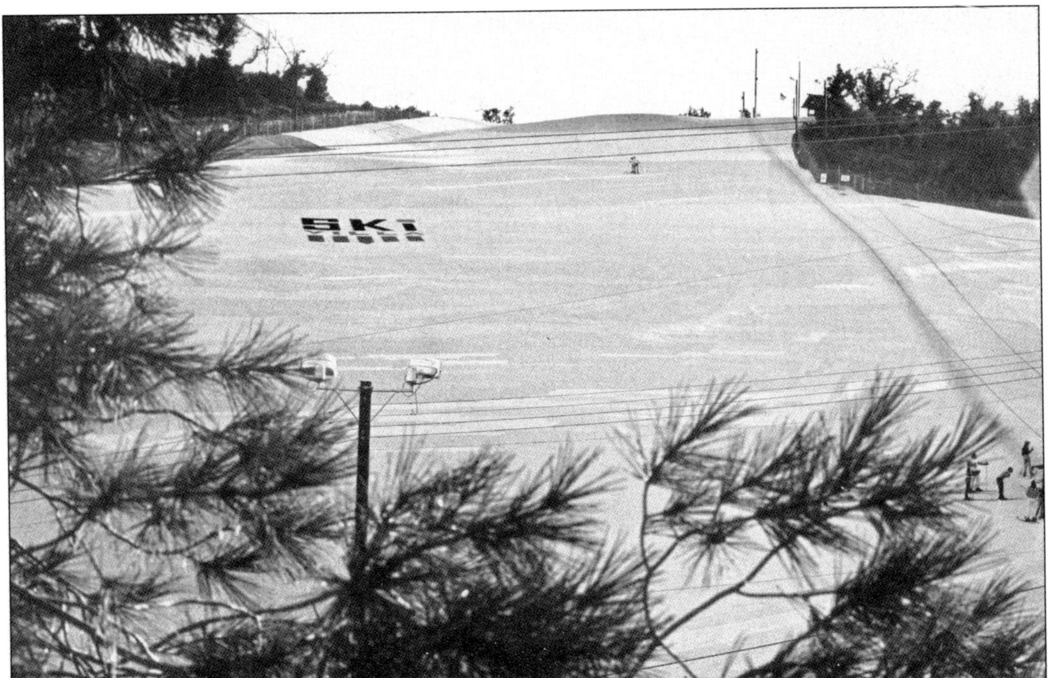

On June 25, 1966, the first and only year-round ski resort in the United States opened for business. Ski Villa was located in the hills of Carbon Canyon, about a 40-minute drive from Los Angeles. The slope, covered with 1.5 million plastic bristle tiles, measured 400 yards from top to bottom. It was 200 feet wide at the top and increased to 900 feet wide at the bottom. (Courtesy Elmar Baxter.)

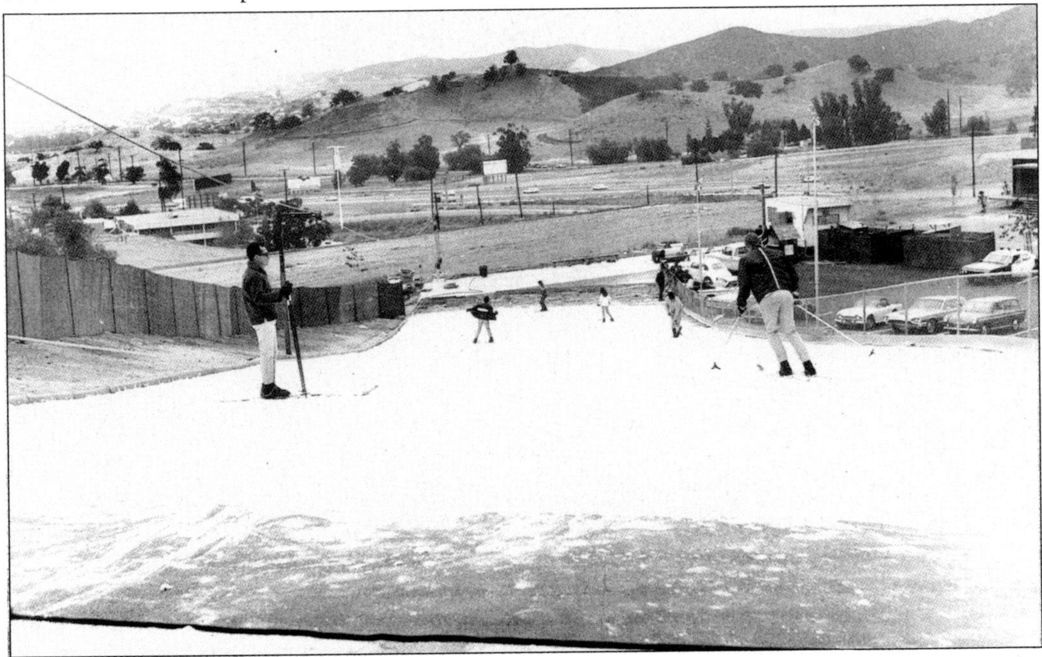

This is a skier's-eye view of Ski Villa. Though it initially seemed to be a promising venture, the area remained in business for only about a year. The surface proved to be too hard and unforgiving during a fall, perhaps hastening the area's demise.

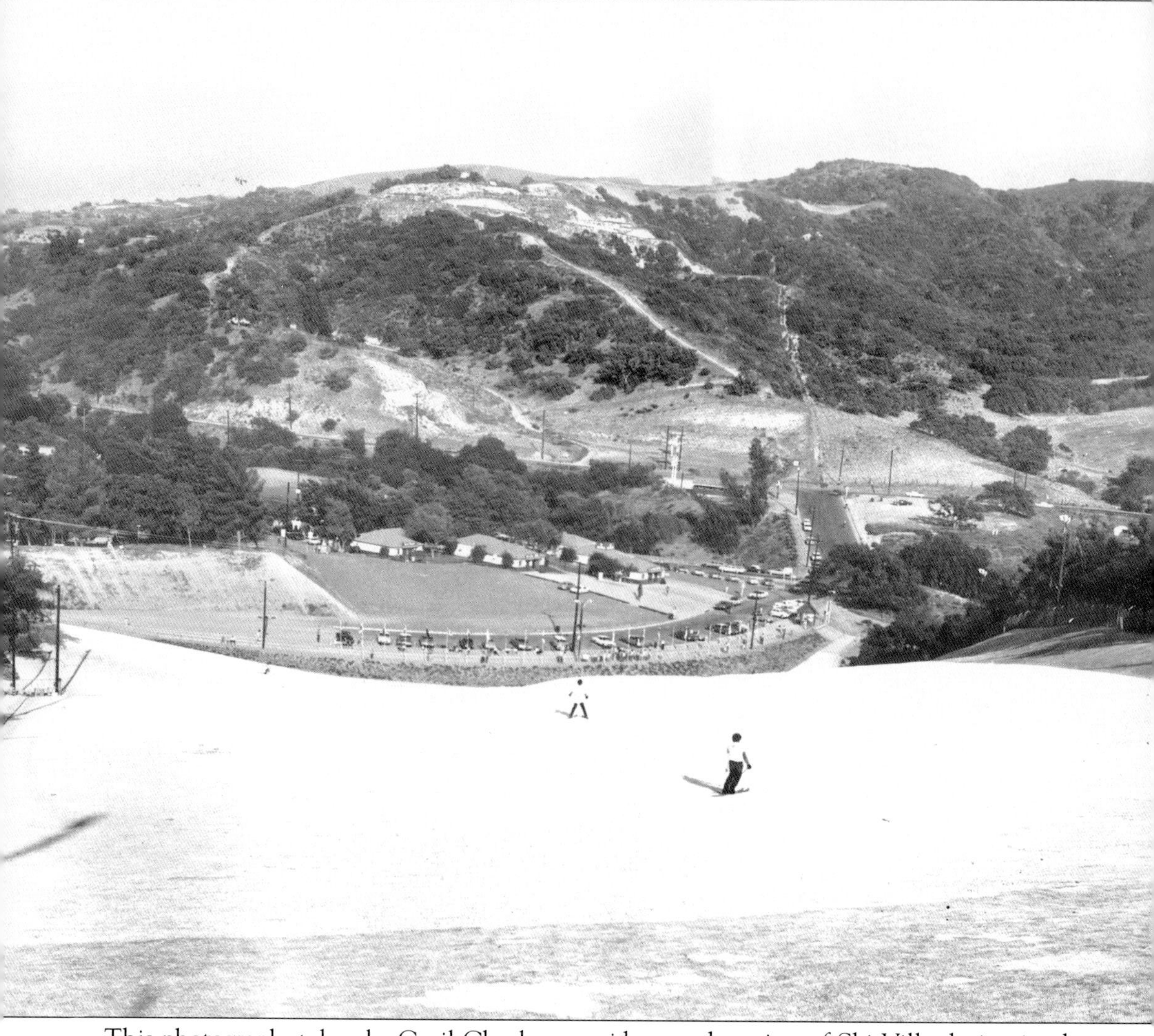

This photograph, taken by Cecil Charles, provides another view of Ski Villa during its short existence. The white, bristle-covered slope certainly made the area stand out among the surrounding rolling foothills, but that did not seem to aid in the area's success.

Five

Ski Clubs and the Far West Ski Association

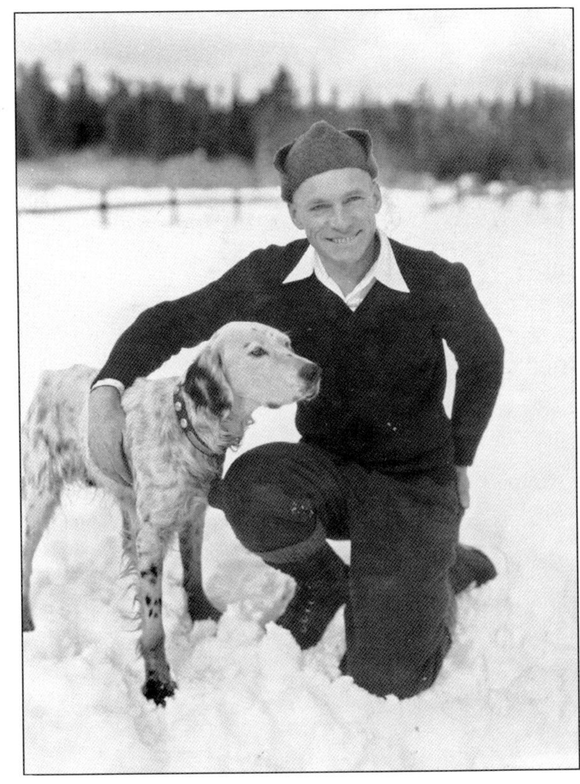

The Far West Ski Association, originally named the California Ski Association, was founded in October 1930. Wendell Robie, shown here, was the inaugural president. Robie, having already been involved with winter sports and the Auburn Ski Club in Northern California, knew that winter access and highway snow removal was critical to the growth of skiing in California. On January 18, 1931, only three months after the birth of the organization, 56 cars loaded with state politicians made their way from the state capital to the end of the narrow, snow-clogged road near Cisco. An additional 2,400 cars arrived with skiers and curious spectators, causing an epic traffic jam. The next day, $750,000 was allocated for equipment and snow removal, providing a huge boost to the development of skiing in California. (Courtesy Western Skisport Museum.)

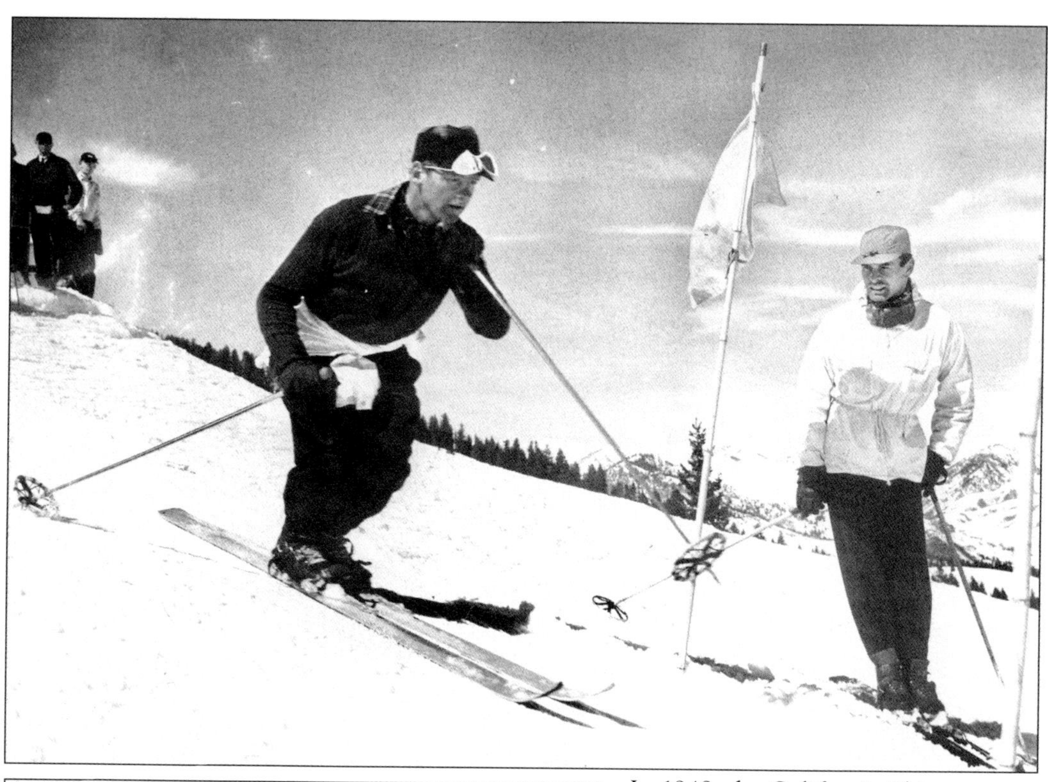

CALIFORNIA SKI ASSOCIATION

CERTIFIED SKI INSTRUCTORS

MEMBERS OF

California Ski Instructors Association

Name and Resort		Name and Resort	
Aro, Arvo Edvin	Soda Springs	Klein, Bill	Sugar Bowl
Brelsford, Robert	Soda Springs	Law, Bob	Mt. Rose
Brooks, Paul L.	Yosemite	Lint, Robert	Yosemite
Benedikter, Sepp	Wrightwood	Mabery, Slim	Soda Springs, Calif.
Brook, Herbert	Strawberry Lodge	Milici, Toni	McGee Creek
Burch, Arnold	Yosemite	Neely, James F.	June Lake
Clark, David	Yosemite	Olson, Marvin	Yosemite
Duncombe, Frank	Sugar Bowl	Steiner, Otto	Pinecrest
Georg, Hans	Mammoth Mountain	Trubschenk, Lorin	Yosemite
Illiff, Harry	Mt. Waterman	Tyndall, Thomas	Idyllwild
Johansen, John L.	Soda Springs	Krause, Otto	

KNOW THEM BY THEIR PIN

INSTRUCTOR

C. S. A.

In 1948, the California Ski Instructors Association held its first independent annual meeting. Thirty-four ski instructors met to discuss teaching techniques and to certify new instructors. Under the guidance of California Ski Association committee chairman Cortland T. Hill, annual instructors' meetings were held so that improvements in ski instruction could be made and uniformity could be maintained. Hill is shown above observing Sepp Benedikter. At left, an October 1947 advertisement shows that there were only 22 certified ski instructors in California that year.

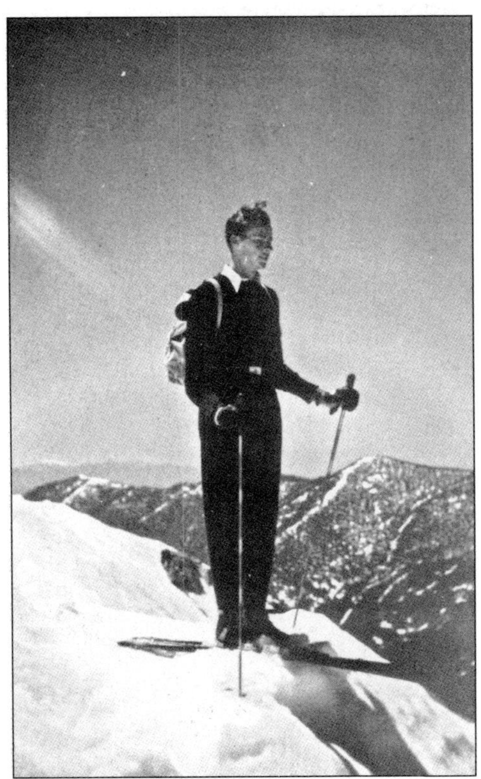

Chris Schwarzenbach, a longtime Pasadena resident, takes in the view from the summit of San Gorgonio in 1941. Below, he shows the racing form that led to his many first-place finishes. He was elected president of the California Ski Association in 1949 and served for one year. (Courtesy Chris Schwarzenbach.)

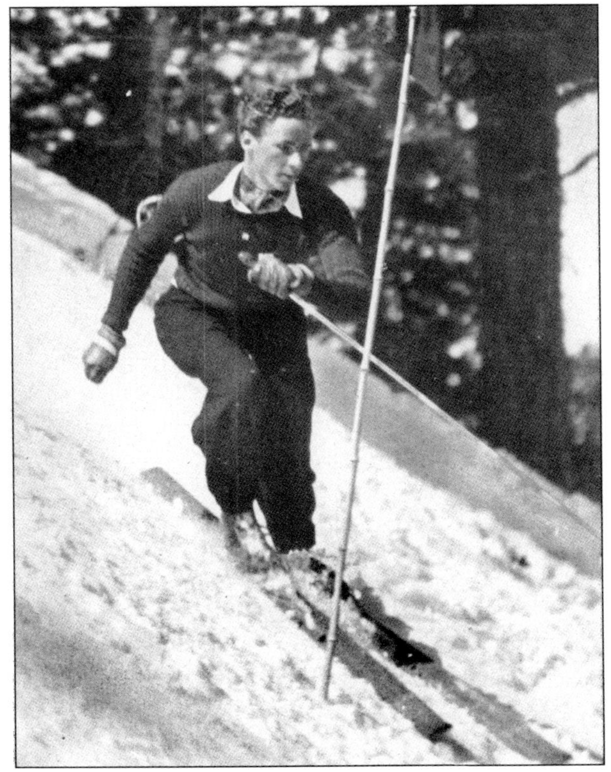

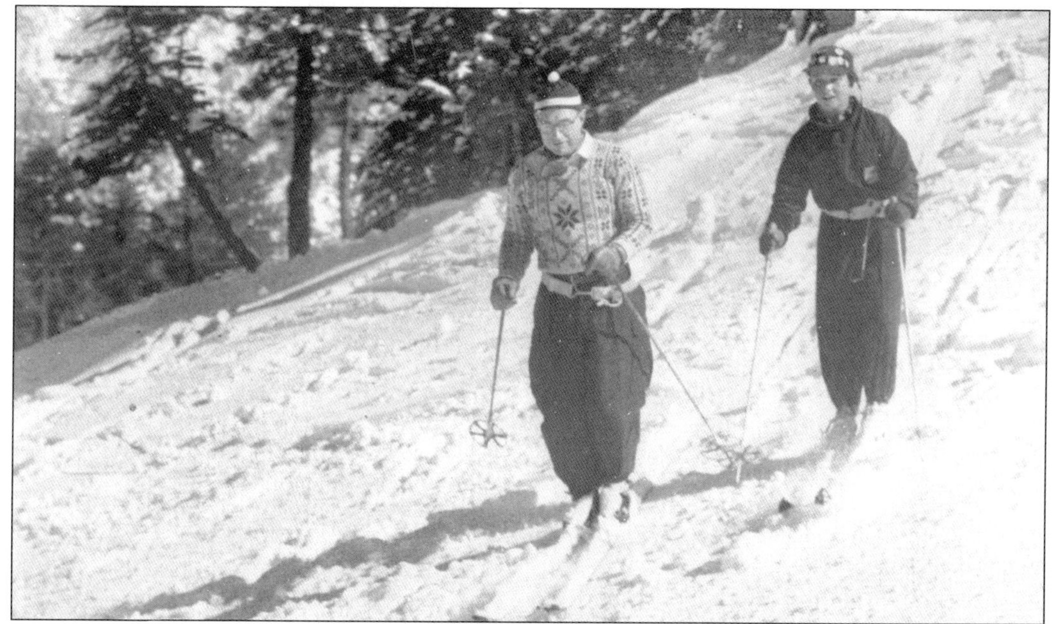

Frank Ferguson, shown here skiing with his son at Kratka Ridge, served as president of the Far West Ski Association from 1951 to 1952. He assumed the presidency when many of Southern California's ski areas had already installed their first chairlifts or were preparing to do so. It was also a time of ever-increasing interest in ski racing, with more than 1,100 classified cardholders in the organization.

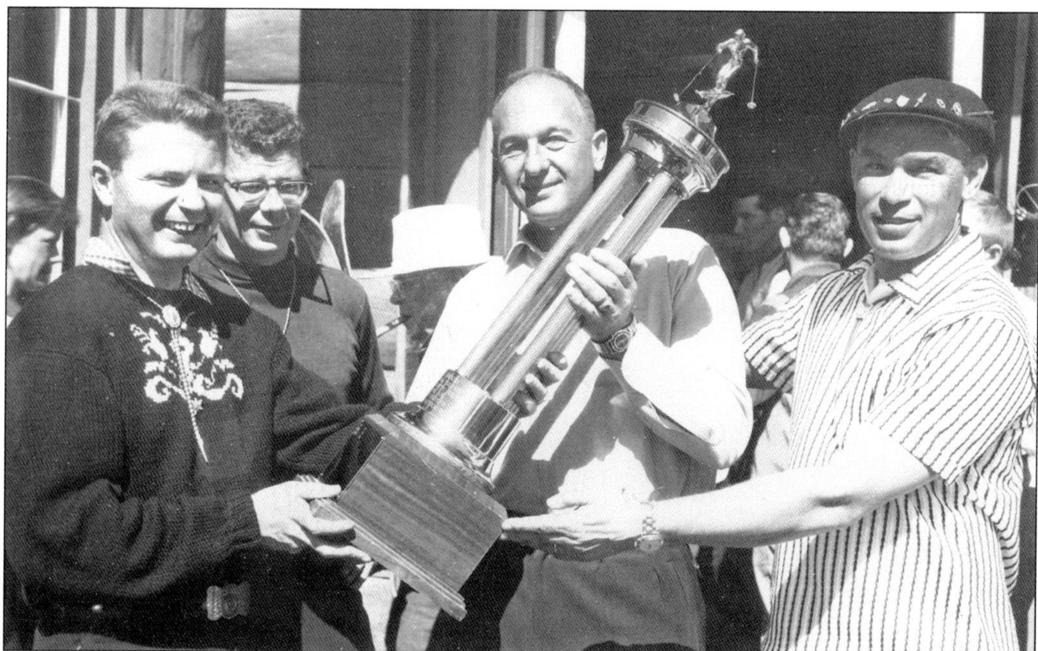

From left to right, Herb Blatt, Chris Coughlan, Byron Nishkian, and Carson White hoist the trophy for the North-South Race held annually in Yosemite. Nishkian served as president of the Far West Ski Association from 1959 to 1961. He also served as president of the United States Ski Association from 1965 to 1968. In 1976, he was elected to the United States Ski Hall of Fame.

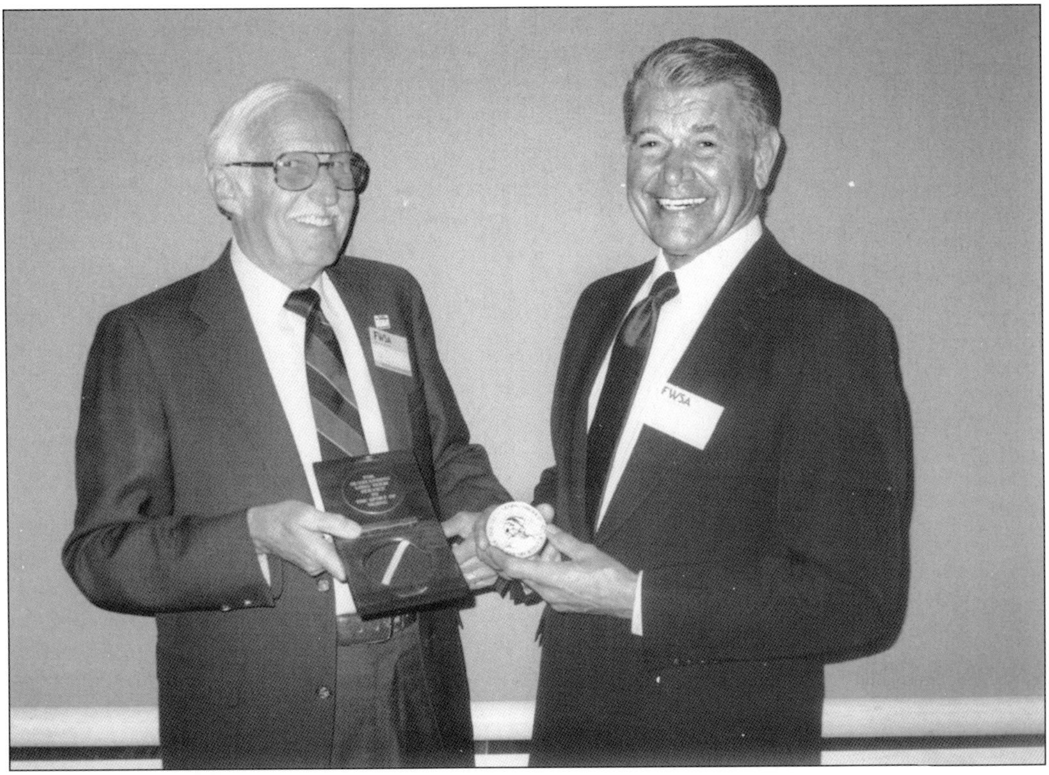

Sutter Kunkel (right) and Louis Buhler are pictured on the occasion of Kunkel's winning the Hans Georg Award, which is given by the Far West Ski Association to an individual who has made significant contributions to skiing. It is the organization's highest award. Sutter founded the Grindelwald Ski Club in 1949 and was president of the Far West Ski Association in the early 1960s. (Courtesy Joan Kunkel.)

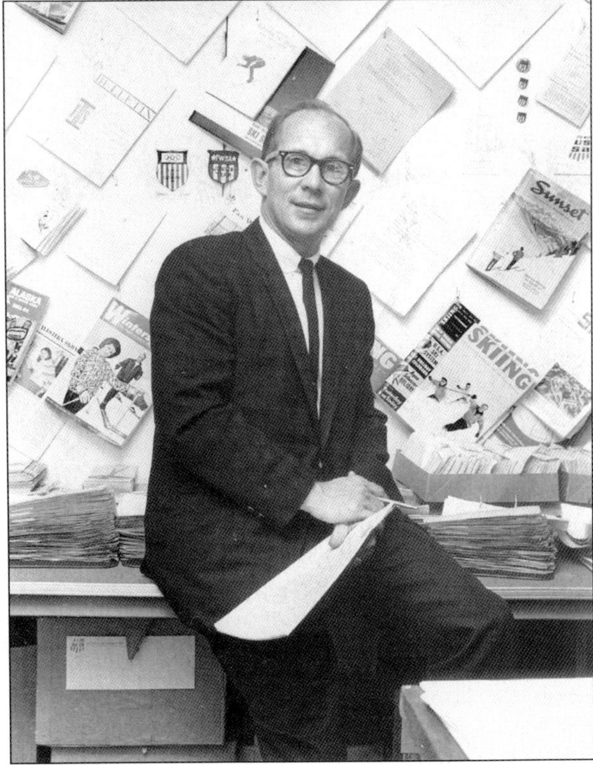

Leonard Speicher served as president of the Far West Ski Association from 1963 to 1966, one of the most turbulent eras in Southern California ski history. The association, as well as many ski-area operators, fought to develop San Gorgonio for skiing. The Far West Ski Association was pitted against the Sierra Club and other environmental organizations. Skiers still visit San Gorgonio, but they are the hardy few who are willing to climb uphill rather than ride.

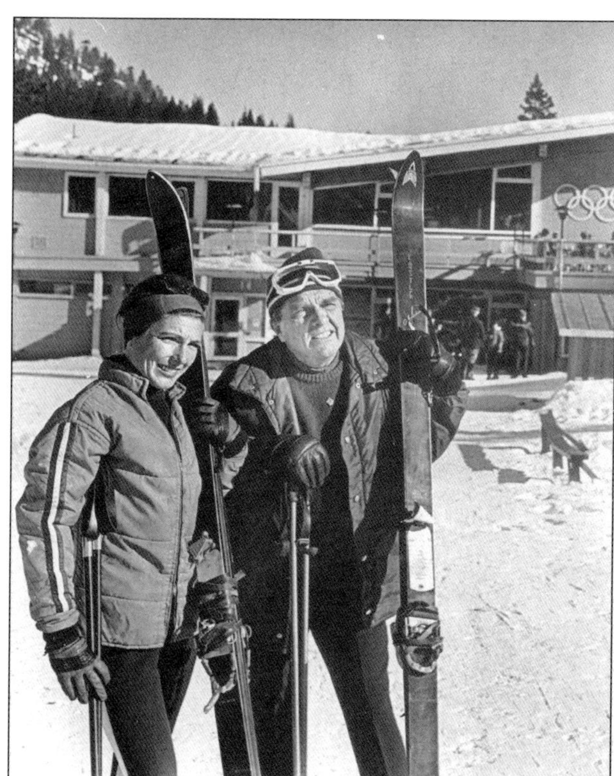

Stanley Walton, shown with his daughter Starr, served as president of the Far West Ski Association from 1966 to 1968. Under his tenure, ski instructors' proficiency tests were developed and adopted by all divisions of the United States Ski Association.

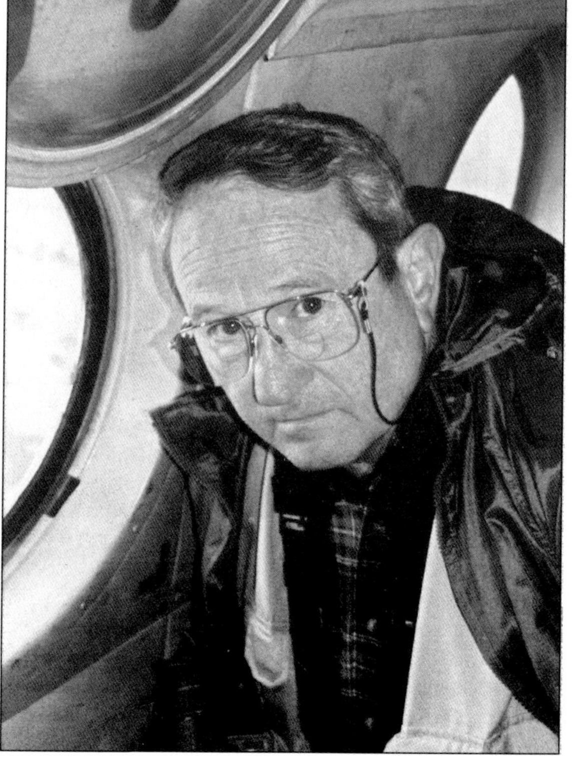

John Watson served as president of the Far West Ski Association from 1971 to 1973. He introduced a number of innovative recreation programs, saw the establishment of the *Far West News*, and increased paid memberships to the highest levels they had ever been. A major innovation under his tenure was the involvement of the ski club councils in the execution of the association's programs. (Courtesy John Watson.)

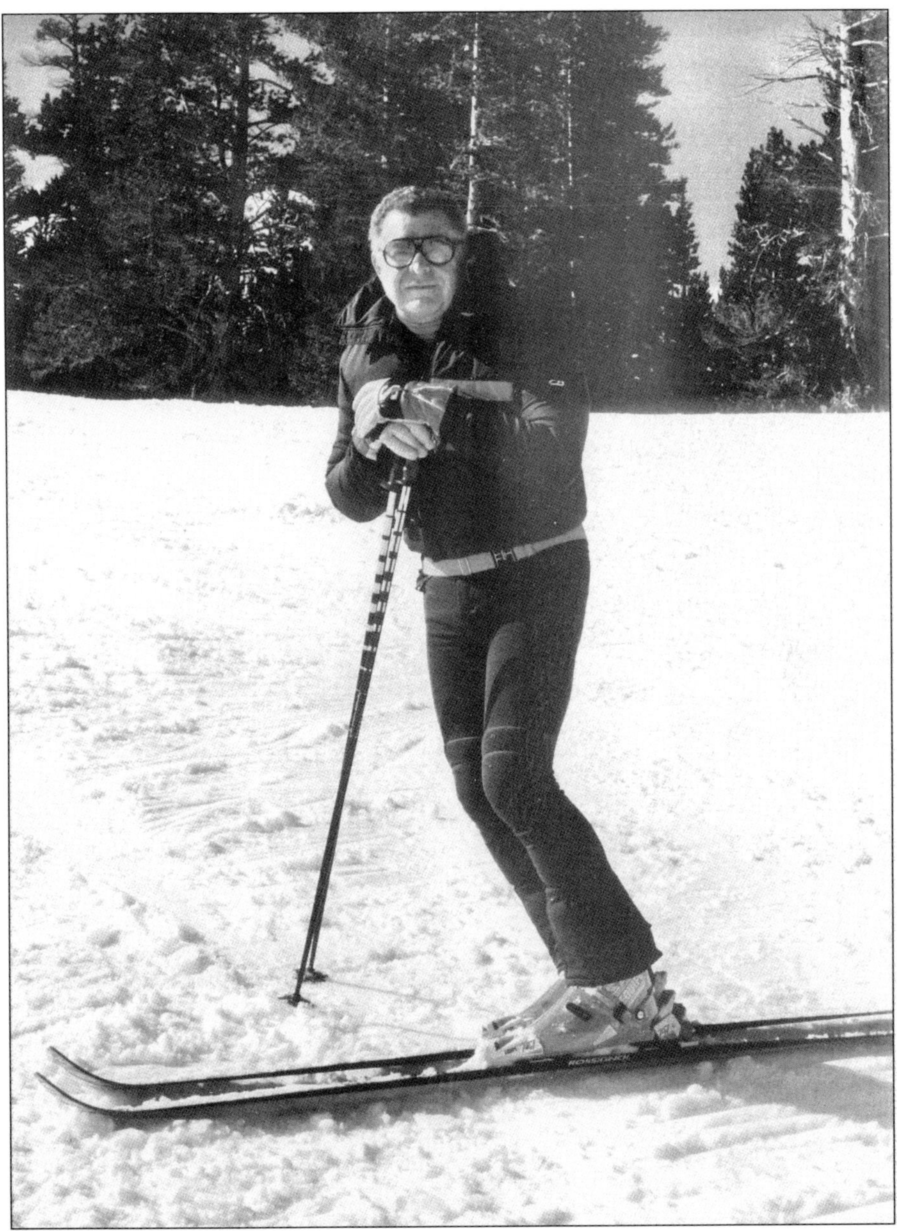

Chuck Morse has been involved in skiing for nearly 40 years. He has created, directed, developed, and coordinated numerous programs for western ski areas and ski organizations. The following are just a handful of his many contributions to skiing: he served as executive director for the Far West Ski Association; co-owned and directed the Mountain High Ski Area; created the first Far West Ski Association Learn to Ski and Race Week; cocreated the Mogul Mike Ski Safety program for the United States Ski Association; served as vice president of the Ski Area Operators of Southern California; coordinated area development projects for Mineral King, Sherwin Bowl, June Mountain, and Peppermint Mountain; served as general manager of Tahoe-Donner Resort; was the western managing director of sales and marketing for Vail Ski Area; and was vice president and director of marketing for Snowbird Ski Resort. The Far West Ski Association awarded Morse its highest honor, the Hans Georg Award, in 1979. (Courtesy Chuck Morse.)

DIRECTORS OF C.S.A. TO CONVENE AT YOSEMITE

Published By The California Ski Association

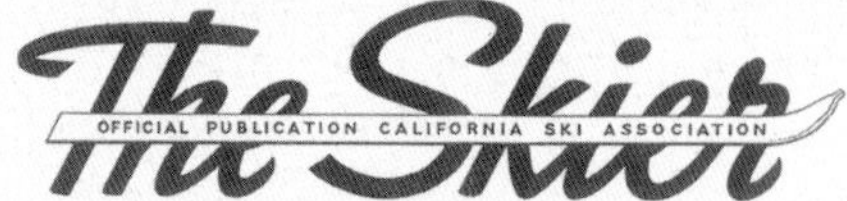

In The Interest Of The Sport Of Skiing

VOLUME I, NUMBER 7 | THURSDAY, OCTOBER 2, 1947 | ONE DOLLAR PER YEAR

Major Changes Proposed In By-Laws Of C.S.A.

Yosemite Winter Club Will Be Host To C.S.A. Delegates

The 1947 convention of the California Ski Asociation will be held at Yosemite National Park on Saturday and Sunday, October 11 and 12, 1947. The Yosemite Winter Club will be host to us at this convention.

Dues Must Be Paid

A member club, to be eligible to participate in the convention, shall have paid its 1947-1948 dues of $25.00 prior to the convention (see By-Laws, Sec. 2.6). If you have not already done so, see that your dues are paid to C. T. Hill, Treasurer, California Ski Association, 960 East 61st Street, Los Angeles 1, California.

Official Delegates To Be Reported

The names of official delegates and alternates (if any) shall be set forth on the enclosed registration form and forwarded to the Secretary as soon as possible,

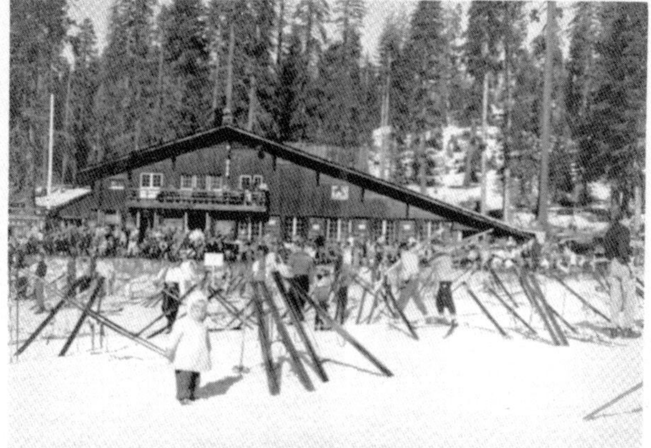

A typical Sunday afternoon at Badger Pass, Yosemite. Youngsters also enjoy the snow and sun at

Activities Of C.S.A. Convention To Be Held At Ahwahnee

All activities of the Convention will be held at the Ahwahnee Hotel. The following program will be followed:

Saturday, October 11:

9:30 A.M.—Registration of delegates and guests.

10:00 A.M.—1:00—First business meting.

1:00 P.M. — Special Skiers' Luncheon ($1.55, inc. tax).

2:15-5:00 P.M.—Second Business meeting.

6:30 P.M. — Yosemite Winter Club Cocktail Party for delegates and guests.

8:00 P.M.—Banquet (informal attire or ski togs—orchestra and plenty of folk dancing) ($3.56 including tax).

Sunday, October 12:

9:00 A.M.-12:00 M—Third business meeting.

12:00—Luncheon

The California Ski Association began publishing *The Skier* in January 1947. It provided skiers with the latest news of area developments and ski-race schedules, as well as updates regarding club activities.

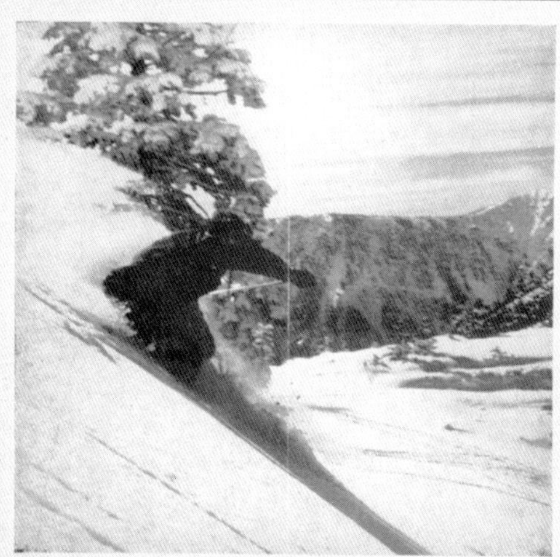

Big Pines Ski Club & Sepp Benedikter

PRESENT

FAR WEST SKI ASSOCIATION

Southern District Championships

Class B (Only) — Downhill & Slalom

COMBINED WITH

Sepp Benedikter Challenge Trophy Race

"Open" (FIS) — Class "A" — Class "B" — Downhill & Slalom

Feb. 19-20, 1949 - Big Pines, Calif.

One of the many significant achievements made by the Far West Ski Association was to provide greater publicity and organization for ski clubs and their races. The association assisted in coordinating club calendars so that important race dates did not conflict, and it publicized races throughout the state. The association also sanctioned district races and oversaw the California State Championship races and meets.

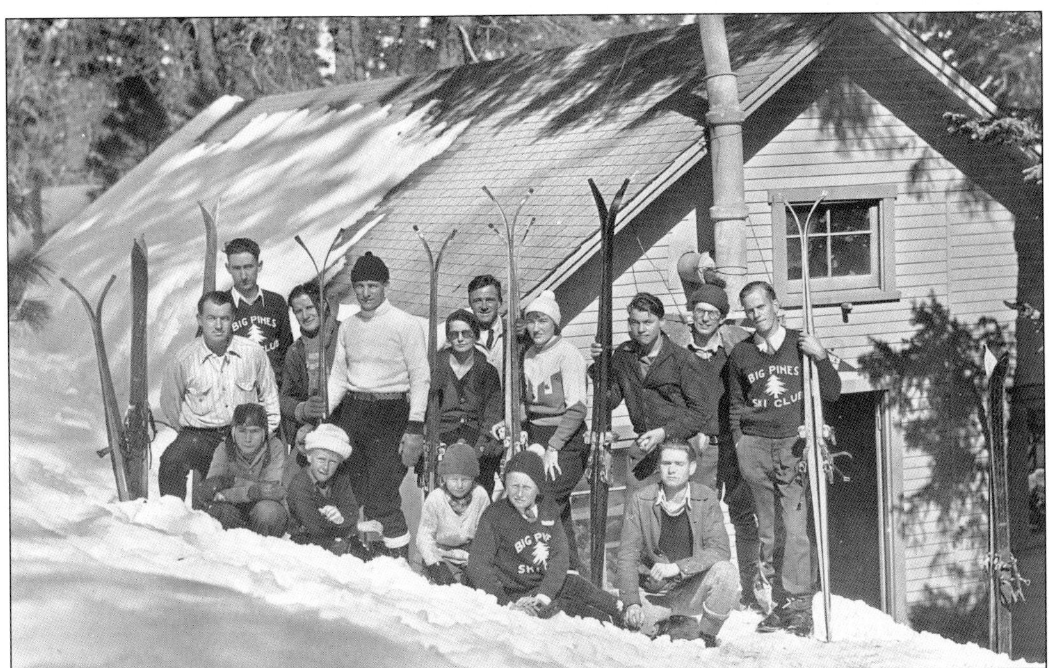

The first ski clubs in Southern California were established in the late 1920s, when skiing was just beginning to attract attention in the Southland. Those early skiers, as few in number as they were, sought the camaraderie and fellowship of other skiers. More than anything, they were simply happy to find someone else who skied or who was willing to try. A club often formed when a group of skiers met on the slopes, discovered they had similar interests, and skied as a group during following weeks. The Big Pines Ski Club, shown in these two photographs, was formed on January 2, 1932. It is one of the few clubs from the 1930s that is still in existence today. (Courtesy Ann Dormer Johnson.)

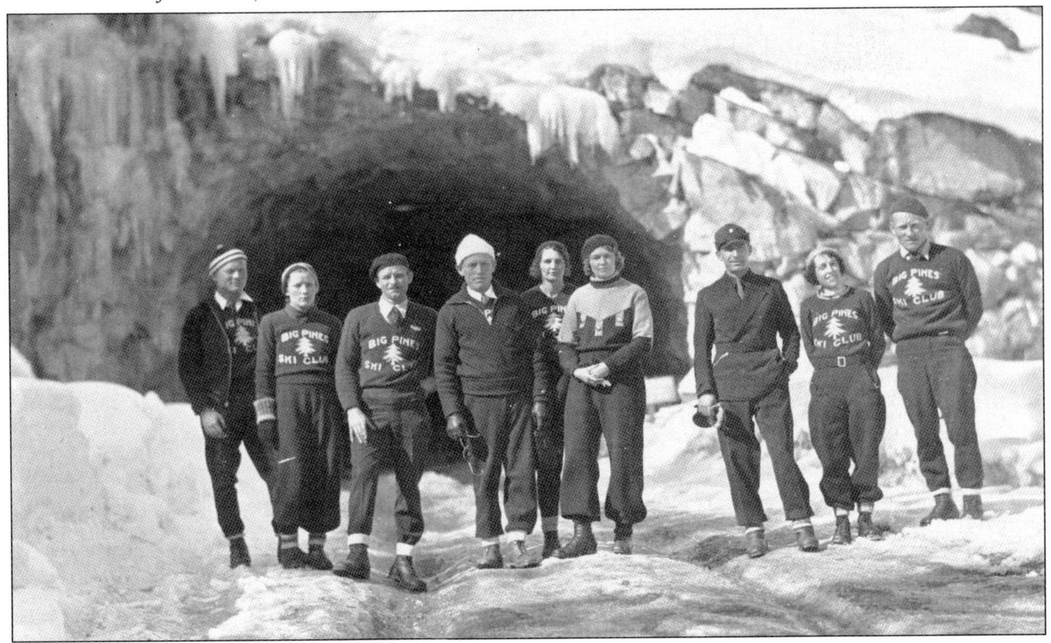

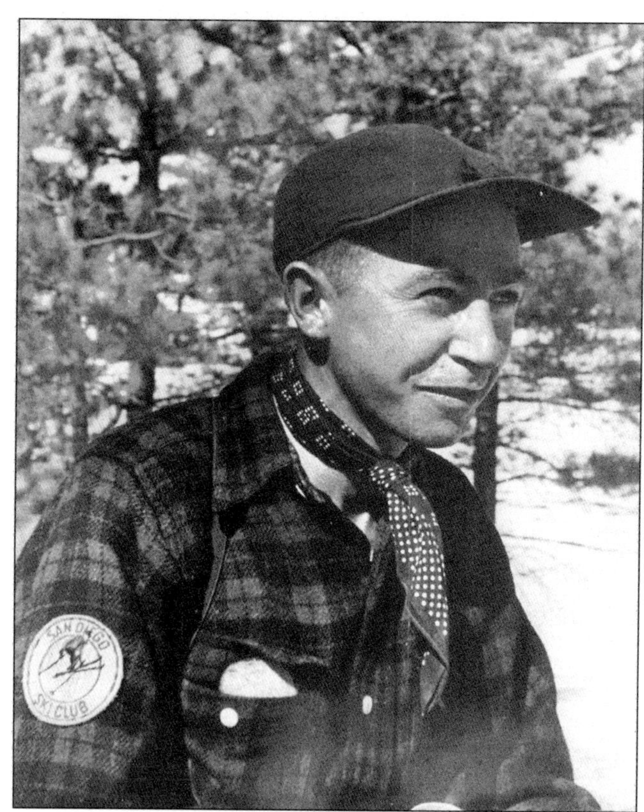

The San Diego Ski Club, founded in the fall of 1937, has the distinction of being the most southwesterly club in the United States. It began with 40 members, many of whom were accomplished skiers and ski patrol members. Art Wullich, shown sporting his San Diego Ski Club patch and racing in the San Antonio Downhill, was an active and prominent member of the club. (Courtesy Karen Wullich Herbst.)

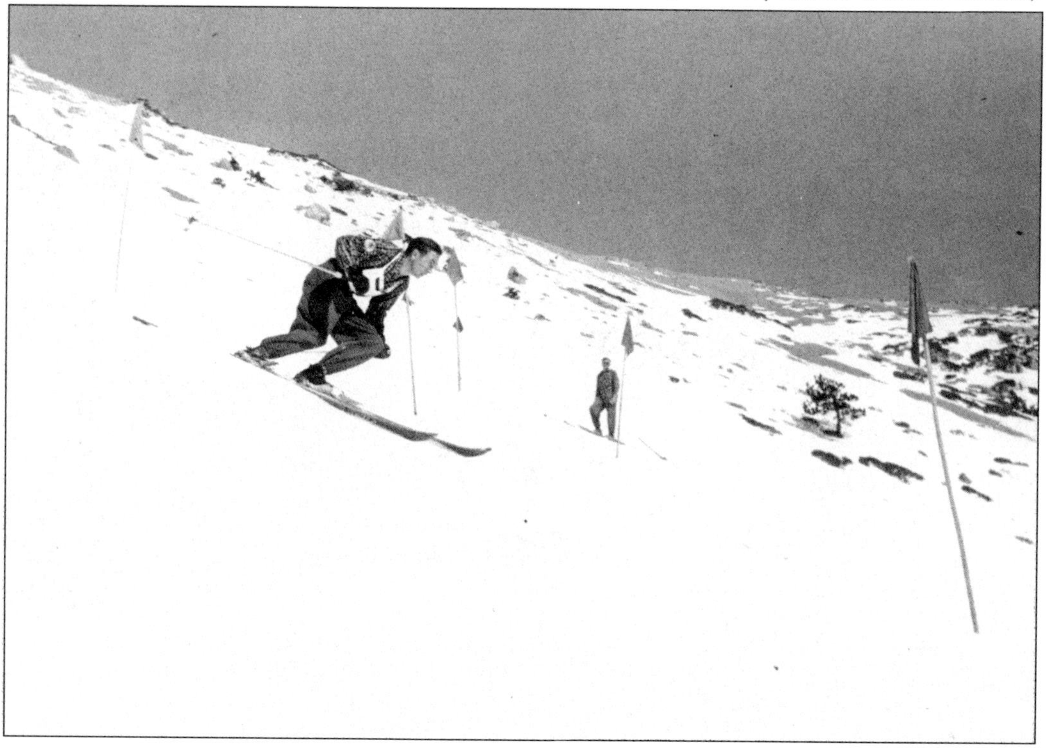

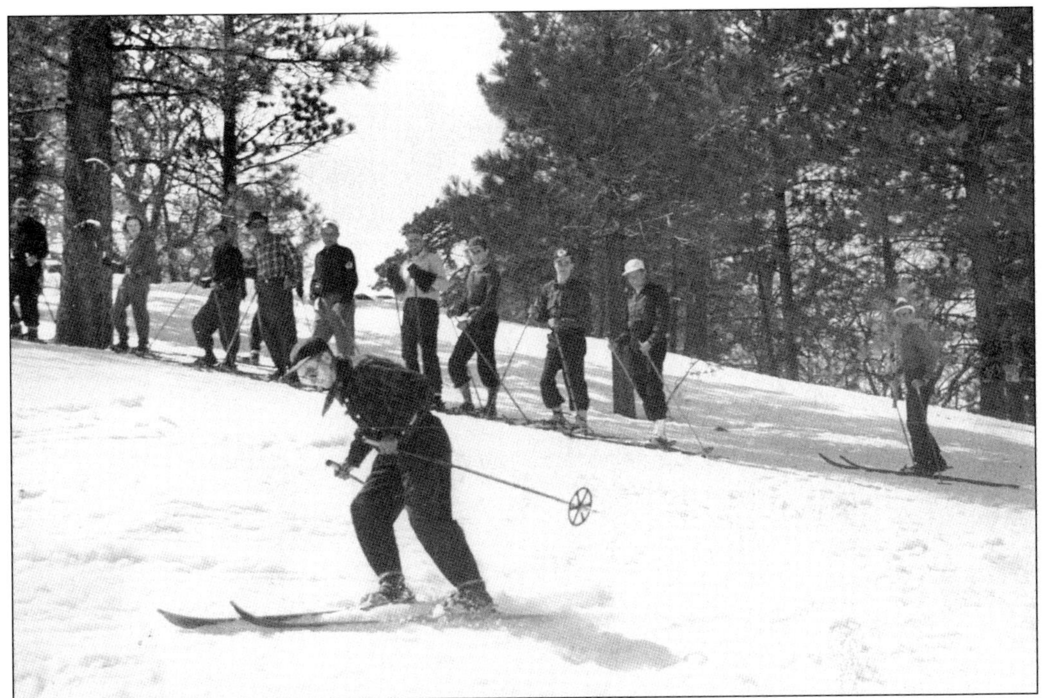

In 1939, the San Diego Ski Club realized two of its dreams: the formation of a ski school and the installation of a rope tow on the slopes of Cuyamaca. In the photograph above, Art Wullich instructs a group of San Diego Ski Club members on the finer points of making a stem turn. Below, Dorothy McClung, gripping the rope tow, is pulled upslope from the base of the new tow. The club also built a tow house and a shed for storing ski patrol equipment. (Courtesy Karen Wullich Herbst.)

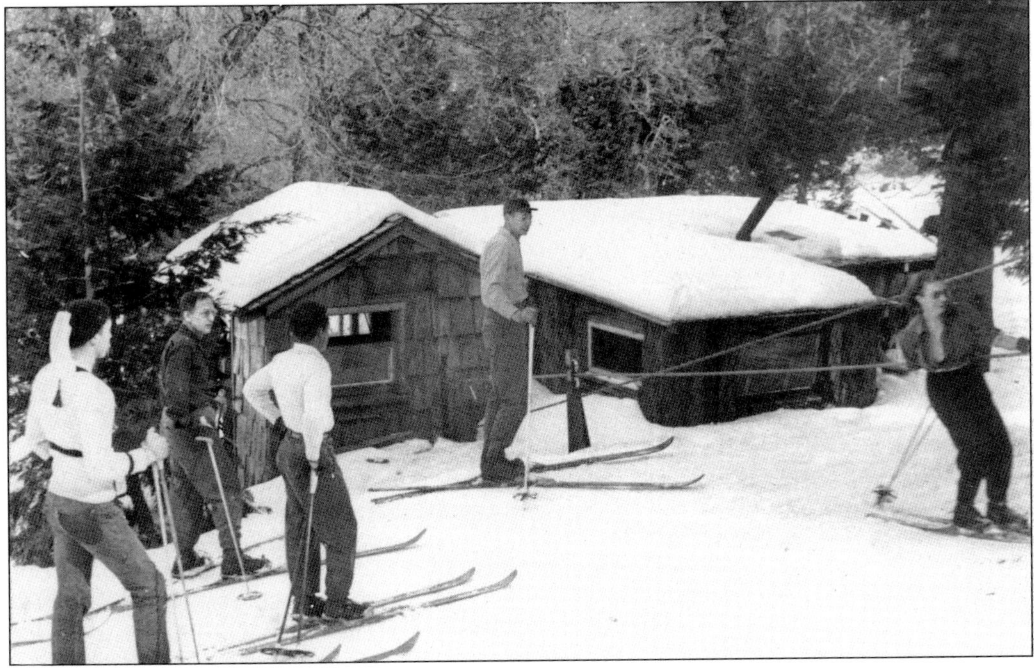

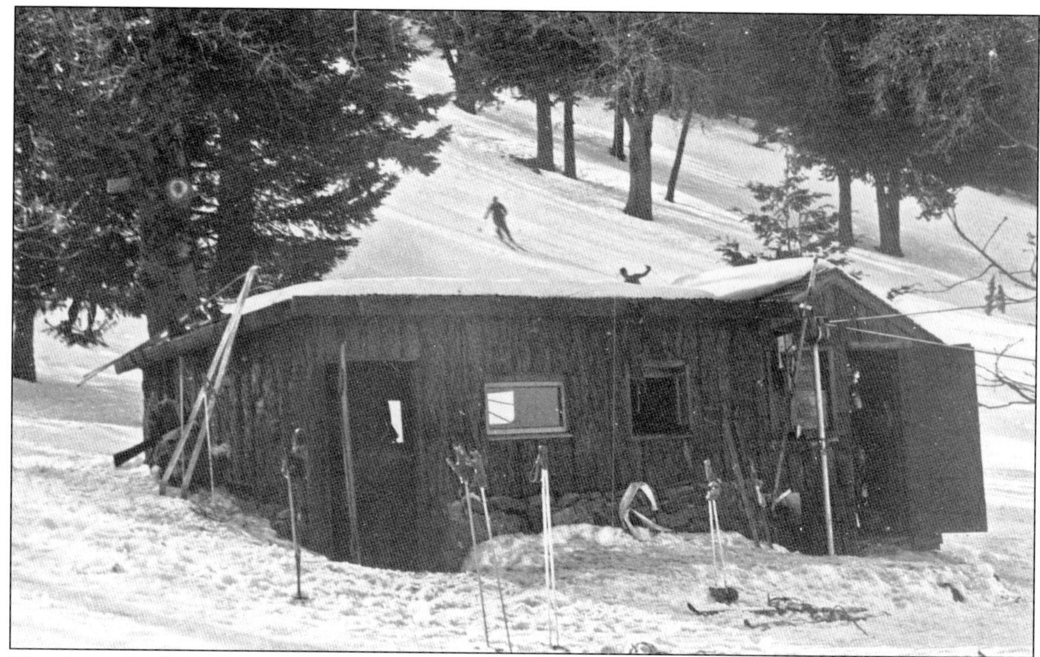

The State Park Commission of California gave the San Diego Ski Club permission to clear a portion of the slopes on Cuyamaca Peak for ski runs and facilities. Club members spent nine consecutive weekends clearing brush and other obstacles. Their hard work resulted in first-rate ski runs and club buildings, like the one shown here. (Courtesy Karen Wullich Herbst.)

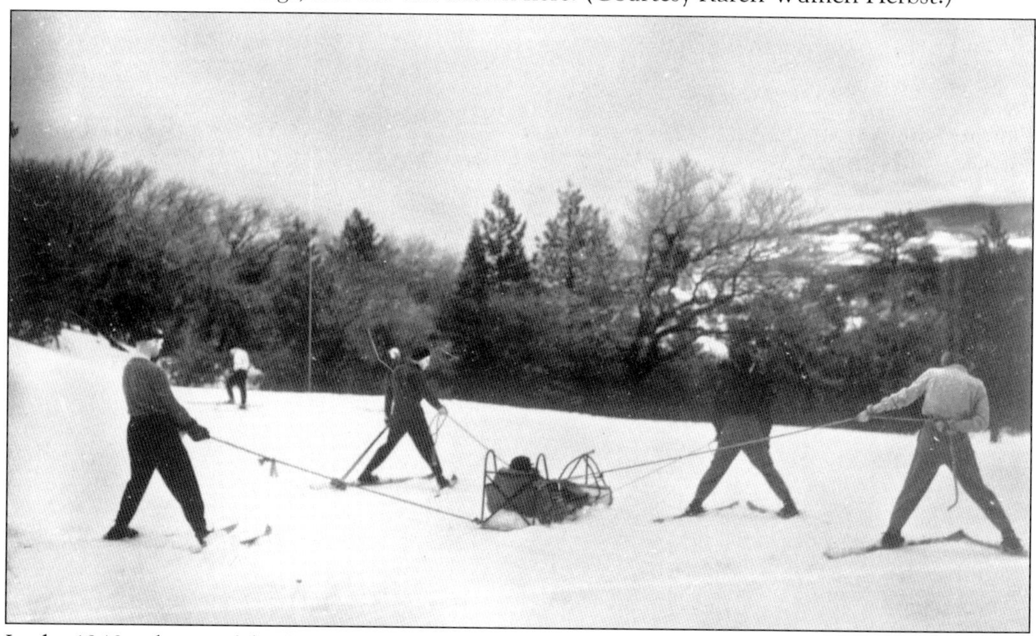

In the 1940s, eleven of the San Diego Ski Club's 60 members were proficient enough to be members of the San Diego or National Ski Patrols. They were Milton S. Jackson, Eugene Van Tibbetts, Gene Muehleisen, Arthur Wullich, George Prentice, Blake Vanderwater, Harry Poschman, Don Horner, Dorothy McClung, Joe C. Miller, and Bill Nelson. Some of them are shown here practicing their skills on Cuyamaca Peak. (Courtesy Karen Wullich Herbst.)

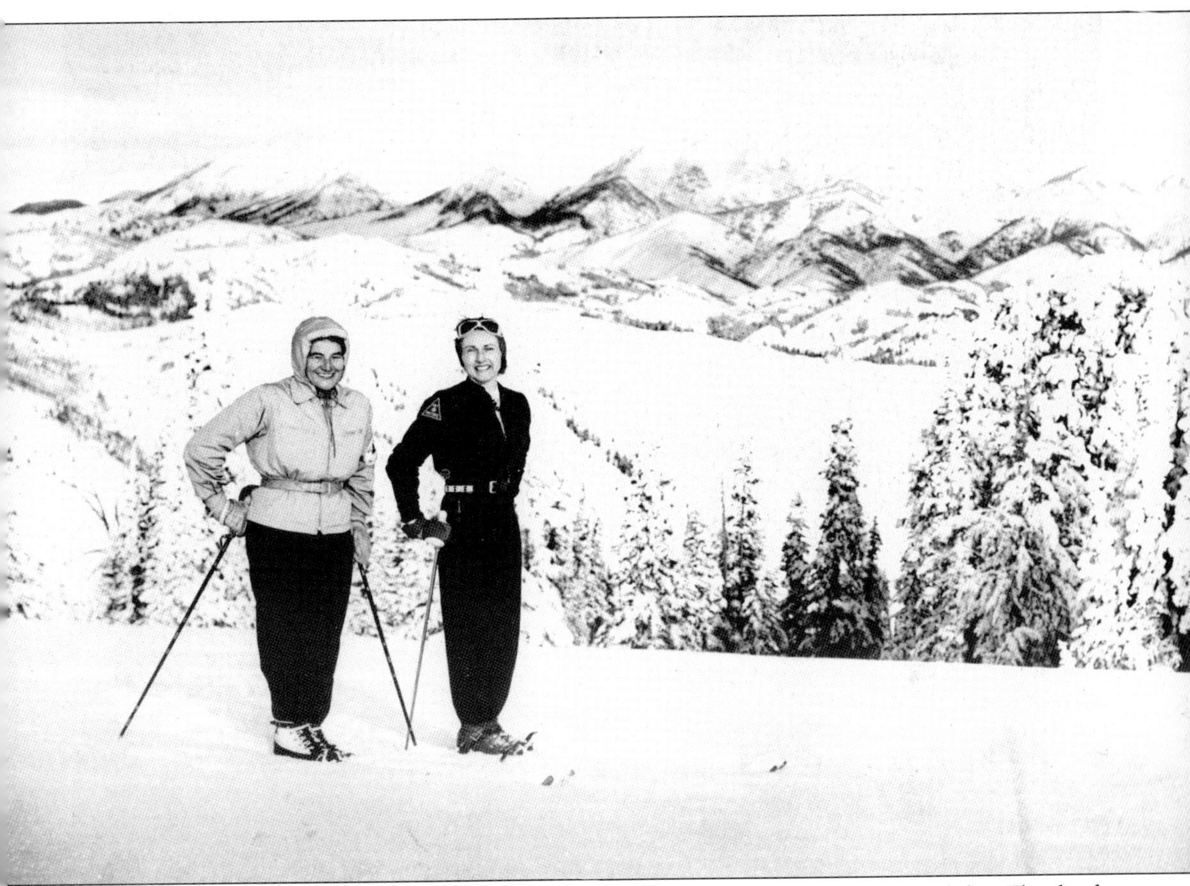

Pictured are two illustrious members of the Big Pines and San Diego Ski Clubs, Elizabeth "Schatzi" Wood (left) and Dorothy McClung Wullich. Both were known as physically strong, competent skiers who were able to hold their own among male skiers. On January 12, 1942, after only three years on skis, Wullich demonstrated the physical strength, first aid skills, and skiing expertise needed to win the honor of being named the first woman member of the National Ski Patrol. Wood, who became the 16th woman member, was made a section chief in 1950, taking responsibility for 27 patrol people at three ski areas in Big Pines. In 1951, Wood was given another well-deserved award, the Yellow Merit Star, for her work as an outstanding patrol person. (Courtesy Karen Wullich Herbst.)

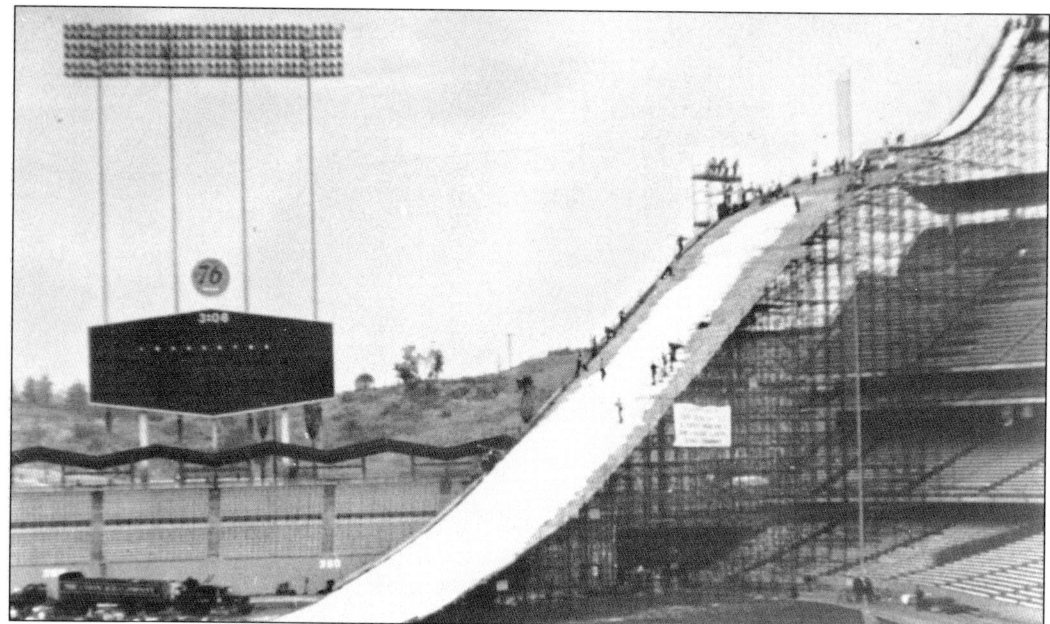

From October 25 to 27, 1963, the Grindelwald Ski Club held a ski jumping tournament at Dodger Stadium. The event was dubbed the Giant International Ski Show and Grindelwald Ski Swap. The 26-story jump was 680 feet long, making possible jumps of 190 feet. The event included a six-session jumping tournament, slalom racing exhibitions, and the annual Grindelwald Ski Swap. Sepp Benedikter, who had put on the 1951 county fair ski jumping meet, designed the jump. (Courtesy Joan Kunkel.)

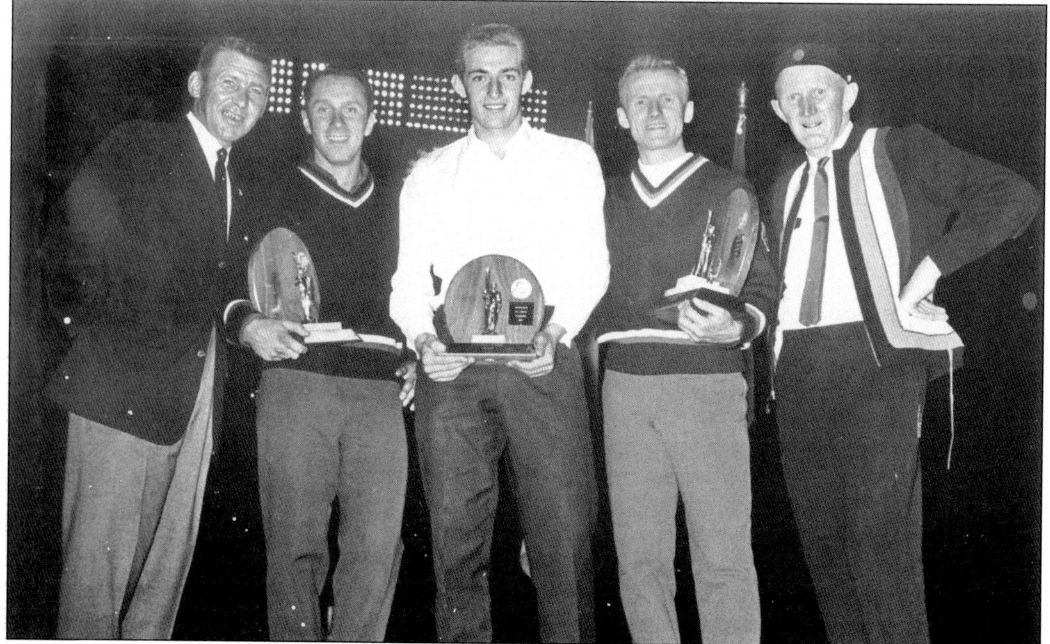

Pictured at the Dodger Stadium ski meet are, from left to right, Olympic Nordic coach Art Tokle, second-place finisher Steve Rieschl, third-place finisher Frithjof Prydz, first-place finisher Ansten Samuelstuen, and jump hill supervisor Gunnar Larssen.

Six

Skiing in the San Bernadinos

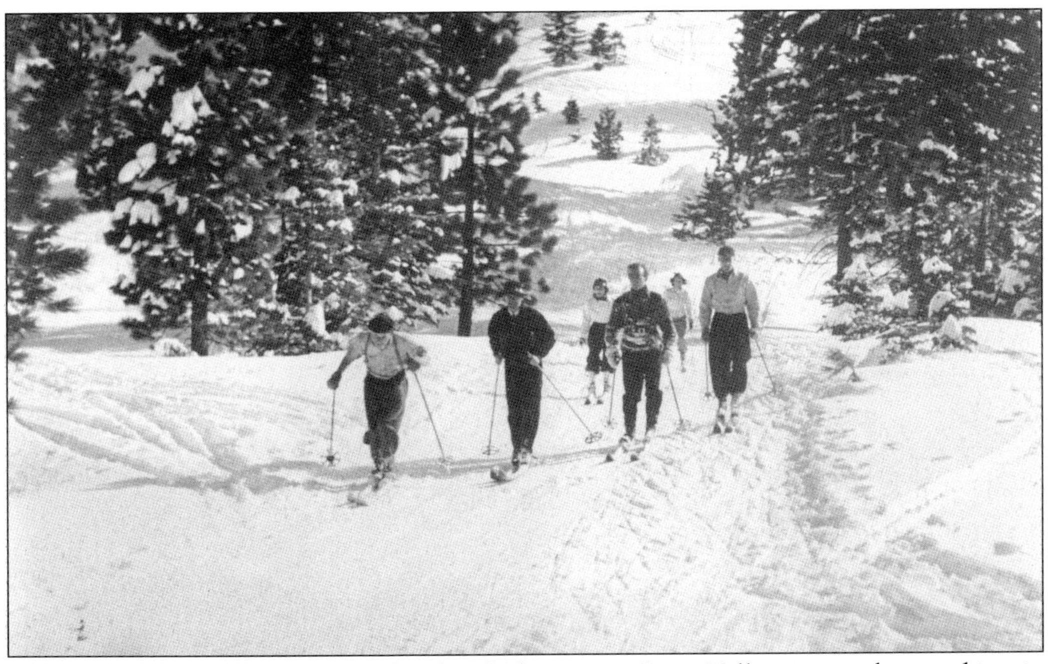

The hills surrounding Lake Arrowhead and what is now Snow Valley attracted many skiers in the 1930s, especially after the sling lift was built at Snow Valley during the 1935–1936 season. The Arrowhead Springs Corporation operated the area from 1939 to 1941. Otto Steiner managed the area, and John Elvrum taught skiing on the weekends. Steiner, second from left, is leading a group of skiers at Lake Arrowhead in the 1930s. David Niven is at the far right. (Courtesy Gina Merz McGloskey.)

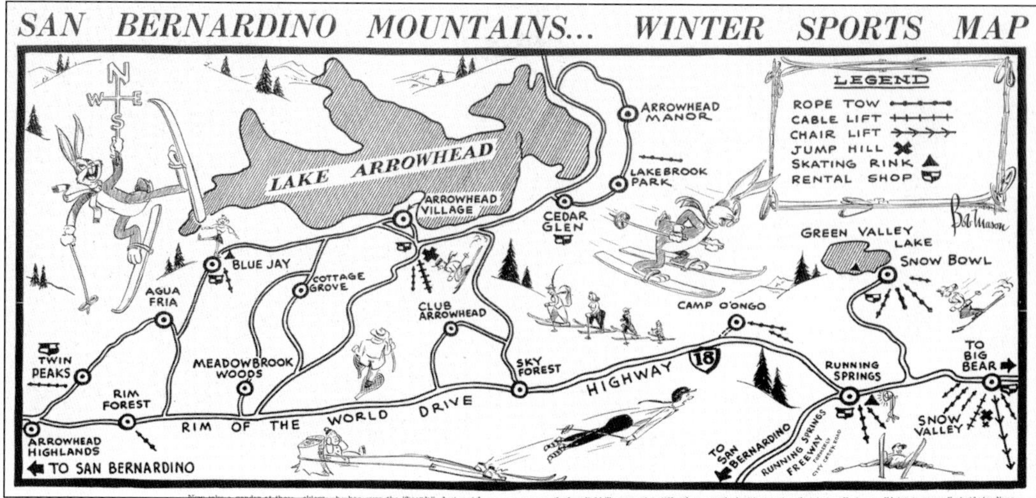

This winter sports map of the San Bernardino Mountains near Lake Arrowhead shows the long-forgotten tows that dotted the slopes throughout the area by the late 1940s.

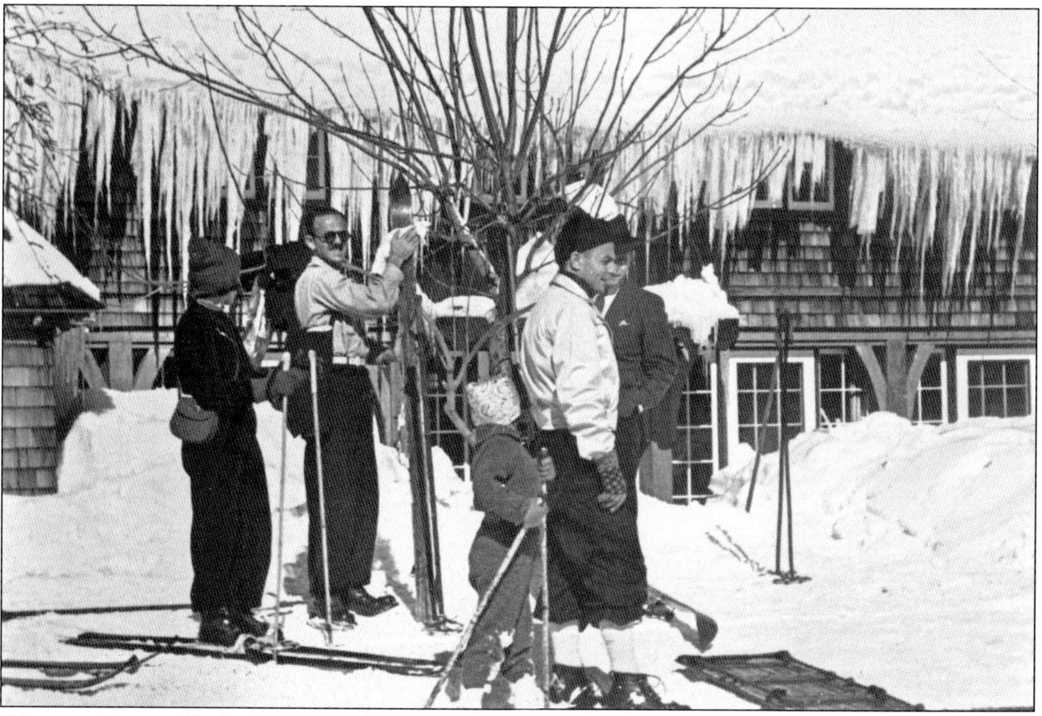

The popularity of Lake Arrowhead in the 1930s drew many Hollywood stars, as well as novice ski enthusiasts wanting to learn and practice the sport. Walter Mosauer, pictured here in sunglasses, frequented Lake Arrowhead and was a much-sought-after instructor and mentor. (Courtesy Gina Merz McGloskey.)

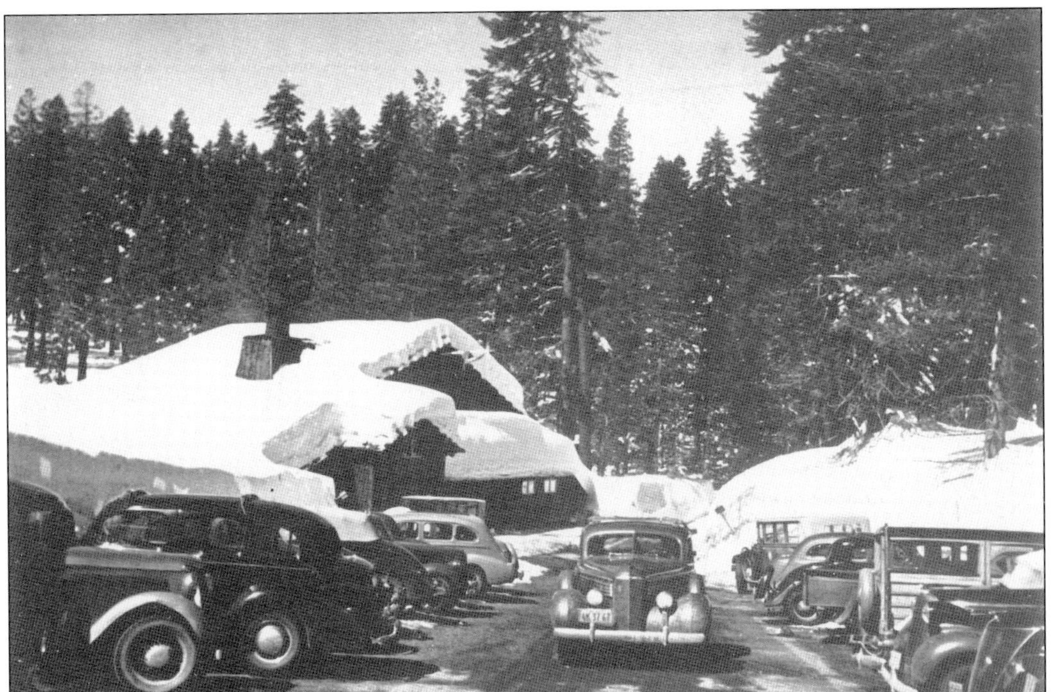

Once winter sports finally caught on in Southern California, Lake Arrowhead became one of the most popular locales for skiing. Crowds visited the area on a typical winter weekend. As winter sports became more popular, extensive preparations were made to accommodate winter visitors. Ice-skating rinks, ski runs, and toboggan slides were built, and winter carnivals became all the rage. (Courtesy Gina Merz McGloskey.)

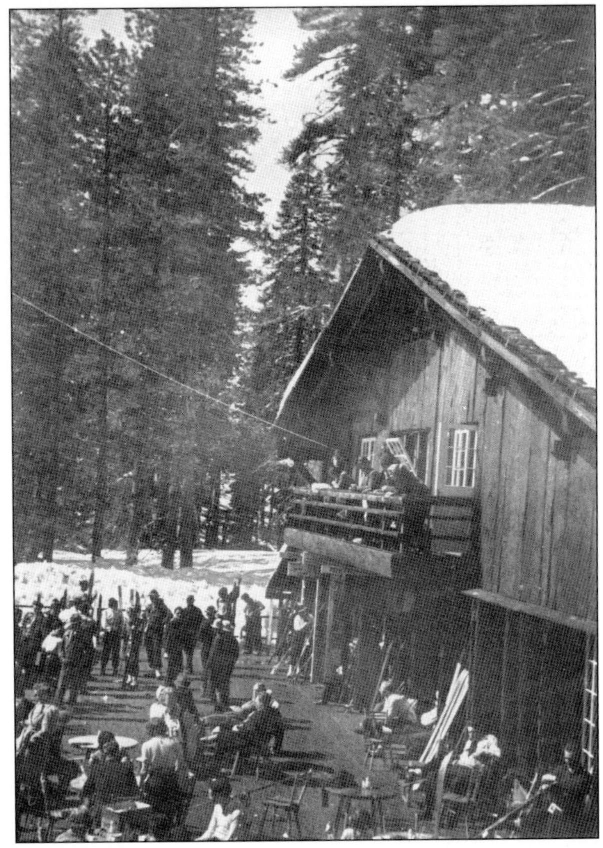

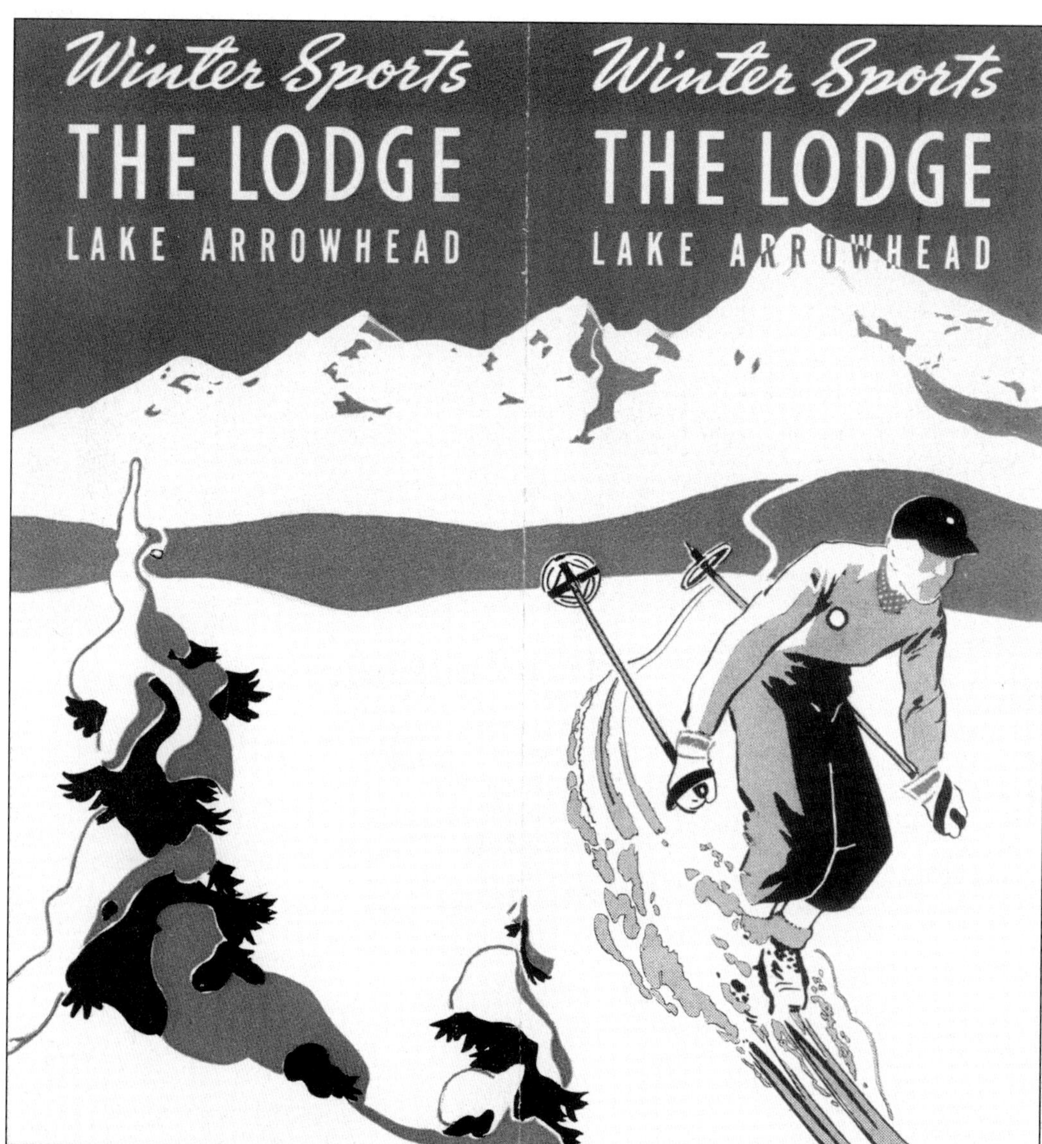

Described as being reminiscent of the Swiss Alps, mile-high Lake Arrowhead was the headquarters for the Ski Runners and the Lake Arrowhead Ski Club. Ethel Van Degrift, describing a typical weekend scene in the 1930s, wrote, "The Snow Valley clubhouses of the Ski Runners, the Ski Mountaineers of the Sierra Club, the Snow Valley Ski Club, and Sverre Engen's Ski Shack all blazed with lights at night, rocked with laughter, reeked of ski wax, and reverberated with argument."

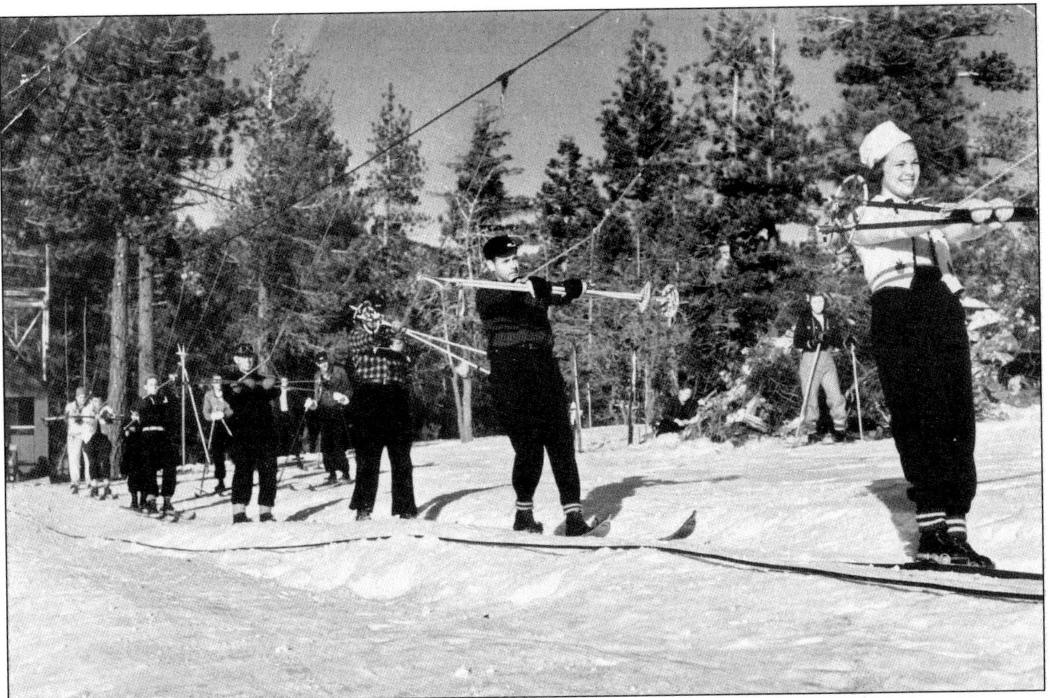

The Big Bear sling lift, built in 1938, carried a series of slings with triangular grips that hung from a cable suspended about 10 feet off the ground. The jig-back sling ran without a hitch for 15 years, giving some of Southern California's earliest skiers, who were used to spending much time and energy skiing uphill, a less strenuous and faster trip up, even though it only had an hourly capacity of 200 skiers.

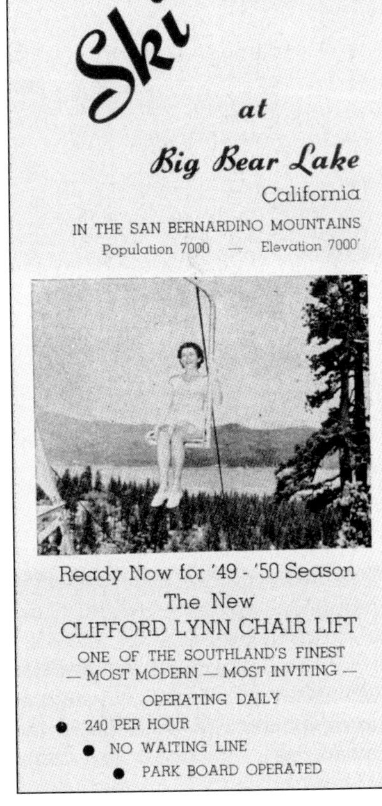

Shown is the original brochure promoting Big Bear Lake's first chairlift. The Lynn Lift was named for Judge Clifford Lynn, who was responsible for its development and completion. It began operating on September 24, 1949.

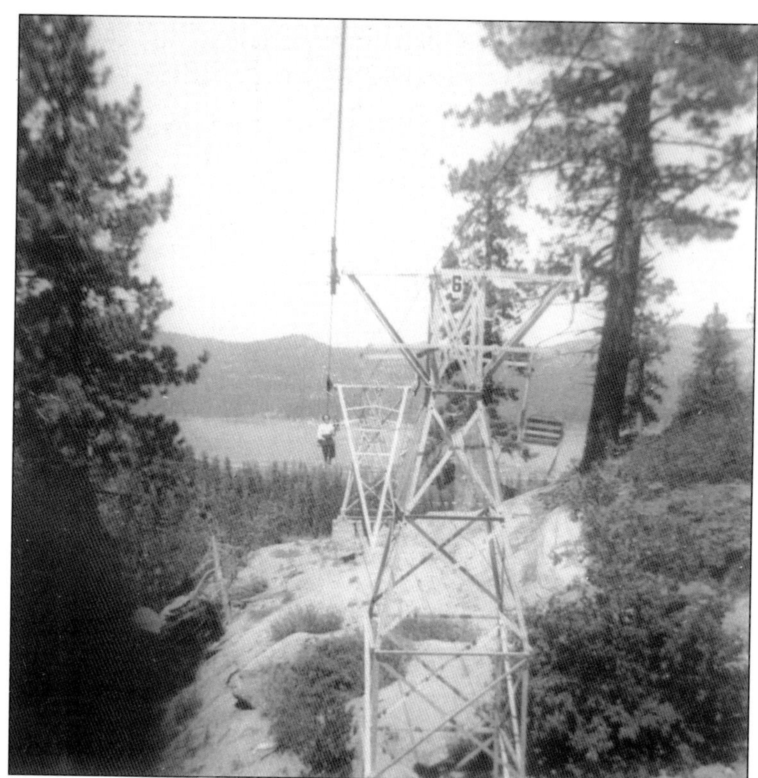

The Lynn Lift was a welcome improvement over the rope tows and sling lifts that skiers were accustomed to. The easier and more comfortable ride of the chairlift led to long lines on busy weekends. Built at the south end of Pine Knot Boulevard in Big Bear Lake Village, it was one of fewer than 10 chairlifts in the nation.

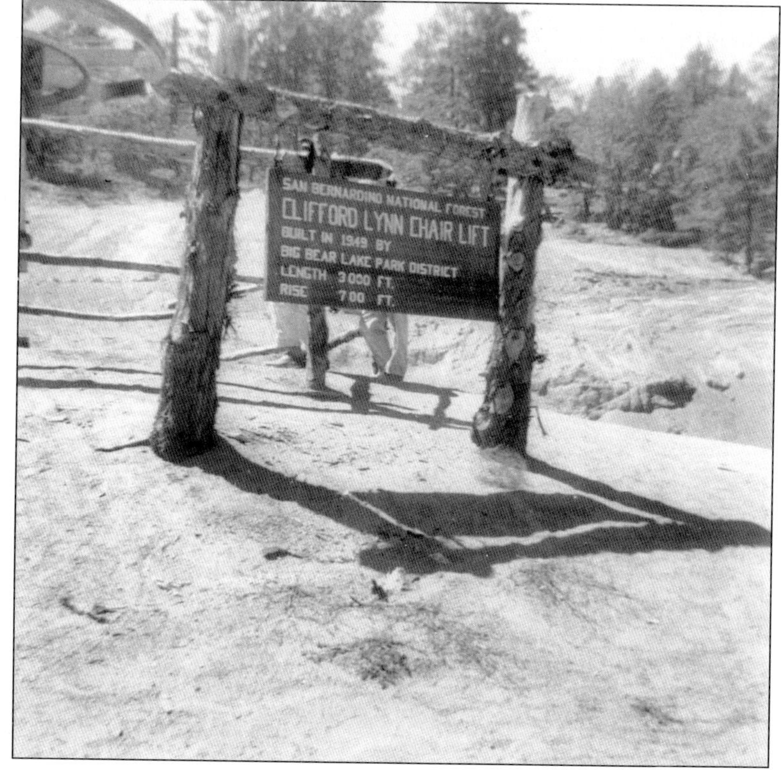

San Bernardino County owned and operated the Lynn Lift until the area was sold to Dave and Dan Platus in 1963. The brothers renamed the area Snow Forest. Tommi Tyndall once commented that the lift was "one of the finest little lifts in the west," but by the mid-1970s, it was idle due to its age and limited capacity. The lift was dismantled during the 1980–1981 season.

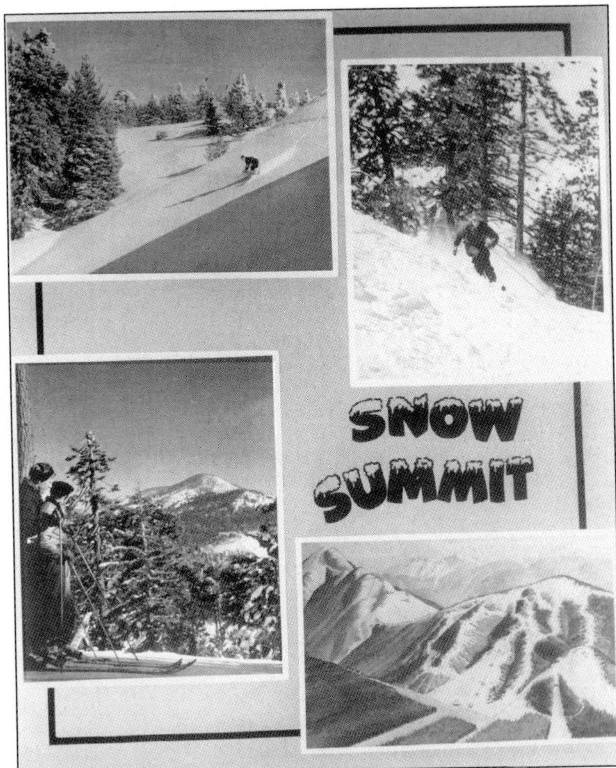

Not long after arriving in Big Bear in 1947, Tommi Tyndall established ski schools at the sling lift and the Lynn Lift, later consolidating them under the name Mill Creek Ski Schools. He also operated ski schools at Mill Creek, Moonridge, the Sugar Loaf area, and the Swiss Ski Tow. The limited potential for growth at the Lynn Lift and the increasing number of skiers gave him the impetus to develop his own area. Snow Summit was born in January 1953, featuring what was then the highest chairlift in Southern California. Tyndall was Big Bear Lake's most vocal and enthusiastic advocate of winter sports. He was a promoter, instructor, and ski-area developer, and he had the greatest impact on the growth of skiing in the Big Bear area during the formative years. In 1963, he installed the largest snowmaking system in the West. Sadly, Tyndall was killed in 1964 in a tractor accident at the area. After his death, his wife, Jo, managed the area until her death in 1980. (Courtesy Snow Summit.)

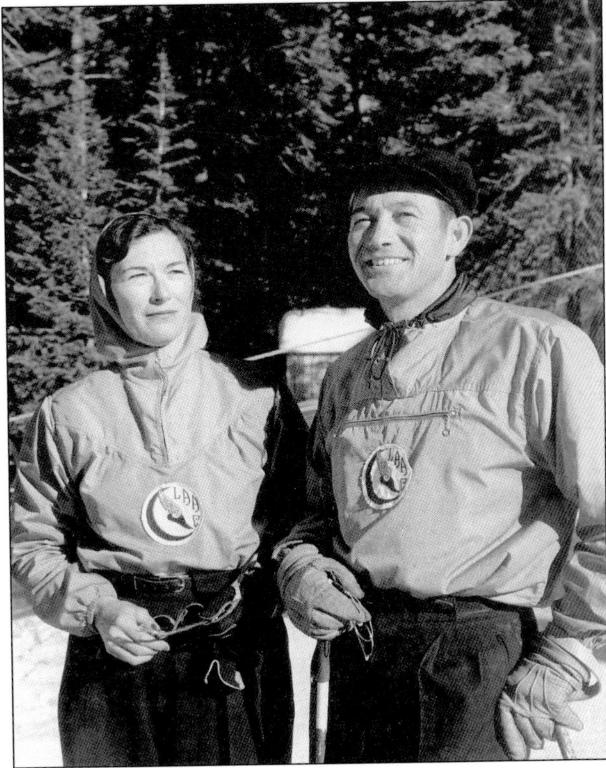

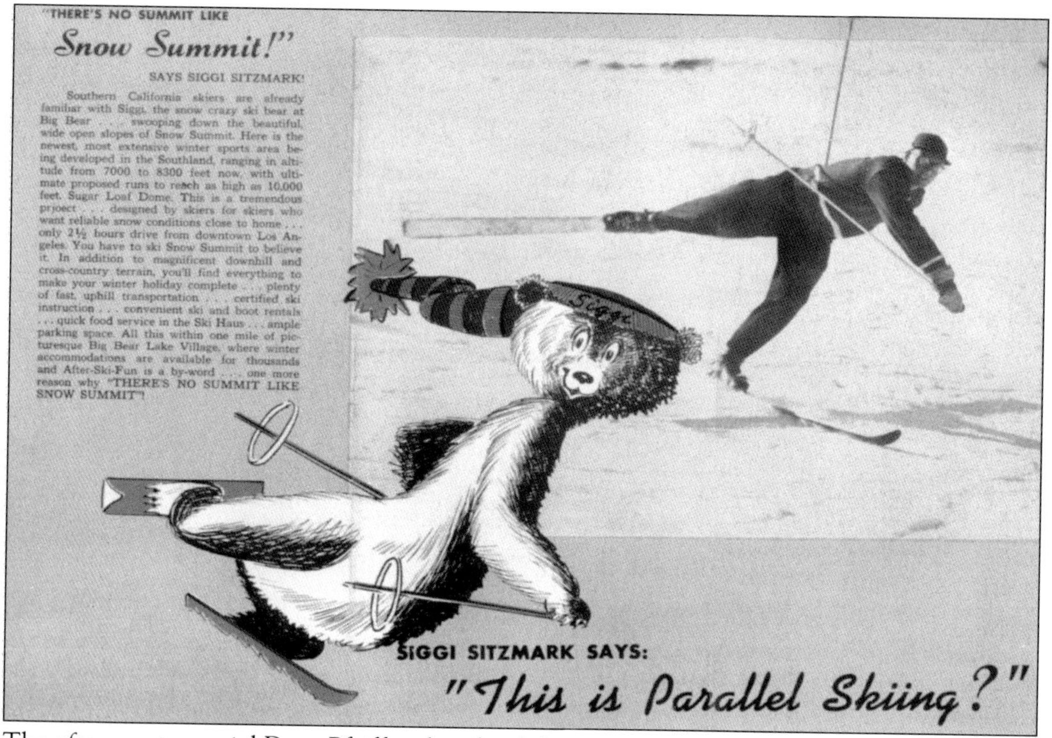

"THERE'S NO SUMMIT LIKE

Snow Summit!"

SAYS SIGGI SITZMARK!

Southern California skiers are already familiar with Siggi, the snow crazy ski bear at Big Bear . . . swooping down the beautiful, wide open slopes of Snow Summit. Here is the newest, most extensive winter sports area being developed in the Southland, ranging in altitude from 7000 to 8300 feet now, with ultimate proposed runs to reach as high as 10,000 feet, Sugar Loaf Dome. This is a tremendous prjoect . . . designed by skiers for skiers who want reliable snow conditions close to home . . . only 2½ hours drive from downtown Los Angeles. You have to ski Snow Summit to believe it. In addition to magnificent downhill and cross-country terrain, you'll find everything to make your winter holiday complete . . . plenty of fast, uphill transportation . . . certified ski instruction . . . convenient ski and boot rentals . . . quick food service in the Ski Haus . . . ample parking space. All this within one mile of picturesque Big Bear Lake Village, where winter accommodations are available for thousands and After-Ski-Fun is a by-word . . . one more reason why "THERE'S NO SUMMIT LIKE SNOW SUMMIT"!

Siggi

SIGGI SITZMARK SAYS:

"This is Parallel Skiing?"

The often-controversial Doug Pfeiffer, ski-school director at Snow Summit, loved to poke fun at the dogma of ski teachers by doing this Reuel (pronounced Royal) Christie and commenting, "Oh, yeah. It's very important to always keep your weight on the outside ski." Pfeiffer's fun-loving antics led him to create and promote the concept of freestyle skiing competitions, which eventually became an Olympic Winter Games event.

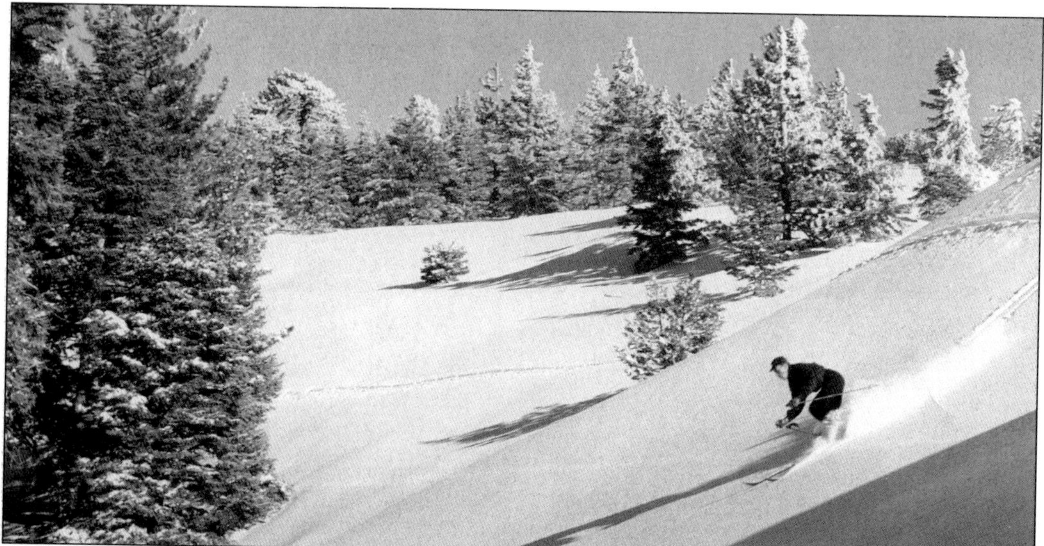

This skier is enjoying a fresh-powder day on some untracked slopes at Snow Summit. When Tyndall decided that he wanted to open his own area, he began exploring the slopes east of Big Bear Village. He decided upon a location that would become one of Southern California's most popular ski areas.

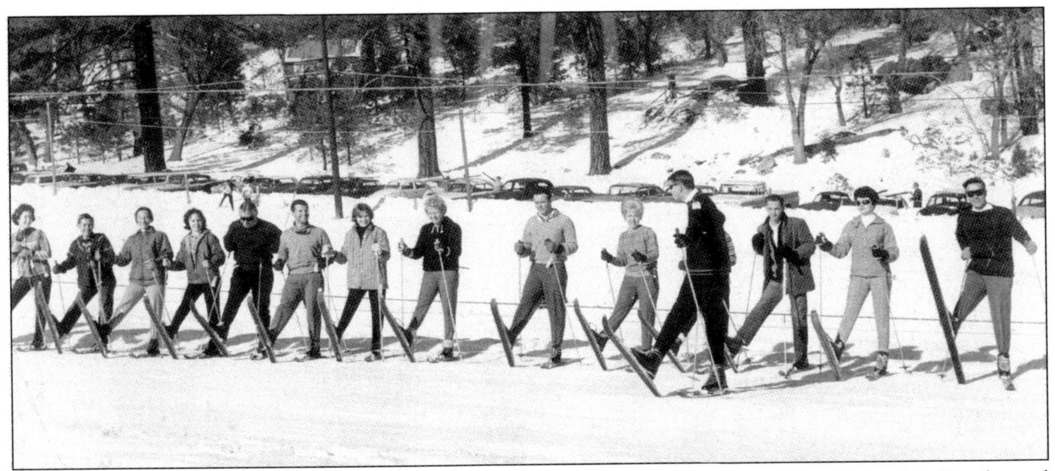

Moonridge was one of the first Southern California areas to offer ski instruction in the Graduated Length Method. The short skis, as seen on this class, were popular with students. Novices learned to ski in less time than with traditional methods, inspiring most ski schools to adopt this method of instruction. (Courtesy Elmar Baxter.)

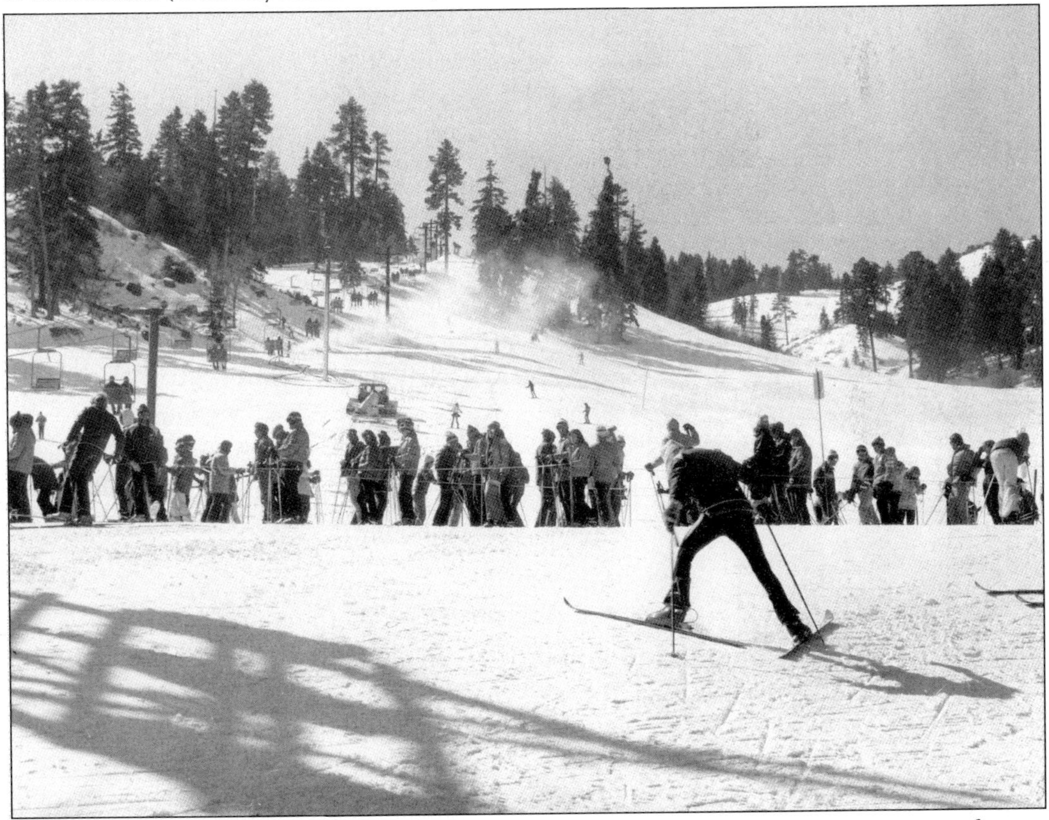

Moonridge, which began with a couple of rope tows in 1943, has undergone a series of name changes over the years. In 1970, it was renamed Goldmine by new owners Bill Strickland and Fred Goldsmith. They installed the area's first chairlift in 1971. In 1988, the area was renamed Bear Mountain, then Big Bear Mountain, and it continues by that name today. (Courtesy Elmar Baxter.)

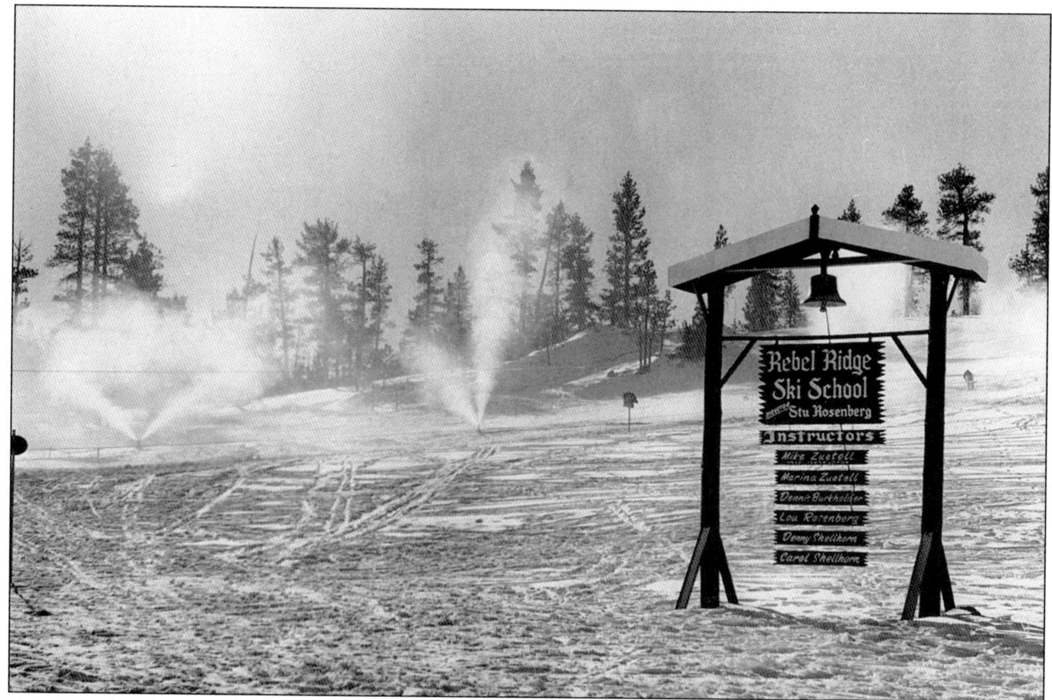

Rebel Ridge, founded by Chuck Smith in 1953, was the first California ski area to have a successful snowmaking operation. Smith was a trailblazer, and other ski-area operators began to take notice. They realized that snowmaking could be the answer to Southern California's fickle weather and could increase the length of a sometimes very short ski season. (Courtesy Snow Summit.)

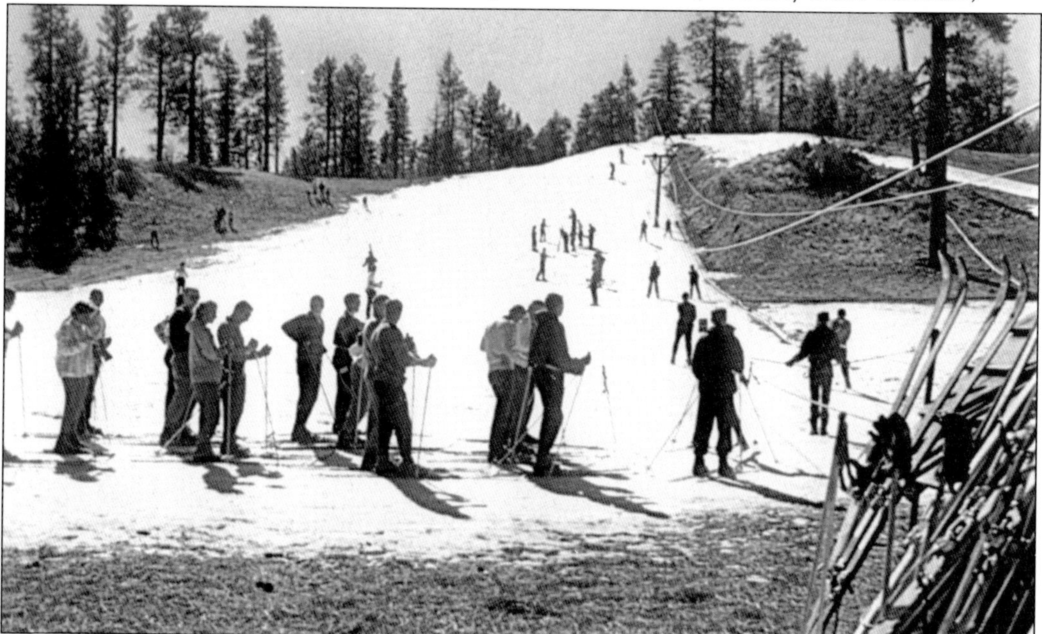

Smith began experimenting with snowmaking as early as 1955. On New Year's weekend in 1961, Rebel Ridge was the only ski area west of the Mississippi open for business. These skiers would not have been skiing were it not for Smith's snowmaking system.

The long, snow-covered slopes at Snow Valley, originally known as Fish Camp, attracted skiers and winter sports enthusiasts as early as the 1920s. The slopes later became home to Southern California's first ski tow. The Fish Camp sling lift (below) was designed and built by Jack Northrop during the winter of 1935–1936. It was a 1,400-foot cable that used triangular slings to pull eight people 350 feet to the top of the hill. This was the model for the Big Bear sling lift that was built in 1938. The tow was slow and primitive, but skiers were happy to have any form of uphill transportation. (Below, courtesy Jarle Eldevik.)

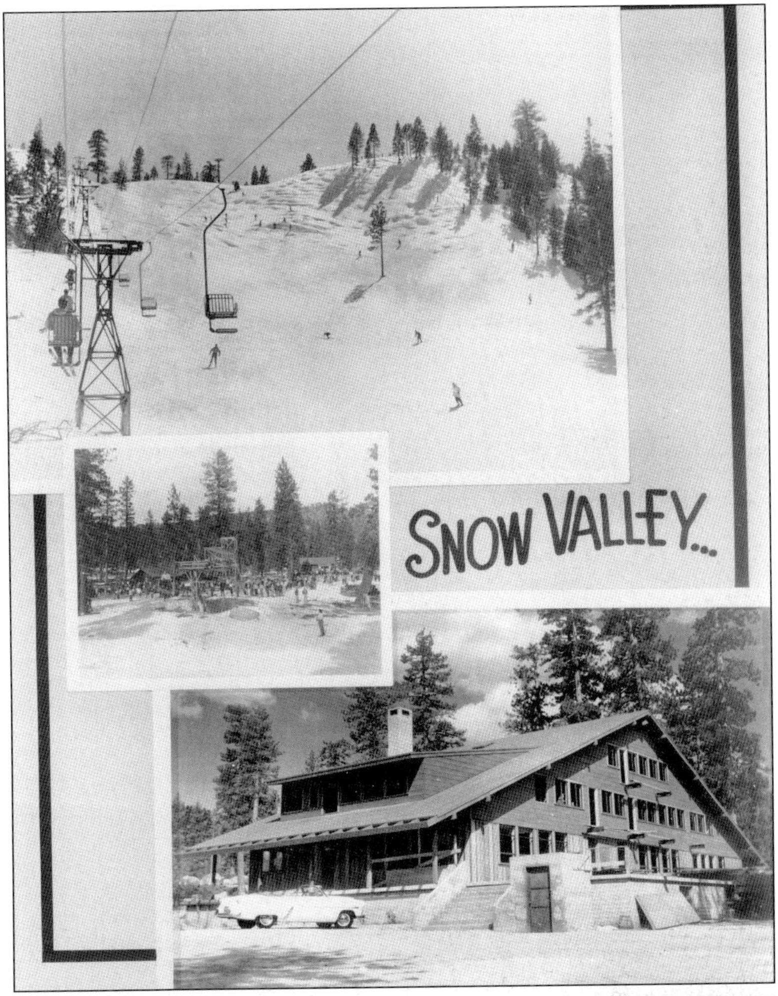

SNOW VALLEY...

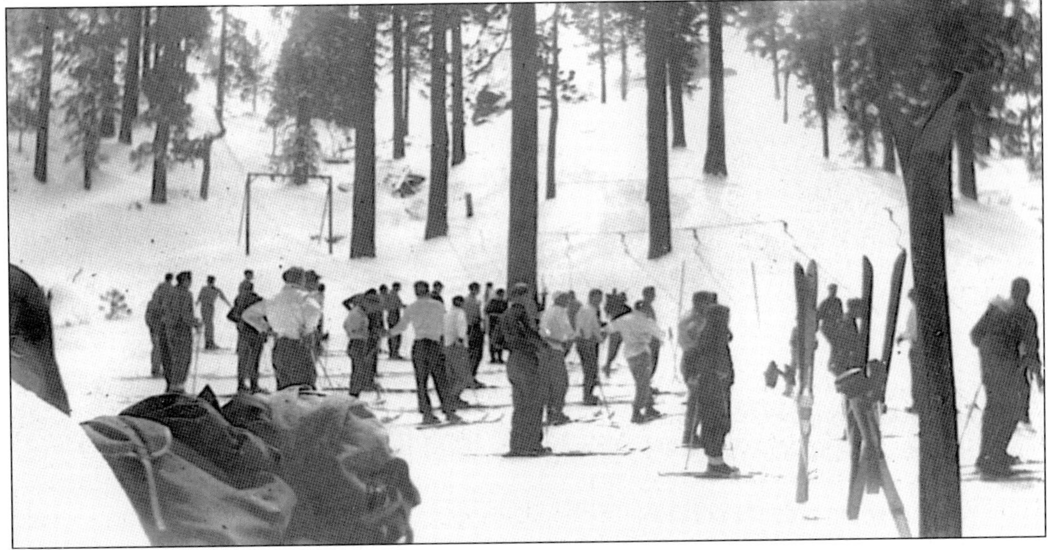

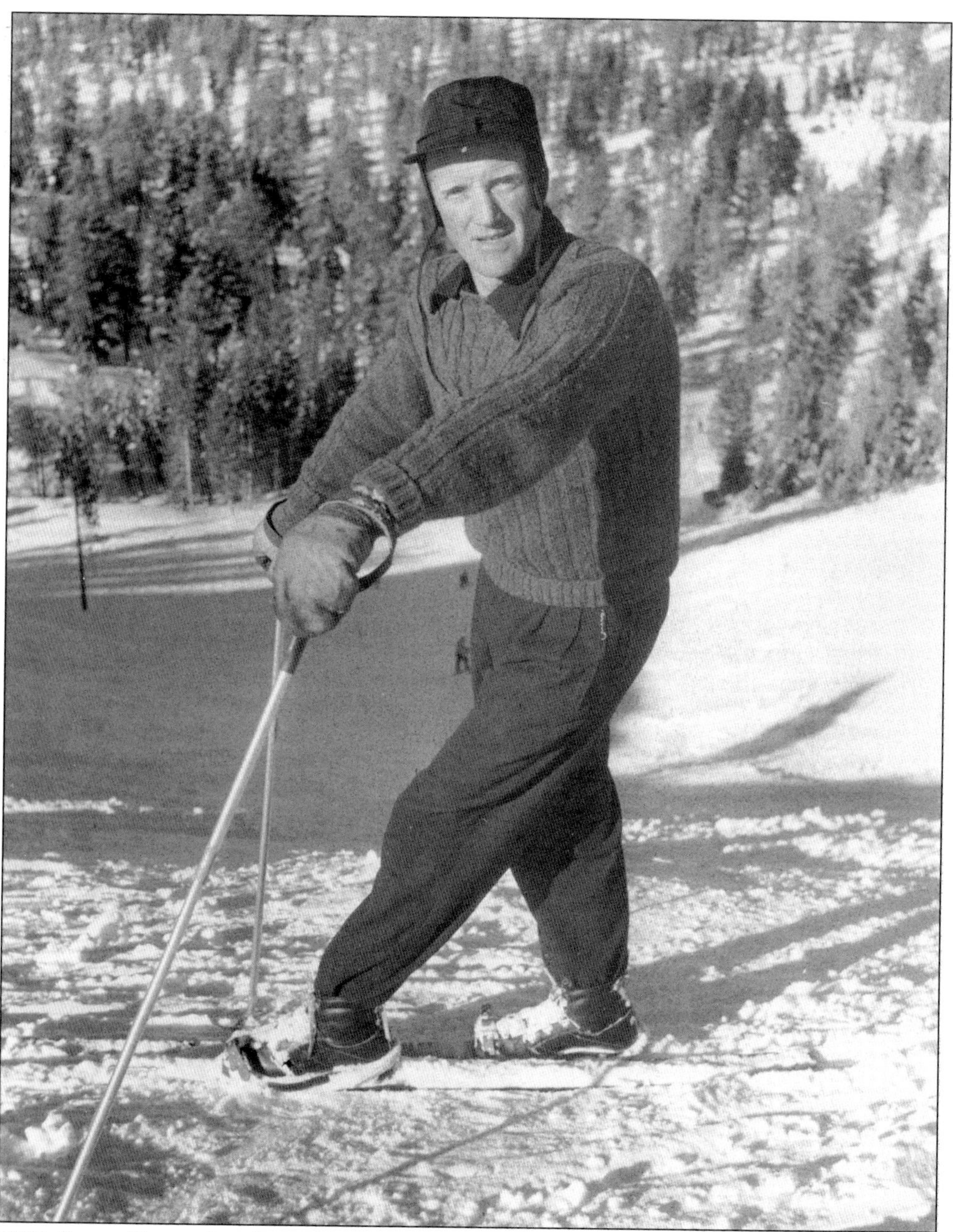

In 1937, Sverre Engen, brother of famous ski jumper Alf Engen, came to Lake Arrowhead with his wife. He had a food concession at his "Ski Shack" at Fish Camp, and he became the local ski expert. In 1939, the Lake Arrowhead Corporation purchased the area from the Engens and hired Otto Steiner to manage and promote the area. Steiner hired John Elvrum, seen here, to teach skiing on the weekends. Elvrum purchased the area from the Lake Arrowhead Corporation in 1941. Elvrum had come to the United States from Norway in 1930 and quickly made a name for himself as a ski jumping champion. He served in the 10th Mountain Division during the war, and upon returning home, he resumed the ownership and development of Snow Valley. He owned the area for 30 years, earning the nickname "Mr. Snow Valley." He passed away in July 2006 at age 97.

Though Green Valley Lake Snow Bowl was not developed until the winter of 1945–1946, winter sports enthusiasts began frequenting the area as early as the 1920s. There was ice-skating on the lake and a toboggan slide, and a ski jump hill was planned. Many local residents built their own tows for friends and family to use.

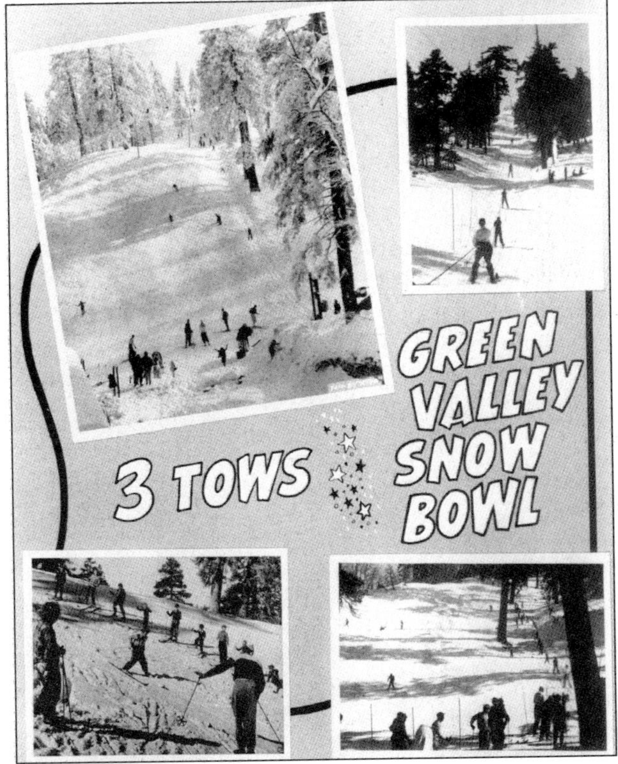

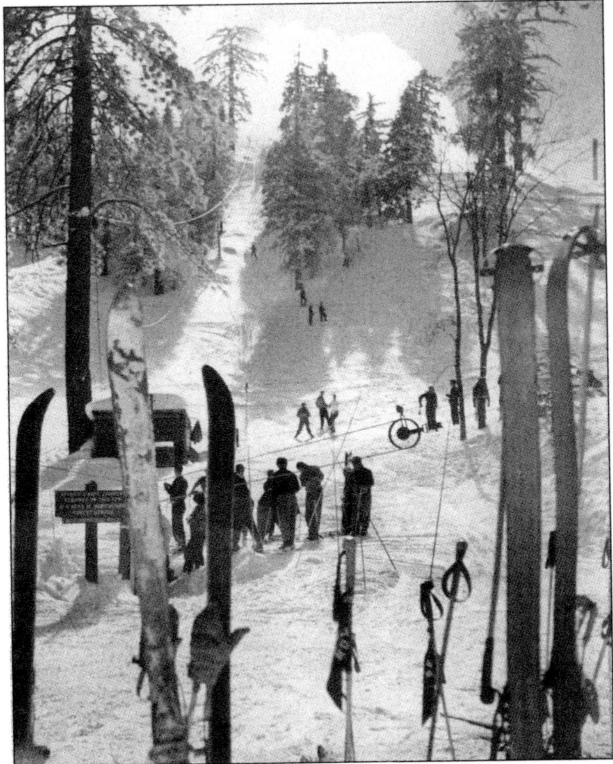

Green Valley Lake Snow Bowl, shown here in 1948, offered the basics for family skiing in a secluded setting. The area has maintained its homey, family atmosphere, but it has gone through numerous name changes over the years. It has been known as Ski Green Valley and Big Air Green Valley (when it operated as the nation's lone "snowboard-only" area), and today it is called Trinity Mountain Resort. (Courtesy Elmar Baxter.)

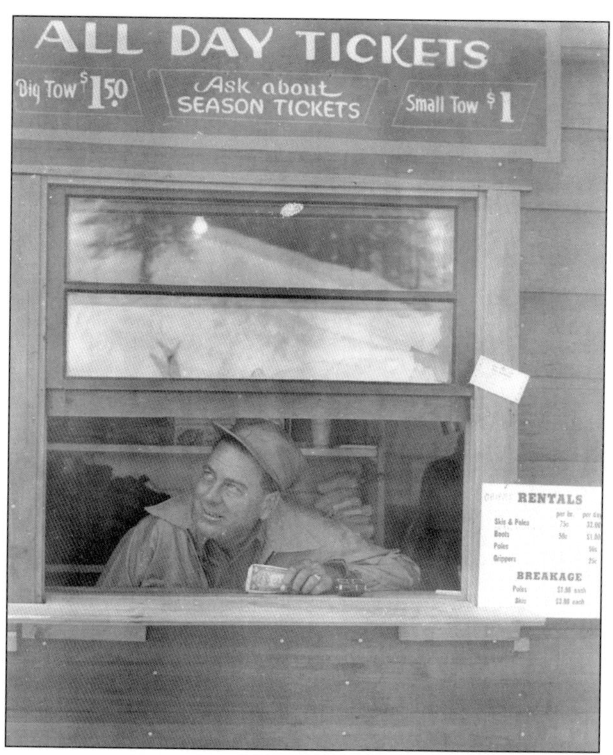

Larry Ferguson (left), Joe Fox, and Ernest C. "Doc" Vawter founded Green Valley Lake Snow Bowl in the winter of 1945–1946. All three men were longtime Green Valley Lake residents, and they wanted to develop an enterprise that would provide recreation for local residents during the winter months. Vawter remained in the partnership until 1960, Fox until 1972, and Ferguson until 1974, when he passed away. Ed Heath, noted on the brochure below, was a 10th Mountain Division ski trooper and a longtime ski instructor at the area. (Courtesy Lyle Ferguson.)

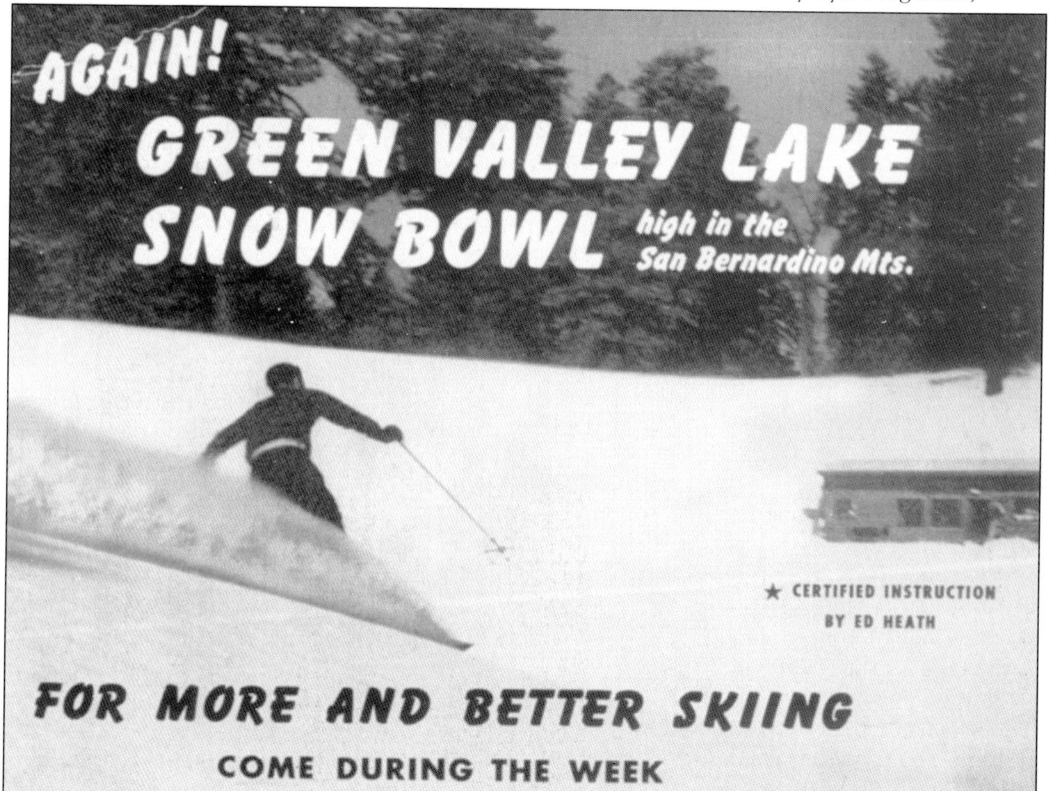

AGAIN!
GREEN VALLEY LAKE
SNOW BOWL high in the San Bernardino Mts.

★ CERTIFIED INSTRUCTION
BY ED HEATH

FOR MORE AND BETTER SKIING
COME DURING THE WEEK

Seven

Skiing in the San Gabriels

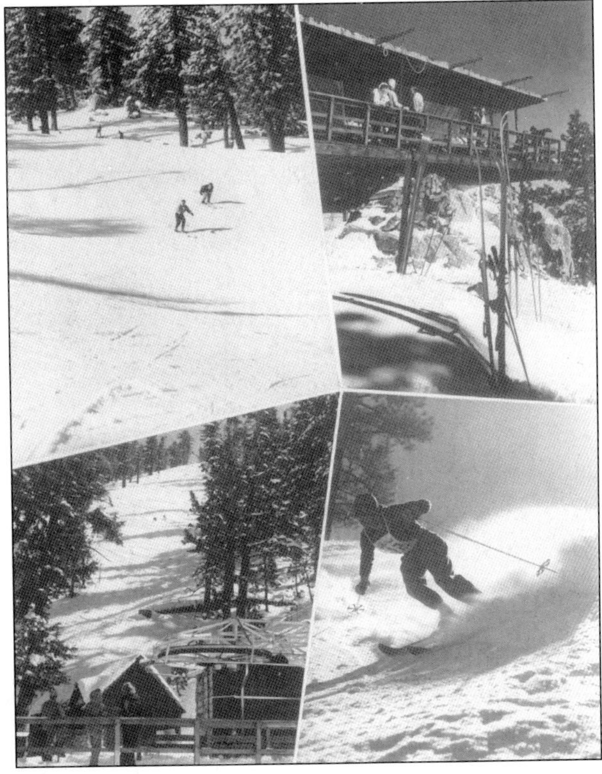

Mount Waterman has long been a favorite of Southern California skiers. Lynn Newcomb Sr. built the area's first rope tow in 1939. The success and popularity of the rope tow inspired him to further the development of the area. The completion of the Angeles Crest Highway in 1941 made Mount Waterman the closest ski area to Los Angeles and added to its popularity with local skiers.

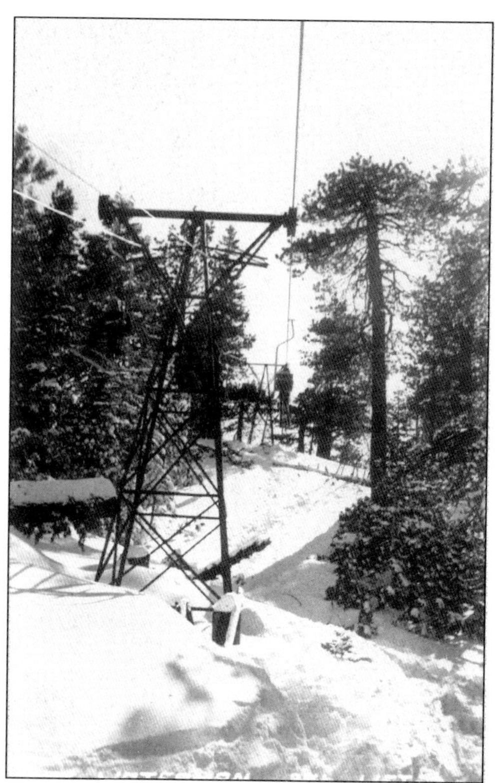

Four months after installing the first rope tow on Mount Waterman, Newcomb began work on Southern California's first chairlift. The 2,100-foot chairlift opened in January 1942 and carried 350 people per hour. Skiers were more than happy to pay $2 for an all-day pass to ride over terrain they previously had to climb. This was California's second chairlift. Sugar Bowl, in Northern California, built the first chairlift in California in 1939.

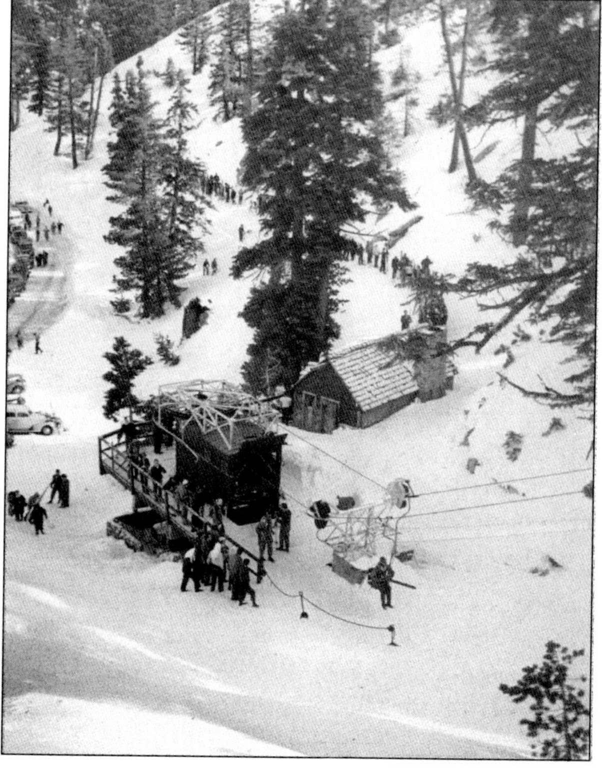

The popularity of Mount Waterman soared with the opening of the Angeles Crest Highway and the completion of the chairlift. Here is a bird's-eye view of a long line of skiers anxiously waiting for their ride on the single chair. Though rope tows were a big improvement over the demands of skiing upslope, they were difficult for many to use, requiring strength and balance to keep hold of the rope for the entire ride.

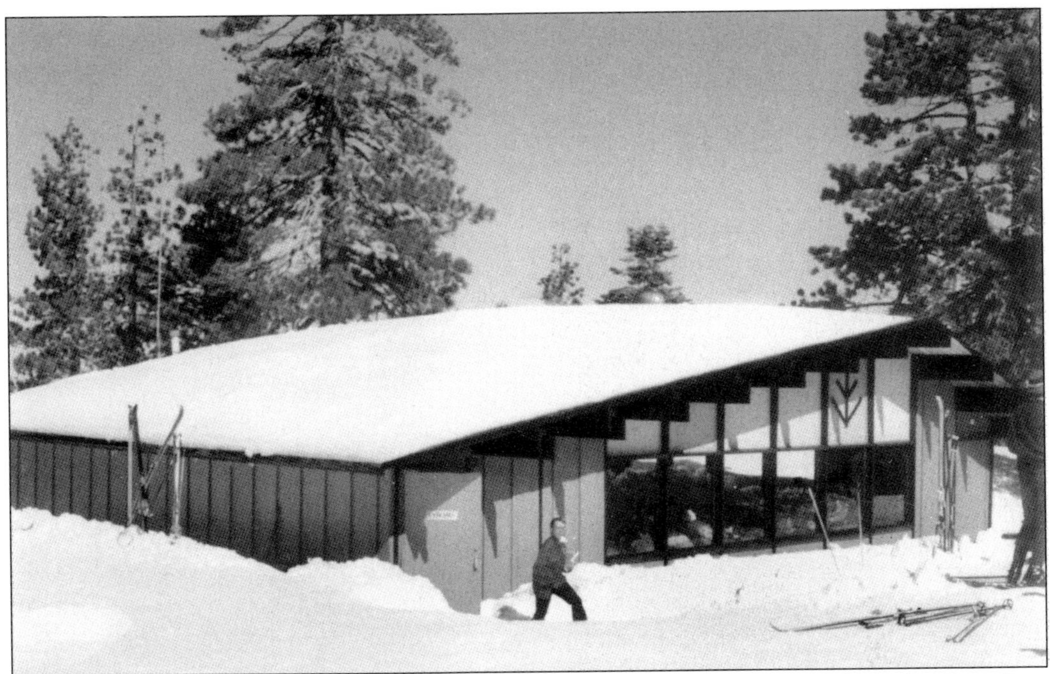

Mount Waterman's warming hut, dubbed the Eagle's Nest, has been serving skiers for more than 50 years. It was equipped with a wax room, a restaurant, and a warming room.

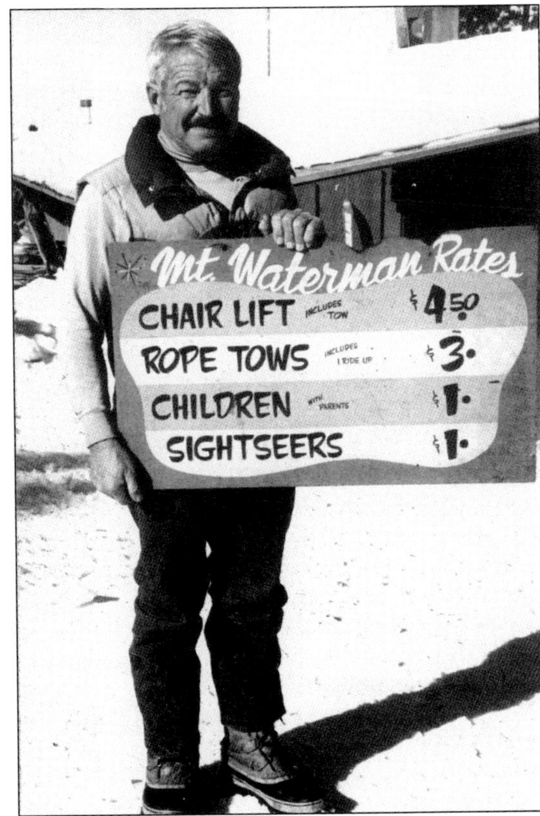

Lynn Newcomb Jr. began managing Mount Waterman in 1945 after his father died. He purchased the area from his mother in 1968 and has continued to own and operate the area for most of the past 68 years. Mount Waterman, though limited by its lack of snowmaking, is still a favorite area for many Southland skiers when Mother Nature provides plentiful snowfall. (Courtesy Elmar Baxter.)

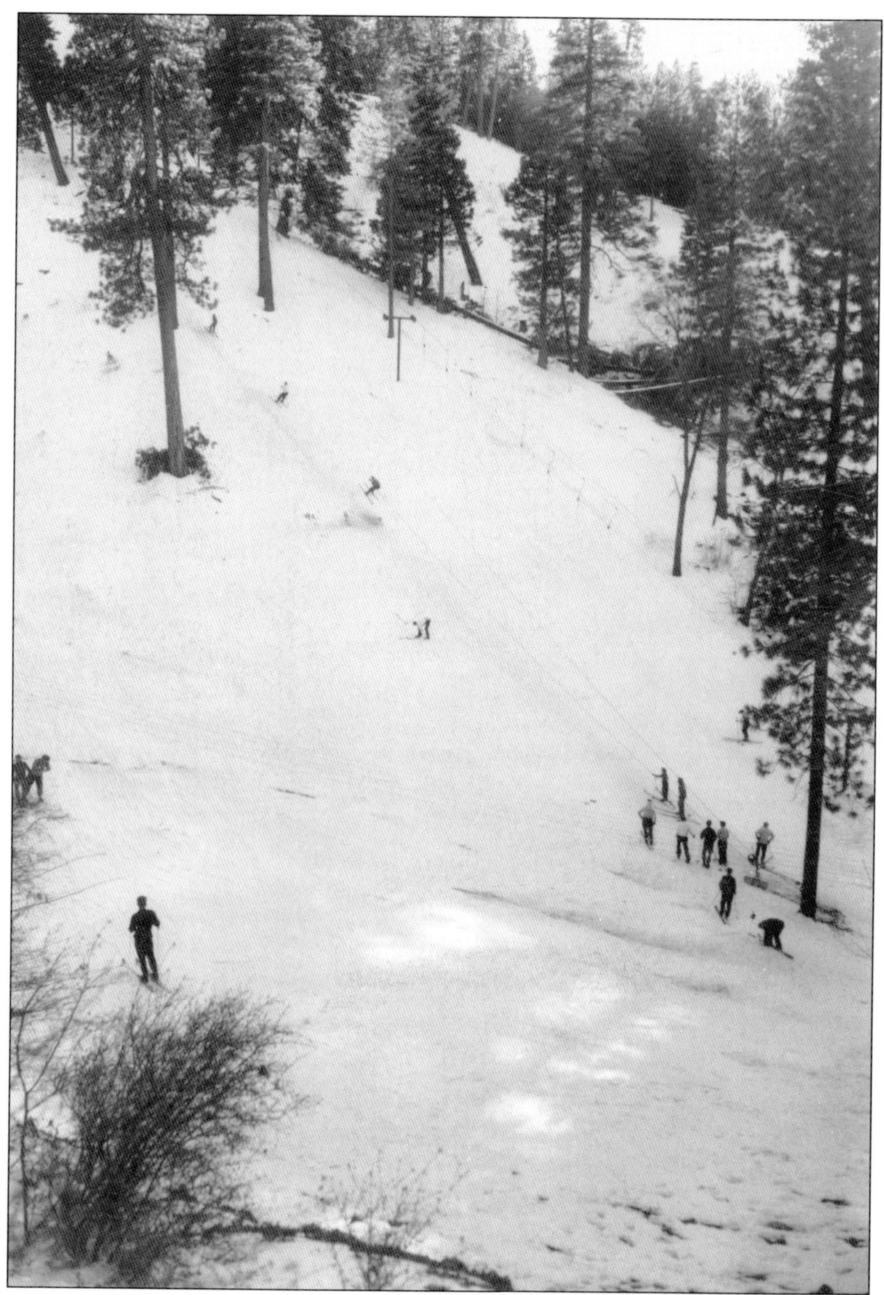

In 1938, Earl "Fuzz" Merritt and members of the Pomona College Ski Club installed the first rope tow on Mount Baldy on Movie Slope, pictured here. The group pulled a 12-horsepower engine up the hill and ran 600 feet of rope back down. The tow could be moved to different locations by toboggan. Herb Leffler and Jim Chaffee installed a rope tow at Movie Slope in 1944. This was the modest beginning of the Mount Baldy Ski Lifts. That first season, the pair made $90. They made a variety of improvements every year and added a second tow during the 1948–1949 season. By the late 1940s, it became evident that Movie Slope had reached its maximum capacity for growth. Chaffee and Leffler looked to the upper slopes of Mount Baldy to expand their area. The hill was steep and skiers had to hold tight to make it to the top of the tow.

In December 1952, Mount Baldy's first two chairlifts opened. Much of the slope clearing and construction in those days was performed by manpower rather than by machine. It took hard work to build and develop a ski area in the 1950s. (Courtesy John K. Adams.)

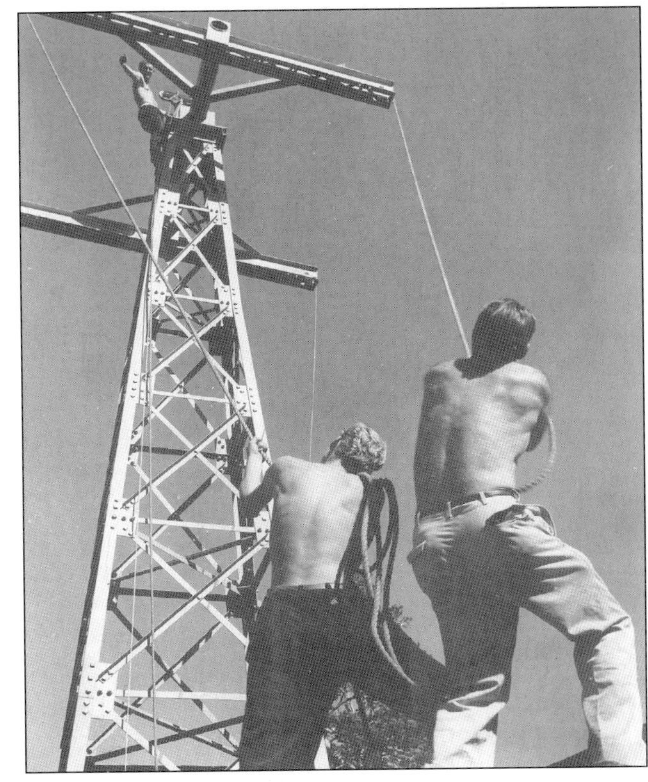

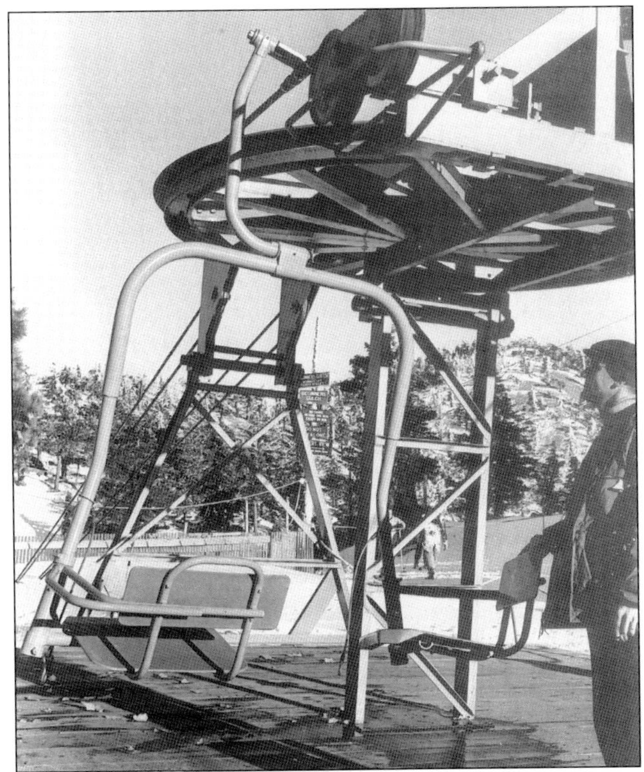

Herb Leffler demonstrates how the Karl Ringer–designed chairs swing back for unloading. He was president and general manager of the Mount Baldy Ski Lifts for 17 years. He ran and maintained tows, supervised personnel, handled rentals and sales, performed construction work, and cleared slopes. His many years of seven-day work weeks resulted in a first-class ski area for Southern California skiers. (Courtesy Jane Leffler.)

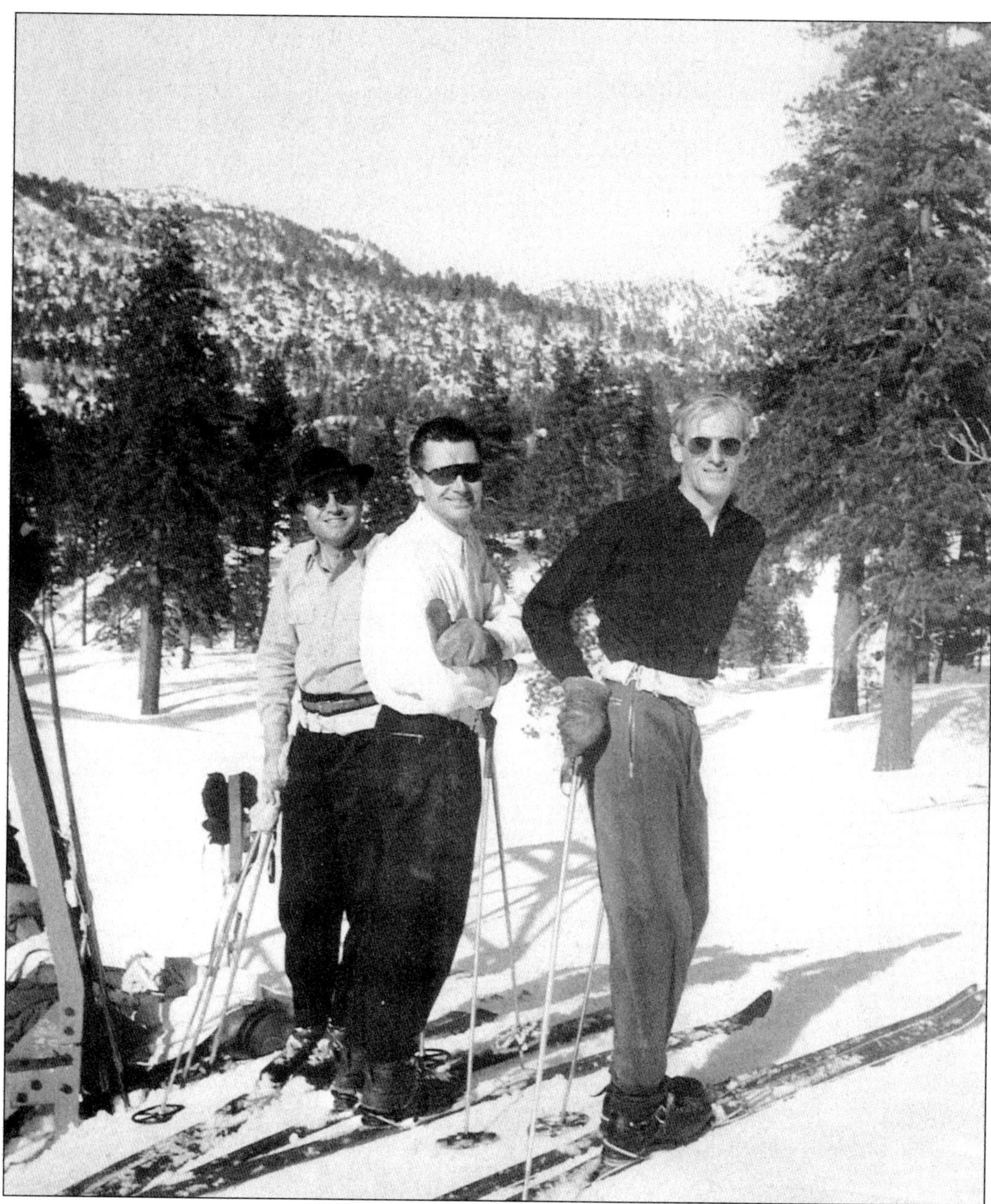

Taking a break from the action at Mount Baldy are, from left to right, Morgan Adams, Larry Jeffries, and Stan Mullin. Mullin, a Los Angeles attorney, was active in the Far West Ski Association, the United States Ski Association, and the International Ski Federation. In 1962, the United States Ski Association awarded him the Julius Blegen Award, its highest service award. He was inducted into the United States Ski Hall of Fame in 1973. Adams supplied much of the financial backing needed to build lifts at Mount Baldy. Jane Leffler once remarked that the Mount Baldy Ski Lifts would not exist were it not for Morgan Adams. (Courtesy John K. Adams.)

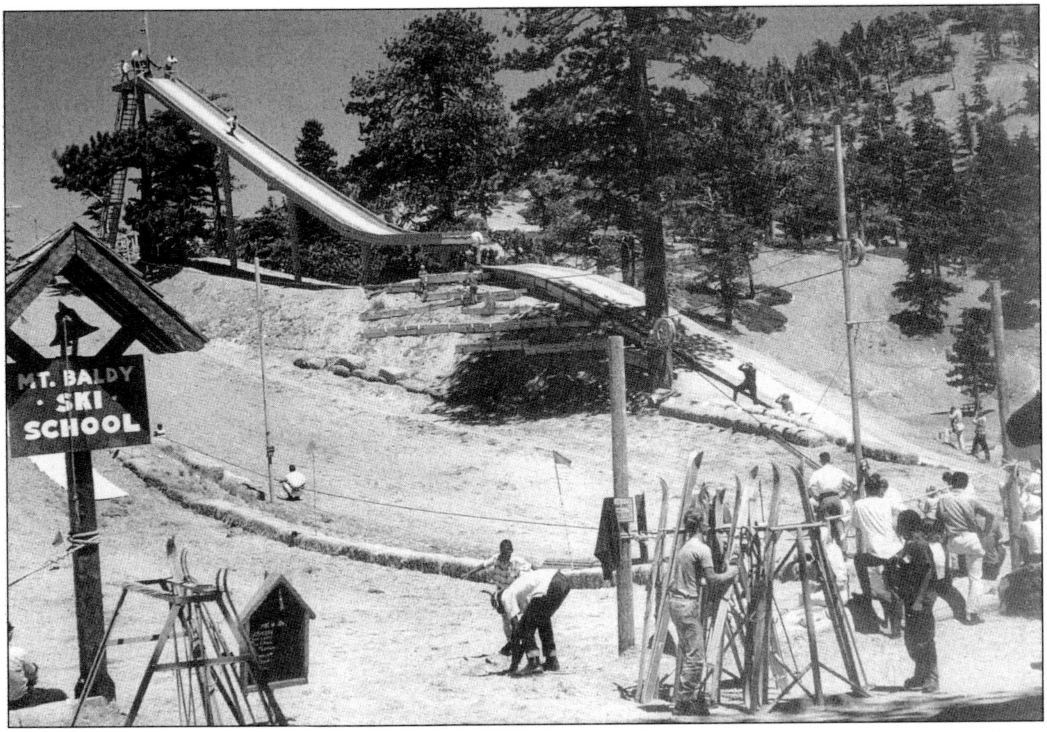

In 1956, Mount Baldy started a summer skiing program. A ski jump was built, and Alf Engen arrived on the scene to give jumping exhibitions. The jump was covered with "artificial snow" that looked like ice-cream salt. Skiers who were not interested in jumping could practice their skills on a straw-covered slope adjacent to the ski jump. The jump provided publicity for the area and began attracting skiers to the slopes. Fuzz Merritt, a longtime skier and football coach at Pomona College, directed the summer ski school. It was estimated that 4,000 to 5,000 people took advantage of the summer ski program each year.

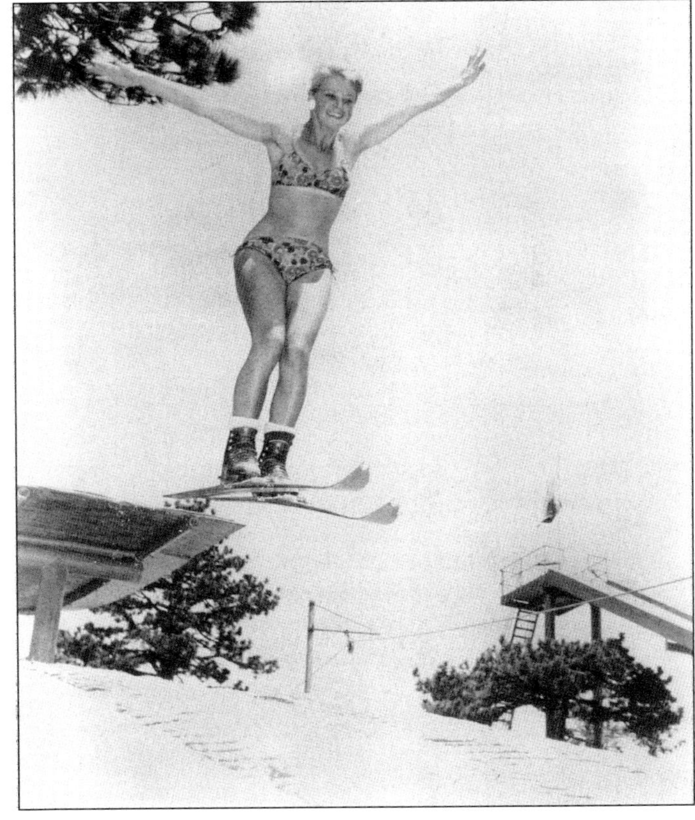

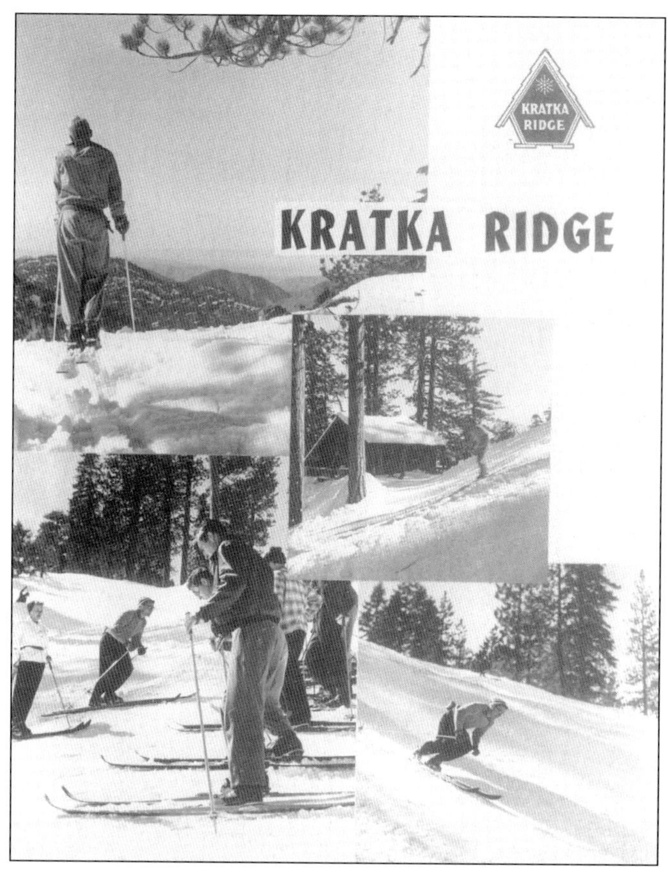

The Angeles Winter Development Corporation, a group made up of 11 members of the San Gorgonio Ski Club, founded Kratka Ridge in 1950. When the area opened for the 1950–1951 season, it was equipped with four rope tows and a day lodge. The first chairlift was installed in 1954. One unique feature in Kratka's history is that each of the 11 founders agreed to contribute an equal amount of money and a minimum of 200 hours of labor in the first year of construction. The fervent men put in an average of 700 hours that year, despite having jobs elsewhere.

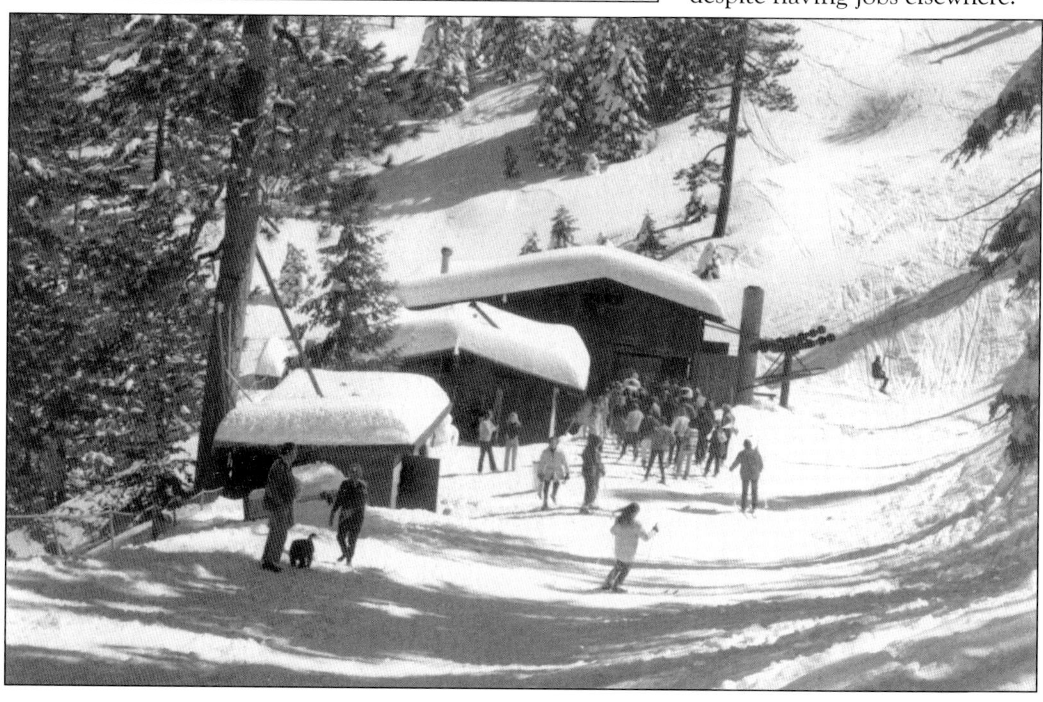

Harlow Dormer, one of the inaugural members of the Big Pines Ski Club, obtained the lease for Table Mountain Ski Area (later named Ski Sunrise) in 1937. He and business partner Craig Wilson began clearing trails and built a warming hut. They installed the first rope tow on Table Mountain that same year. Howard More purchased the lease in 1943, and he owned and operated the area for most of the next 60 years. A unique feature of Table Mountain is that the parking lot and base facilities are at the top of the area.

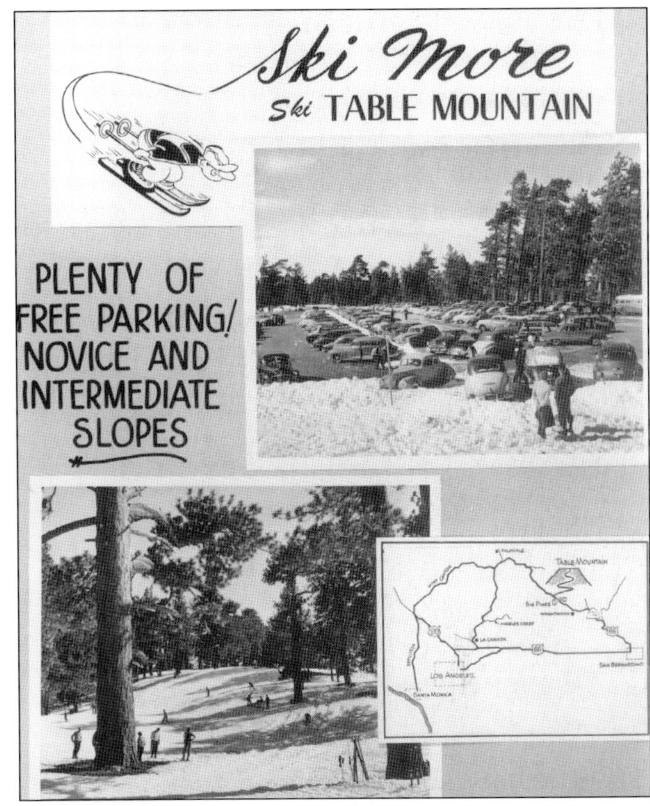

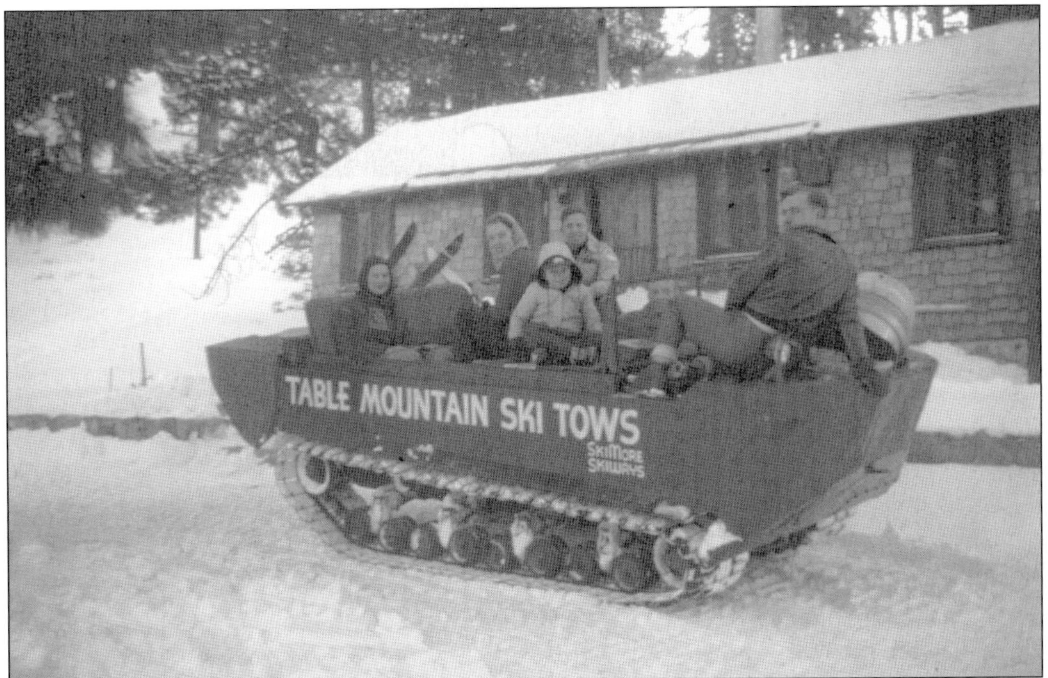

After World War II ended, many ski areas purchased surplus army weasels to assist in transporting skiers. The skiers in this photograph enjoy the ride in Table Mountain's weasel.

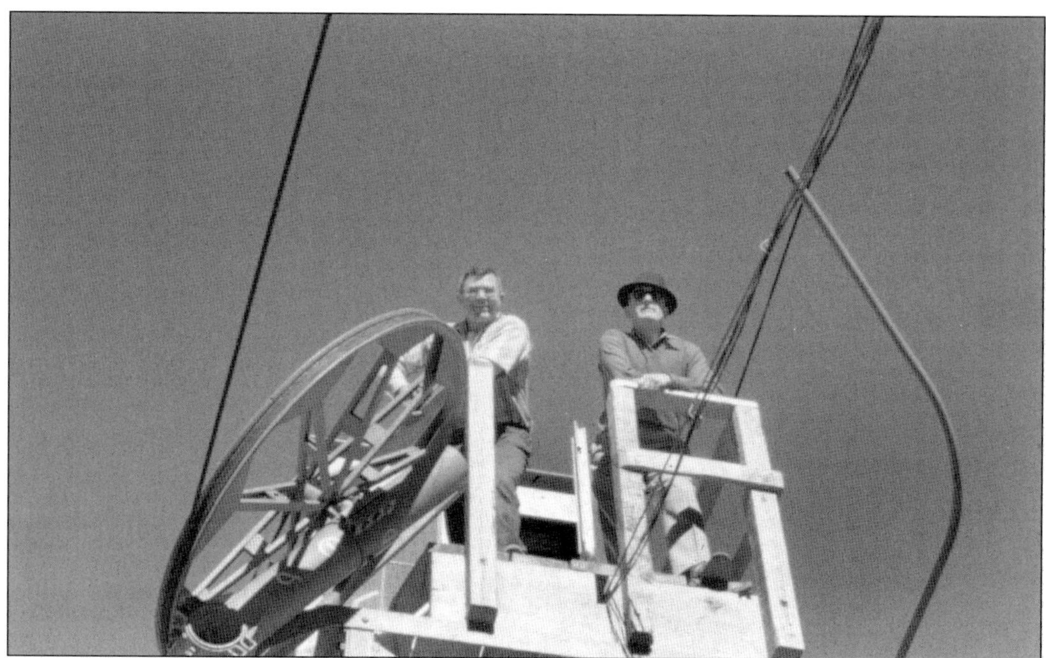

Howard More (above left) first learned to ski in Colorado in 1926. He came to California in 1941 and discovered the slopes at Table Mountain. After More purchased the lease in 1943, the area remained closed for two years while he built rope tows and upgraded the area. The classic day lodge (below) was built during the 1952–1953 season. Much of the timber used in its construction came from the trees that were cleared for the original ski trails.

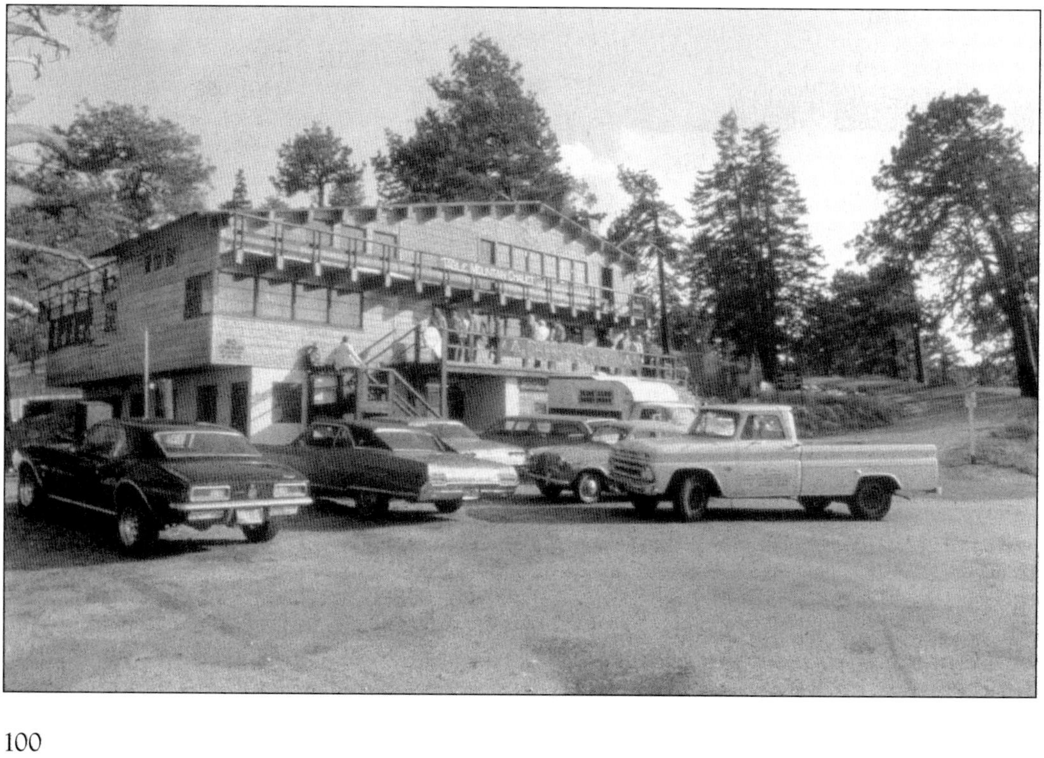

In 1937–1938, Frank Springer and Tom Triol became managers at Blue Ridge, formerly Los Angeles County's Big Pines Park. They built the area's first chairlift in early 1947. On January 30 of that year, after the lift and its 67 chairs was considered complete, Triol threw down his tools and jumped on the first chair. Springer took the second ride. This was California's third chairlift, and the second chairlift in Southern California. Frank and Marcia Springer (below) added lifts and cleared new trails throughout the 1950s and 1960s. Frank Springer sold the area to Dick Woodworth in 1975. (Courtesy Marcia Myers.)

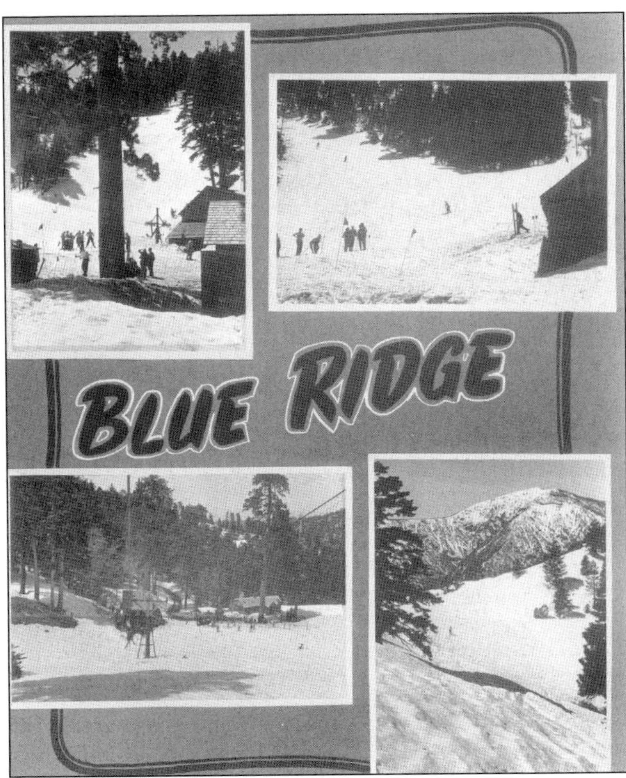

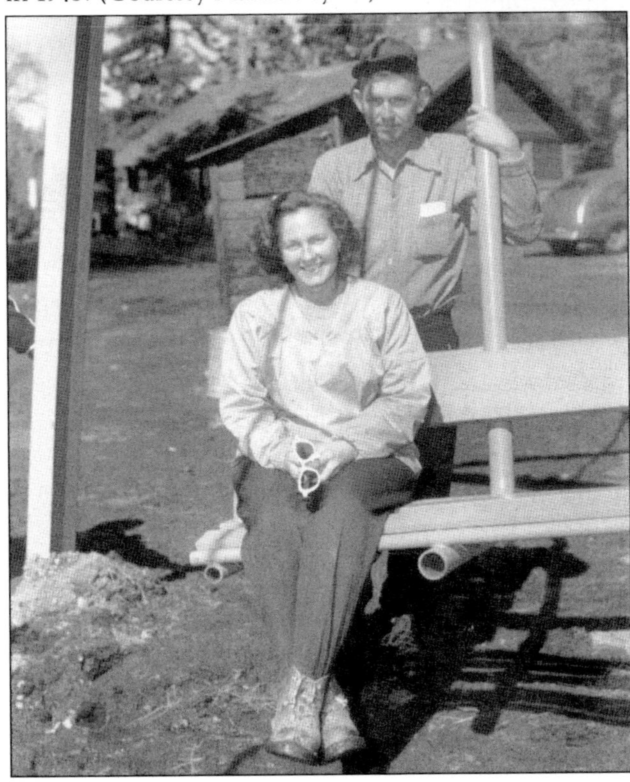

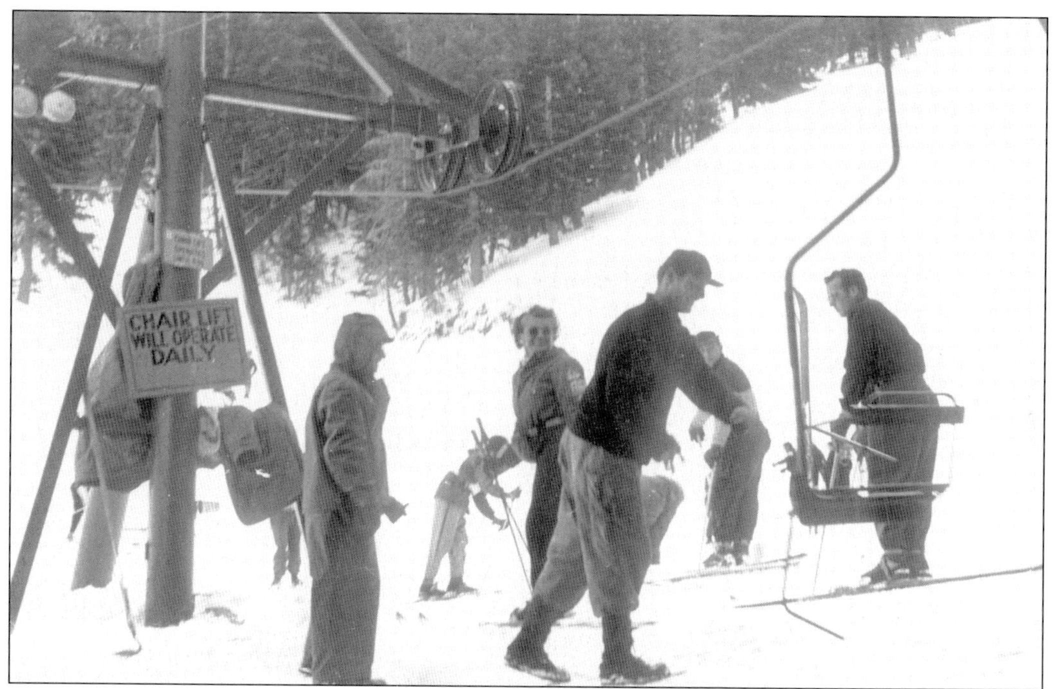

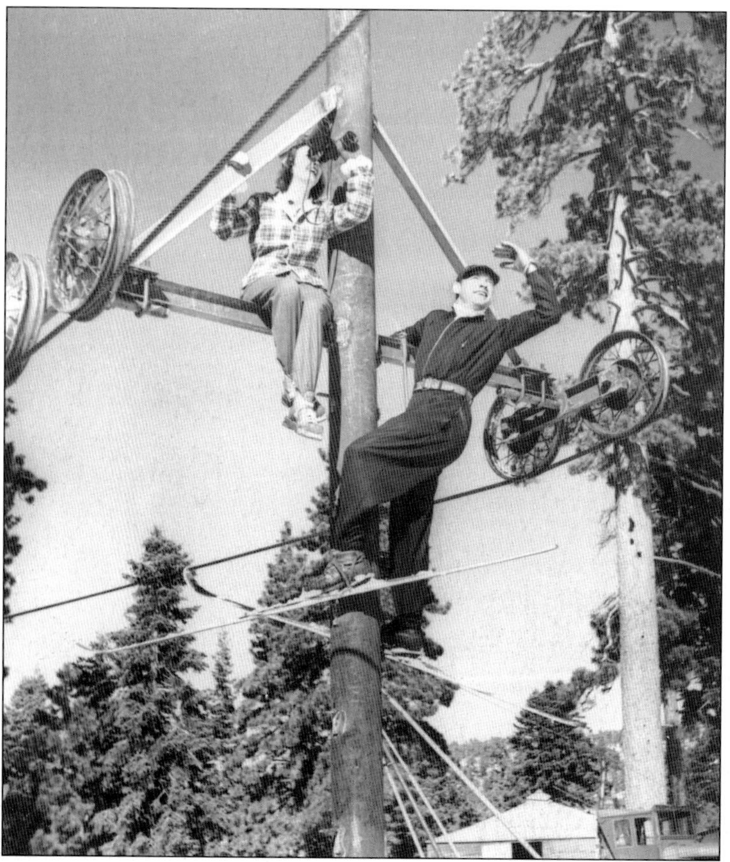

Elizabeth "Schatzi" Wood, center, prepares for a ride on the Blue Ridge chairlift. Big Pines was an extremely popular winter weekend destination, drawing thousands of skiers. The chairlift was an instant hit with skiers weary of the old rope tows. Sepp Benedikter and Ruth Miller, at left, graced the cover of the March 1947 issue of *Western Skiing*. (Photograph above courtesy Marcia Myers; photograph at left courtesy Claudia Benedikter Pedersen.)

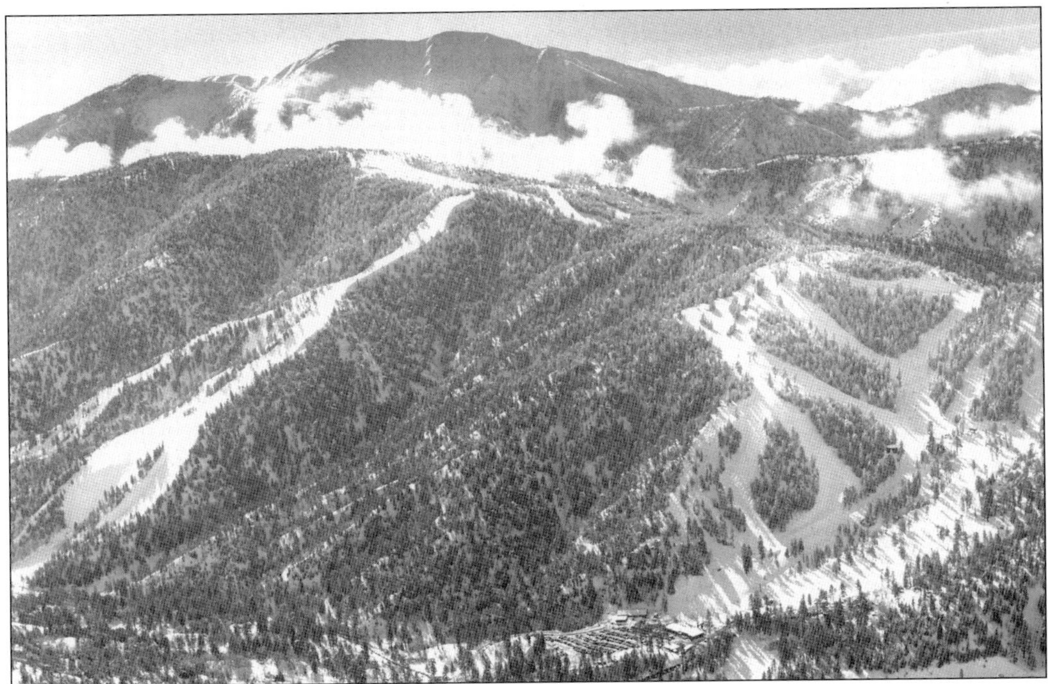

Mountain High, above, is now one area made up of what was formerly Blue Ridge (the ski runs at right) and Holiday Hill. Sepp Benedikter began work on Holiday Hill in the late 1940s. By 1950, several runs had been cleared, as seen below, and he began work on the first chairlift. He and John Steinmann formed a partnership that same year, but it was short-lived. Both were strong-willed and fervent, but they seldom agreed on how to do things. In 1951, they parted ways, with Benedikter selling his share to Steinmann. (Photograph above courtesy Elmar Baxter; photograph below courtesy Claudia Benedikter Pedersen.)

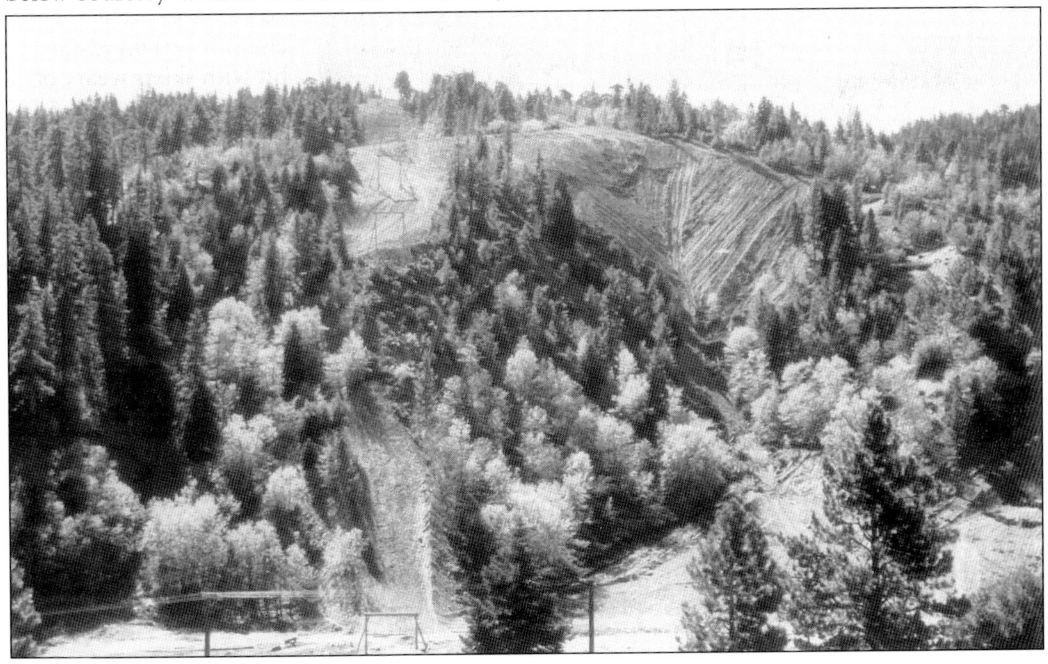

HOLIDAY HILL

is ready for you.
Designed to meet the winter sports needs of your entire family.

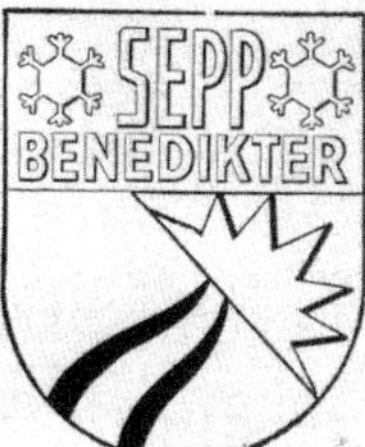

Between Wrightwood and the arch at Big Pines

The SEPP BENEDIKTER SKI SCHOOL will be operating every day. All classes under the personal direction of Sepp and his assistant, Bill Donahower. Every class served by rope tow, no strenuous climbing.

SKIING
SKATING
TOBOGGANING
RENTALS
HOT FOOD
WARMING HUT

HOLIDAY HILL
BIG PINES, CALIFORNIA

Watch for our mid-week ski special!

This is probably the first advertisement for Holiday Hill, published in the January 1, 1950, issue of *The Skier.* It highlighted Benedikter's Ski School, as well as the other activities available for the nonskier.

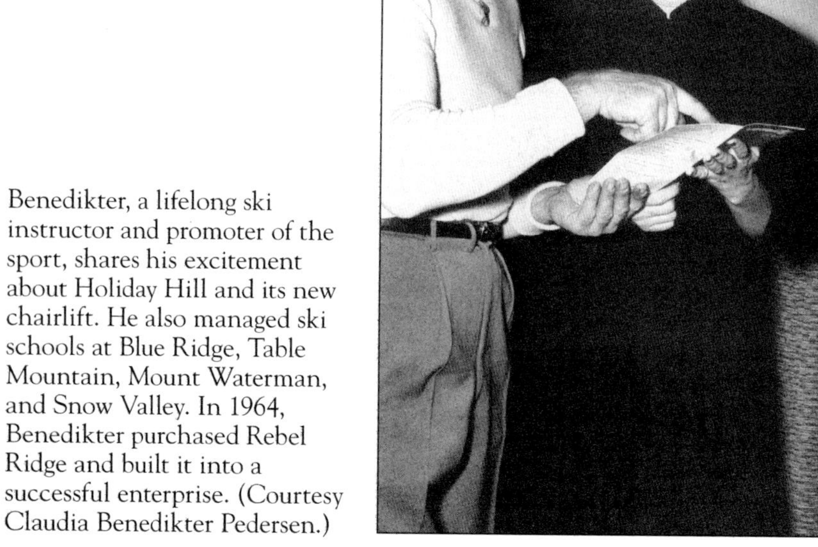

Benedikter, a lifelong ski instructor and promoter of the sport, shares his excitement about Holiday Hill and its new chairlift. He also managed ski schools at Blue Ridge, Table Mountain, Mount Waterman, and Snow Valley. In 1964, Benedikter purchased Rebel Ridge and built it into a successful enterprise. (Courtesy Claudia Benedikter Pedersen.)

With today's high-speed quads and helicopter-installed lift towers, the numerous man-hours and the physical labor that went into the first lifts at many areas is long forgotten. This worker is applying some finishing touches to Holiday Hill's first lift. (Courtesy Claudia Benedikter Pedersen.)

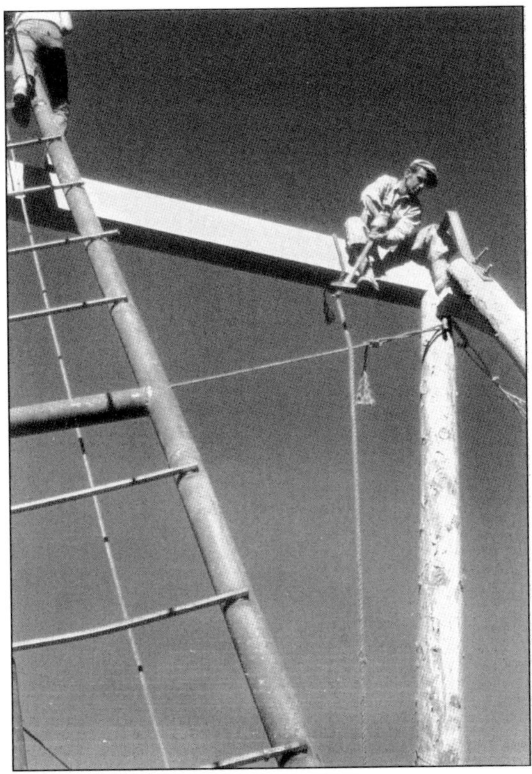

Here are the beautifully cleared slopes of the bowl at the base of Holiday Hill. The original lift towers are on the left. (Courtesy Claudia Benedikter Pedersen.)

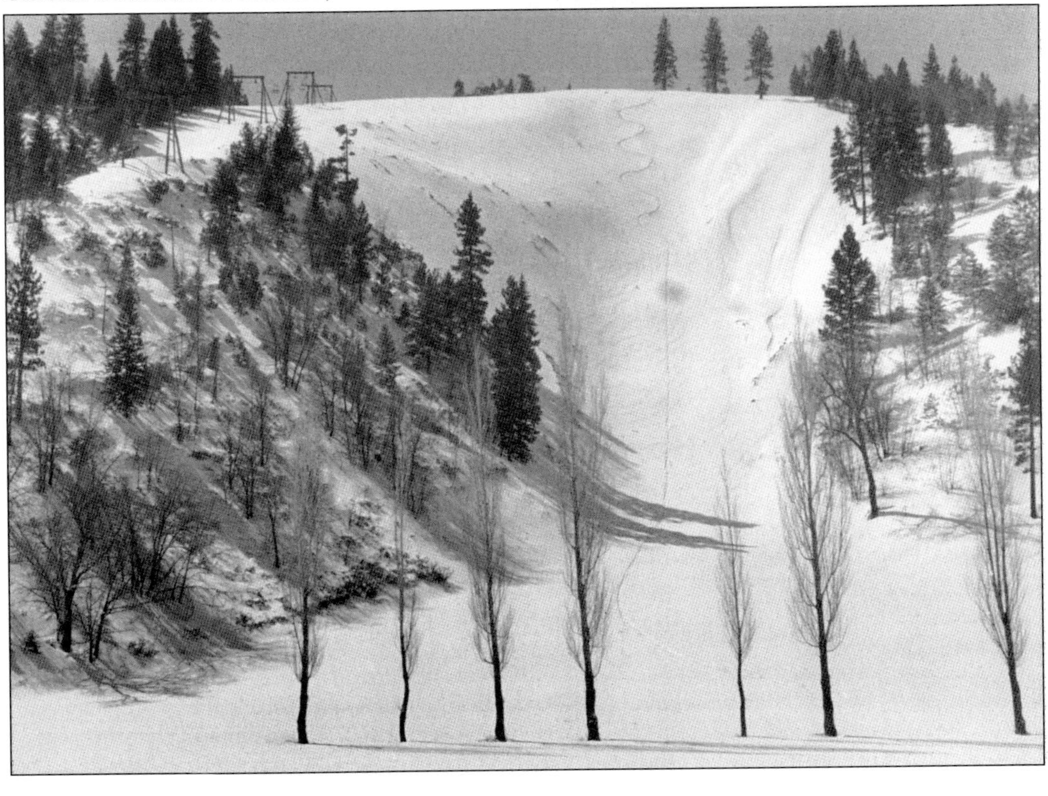

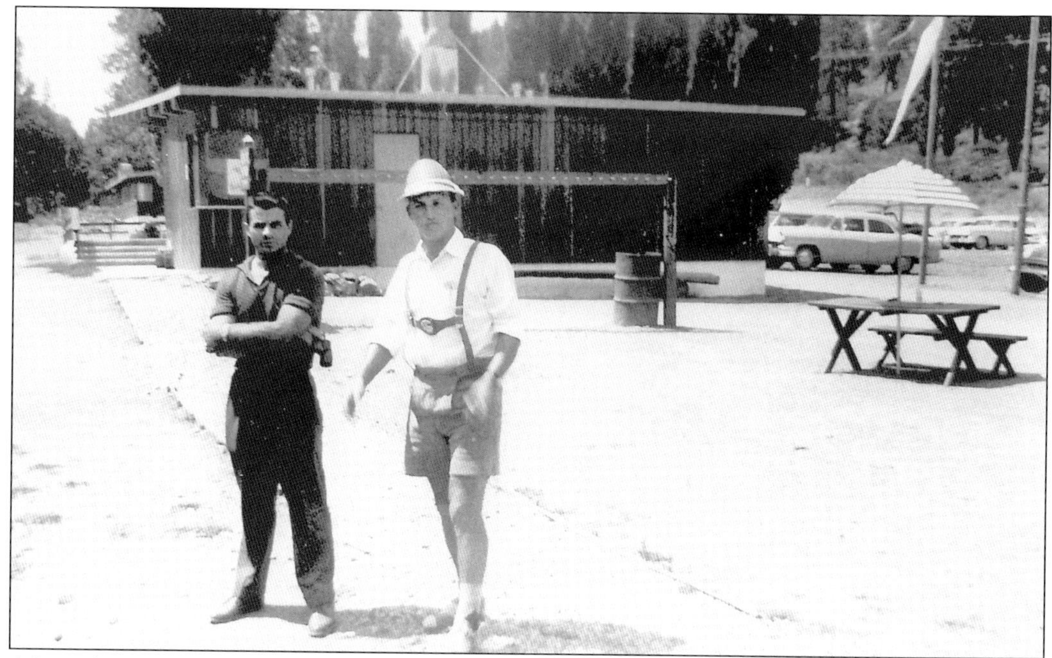

After John Steinmann assumed sole ownership of Holiday Hill, he and his sons owned and operated it for almost 30 years. The family had emigrated from Switzerland in 1948, and their Swiss heritage was sometimes reflected in the facilities and activities at Holiday Hill. Here Heinz Steinmann (right) dons the traditional European lederhosen. (Courtesy Steinmann Collection.)

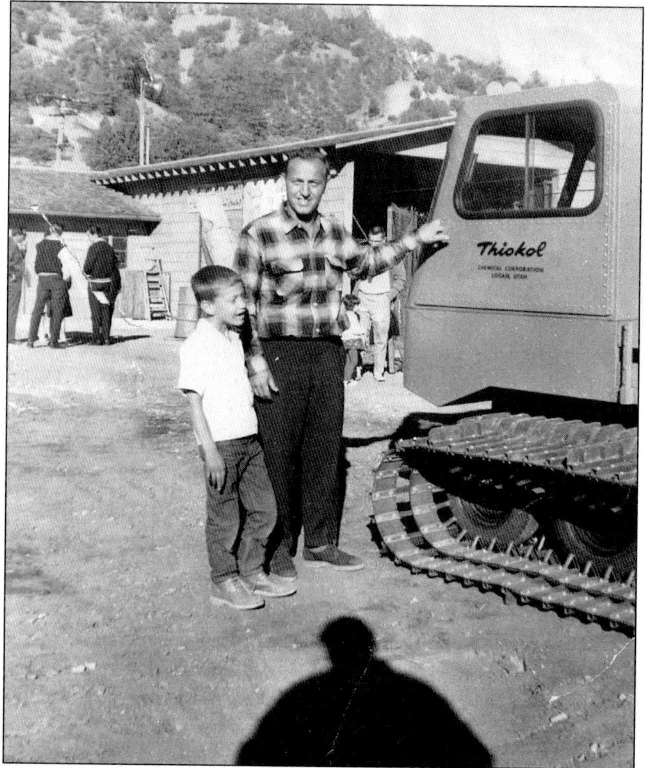

Heinz Steinmann, seen here with son Michael, could certainly be hailed as Mr. Holiday Hill. The Steinmann brothers bought Holiday Hill from their father in 1959, and Heinz bought out his brothers in 1962. He owned Holiday Hill until 1979, when he sold the area. Much of the success and popularity of Mountain High today is based upon the many improvements made during the Steinmann years of ownership. (Courtesy Steinmann Collection.)

Eight

San Gorgonio

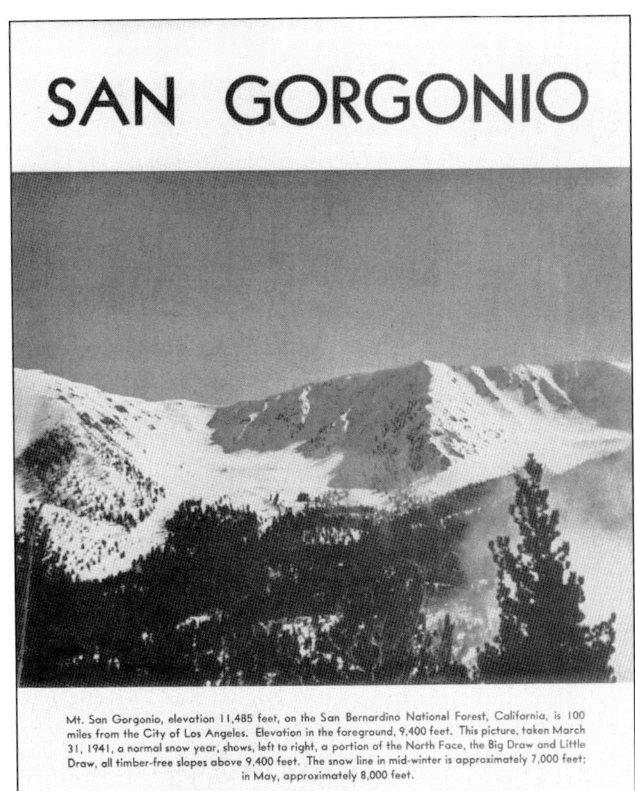
SAN GORGONIO

Mt. San Gorgonio, elevation 11,485 feet, on the San Bernardino National Forest, California, is 100 miles from the City of Los Angeles. Elevation in the foreground, 9,400 feet. This picture, taken March 31, 1941, a normal snow year, shows, left to right, a portion of the North Face, the Big Draw and Little Draw, all timber-free slopes above 9,400 feet. The snow line in mid-winter is approximately 7,000 feet; in May, approximately 8,000 feet.

San Gorgonio, Southern California's highest mountain at 11,502 feet, is blessed with more snow than any other Southland locale. As early as the 1930s, skiers began to call for motorized lifts to allow easier access to the upper reaches of the mountain. In 1942, the San Gorgonio Committee favored reclassification of a small portion of the San Gorgonio Wilderness Area for ski lifts. The outbreak of World War II diverted attention from ski lifts to more pressing needs, but the battle for development really heated up in the 1960s, when ski-area proponents and environmentalists battled long and hard. This is one of the many publications made available to explain the pros and cons of development versus conservation.

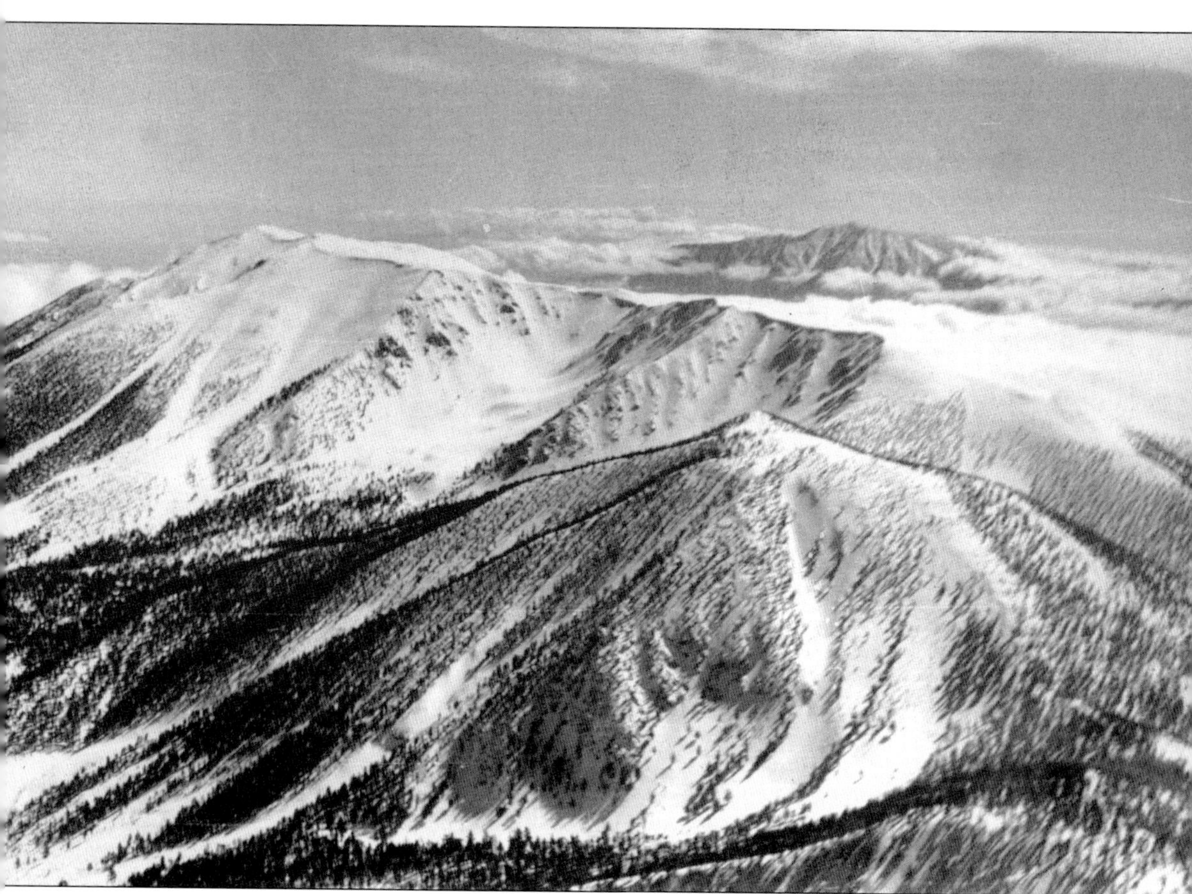

The many snow-covered, north-facing slopes of San Gorgonio, which triggered two generations of skiers to fight for ski lifts on the mountain, are evident in this photograph. Prior to the advent of ski lifts, the abundant snow and the high, open slopes on San Gorgonio became a favorite weekend destination for many skiers and ski clubs. (Courtesy Chris Schwarzenbach.)

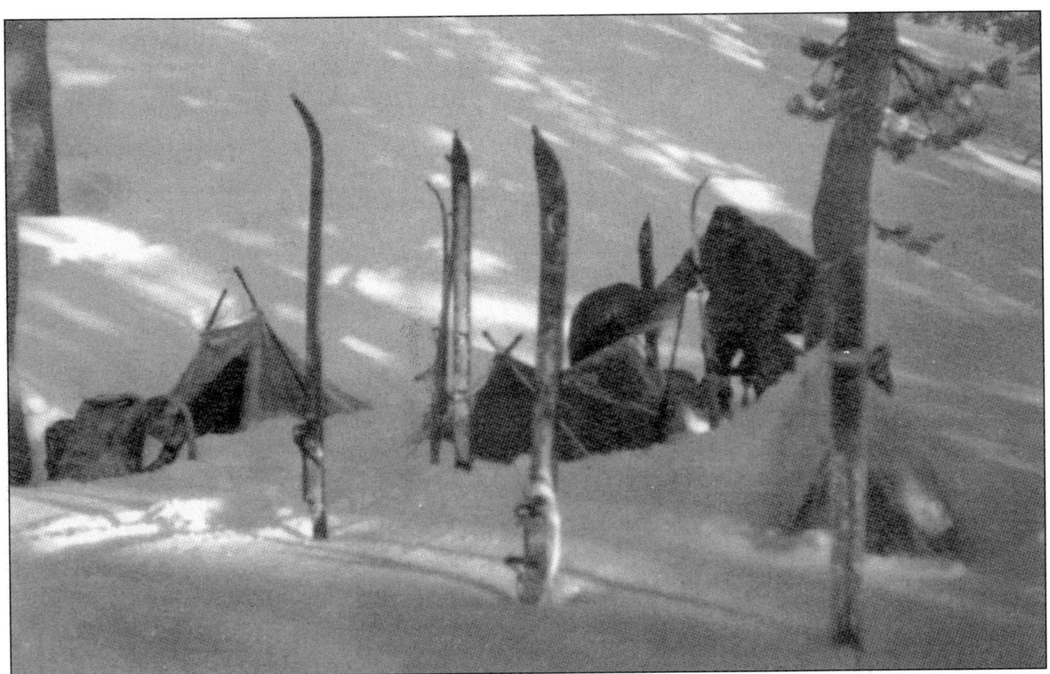

Those intrepid skiers of the 1930s who explored the slopes of San Gorgonio encountered challenging overnight conditions, as seen above. It was difficult to explore the upper reaches of the mountain in just a day; there were no lifts and much time was spent skiing uphill. The Alpenglocke Hut, below, was built was built in June 1940 by Al Wilkes, George Thompson, William H. Baker, Jack Reed, John Hood, Henry Nash, Ray Burns, Maurice Ives, George Johnson, Fred Linder, John Glass, Clem Glass, Bill Schwarzer, and Hugh Herrick. It provided much-needed shelter for 24 years, until the Forest Service removed it in October 1964. The Alpenglocke, in addition to the Edelweiss Hut built in 1934, were probably the two most popular of the improvised shelters that were built on the slopes of San Gorgonio.

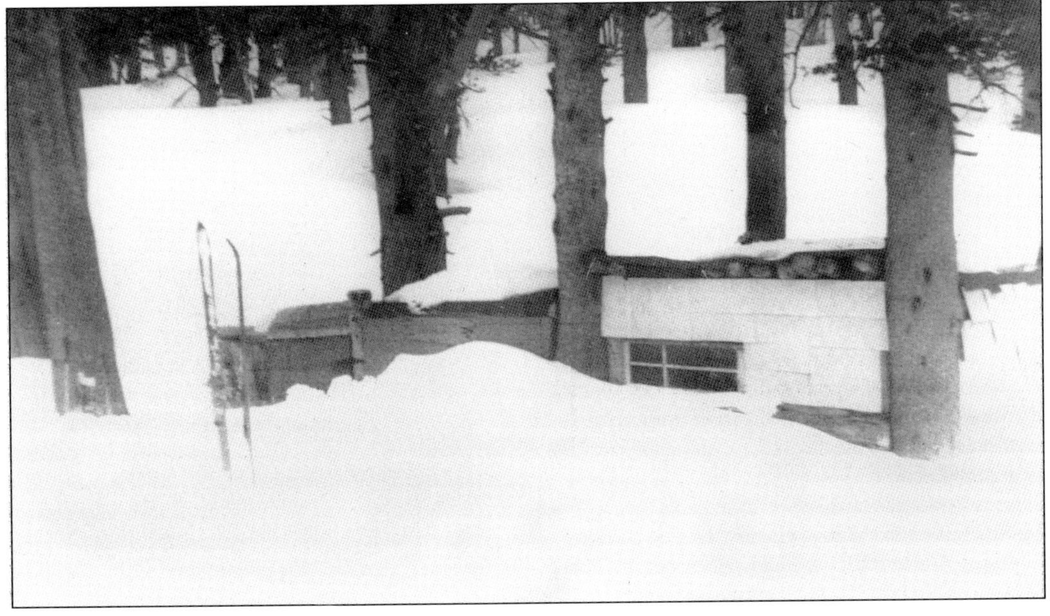

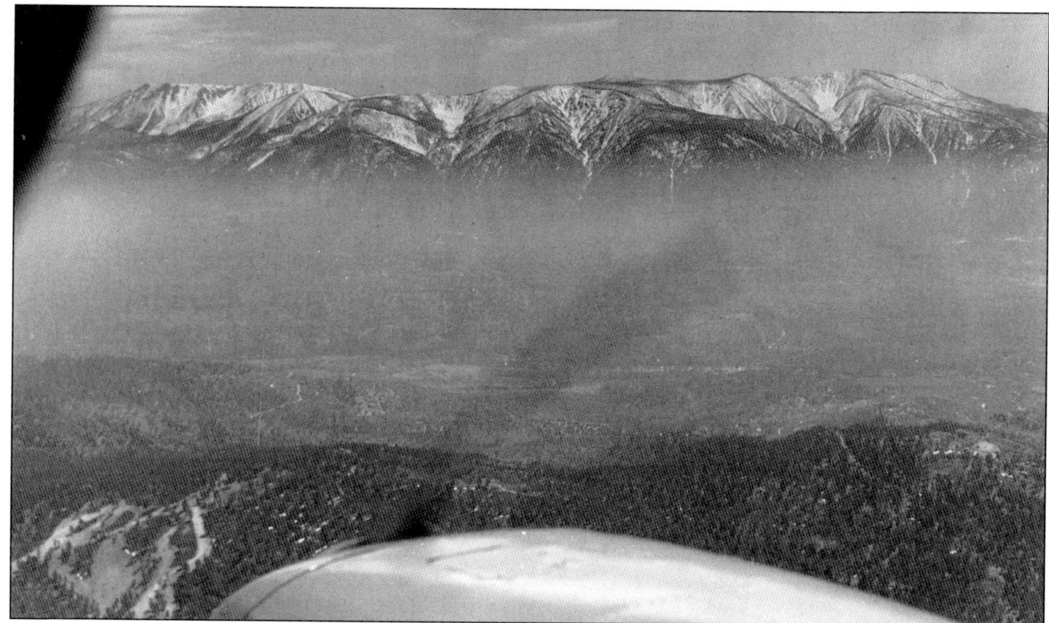

Proponents of the construction of ski lifts on San Gorgonio made extensive aerial photographs to lend graphic support to their arguments for development. This photograph, taken on May 7, 1962, shows Snow Summit's bare slopes in the foreground and San Gorgonio on the left. There was ample snow for good skiing for weeks to come on San Gorgonio. Snow Summit had closed about April 10 that year.

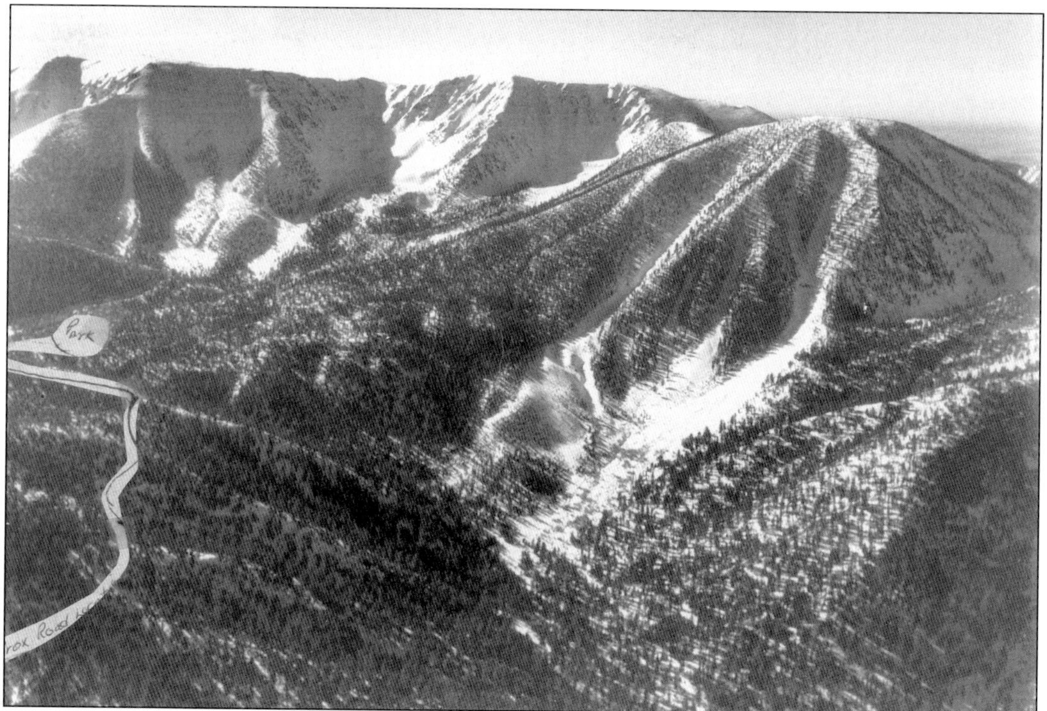

This aerial view shows Christmas Tree Hill and the upper slopes on San Gorgonio. The proposed road and parking area is drawn in on the left.

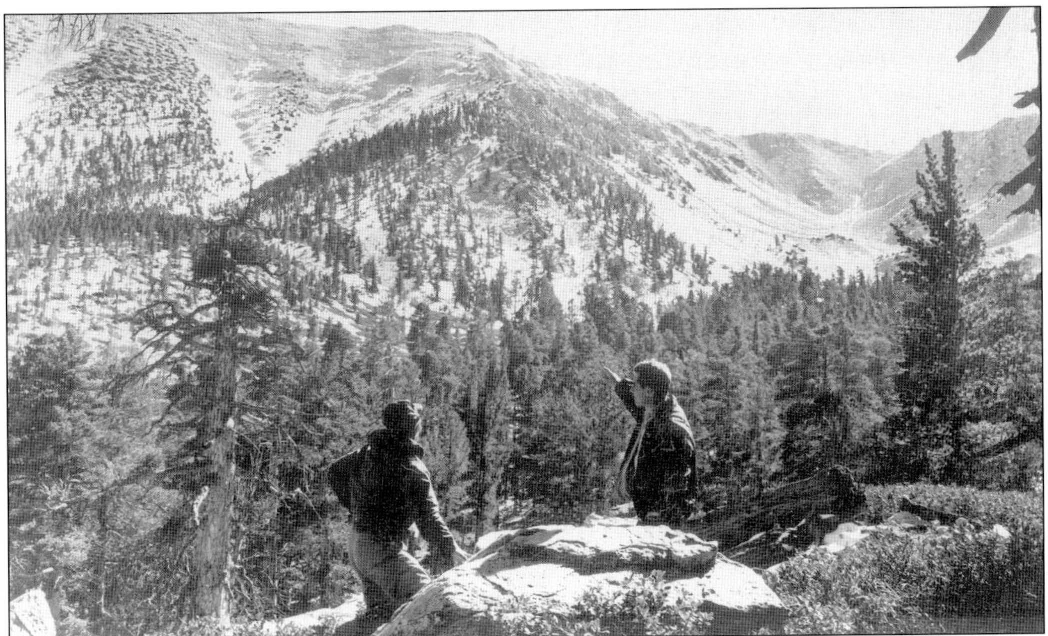

Ken Kaufman and Chandler North look at the north face of San Gorgonio and the Big Draw from above the Edelweiss Hut on November 15, 1961. Chandler North took extensive aerial photographs of San Gorgonio. These images were used to support the arguments for development on San Gorgonio.

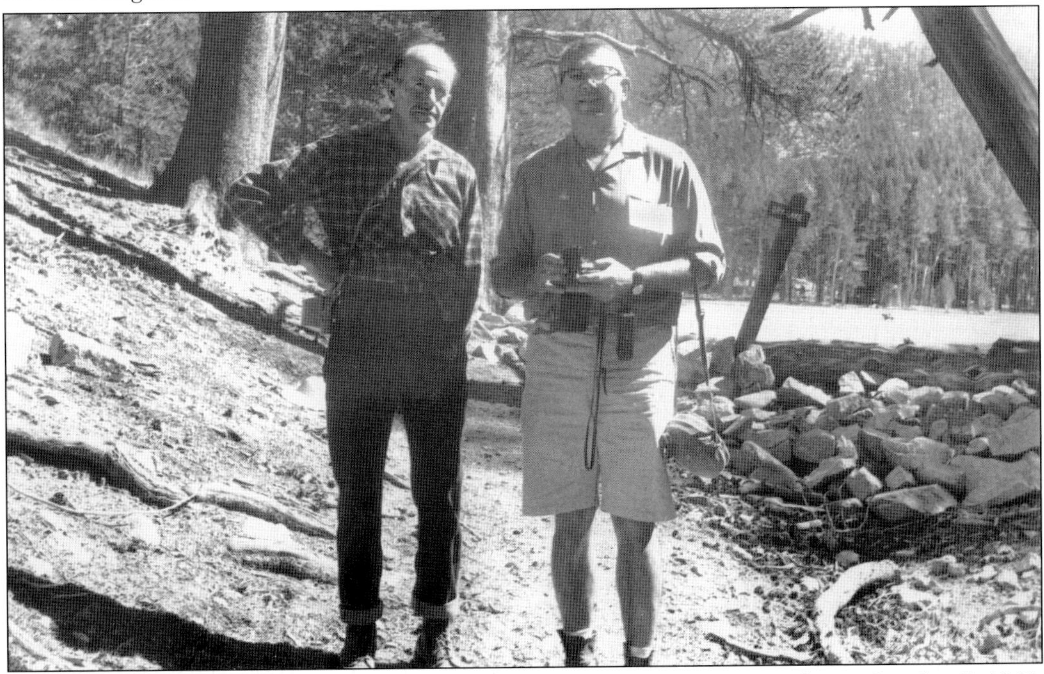

Larry Waag (left) and Howard More are seen here during a visit to Dry Lake on October 5, 1963. More, the longtime owner of Table Mountain (later Ski Sunrise), was a major supporter of the effort to open San Gorgonio to developed skiing. Even in his 80s, More still felt that San Gorgonio should be developed as a ski area.

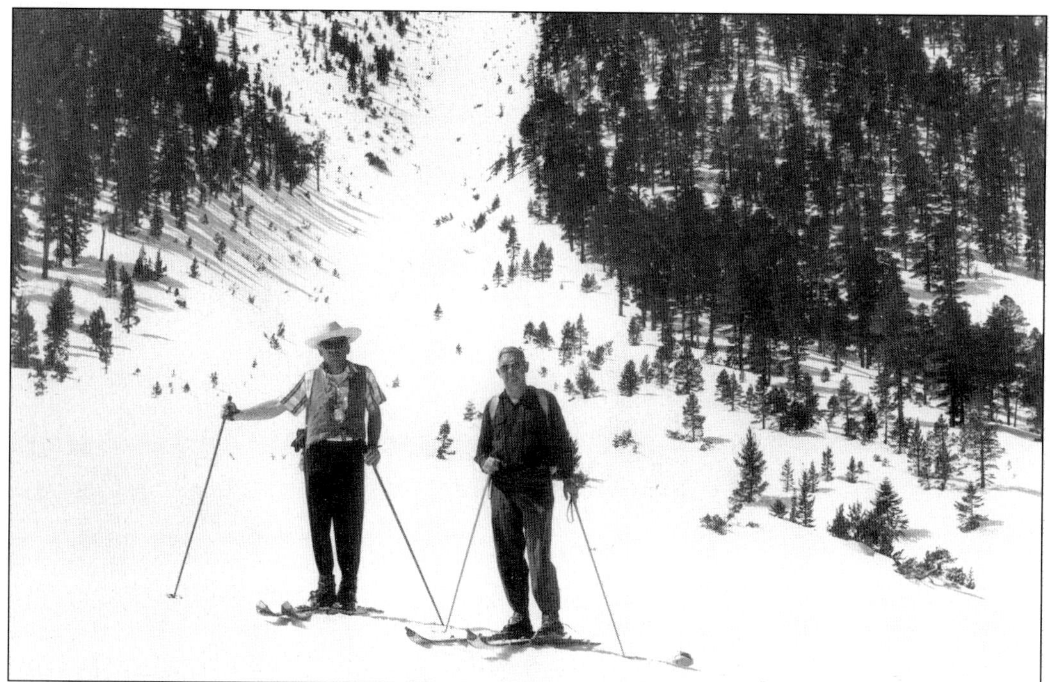

Alex Deutsch (left) and John Surr pose in front of an avalanche path on Charleton Peak in April 1962. About San Gorgonio, Deutsch commented, "Why should the area be denied so many when it was being used by so relatively few?"

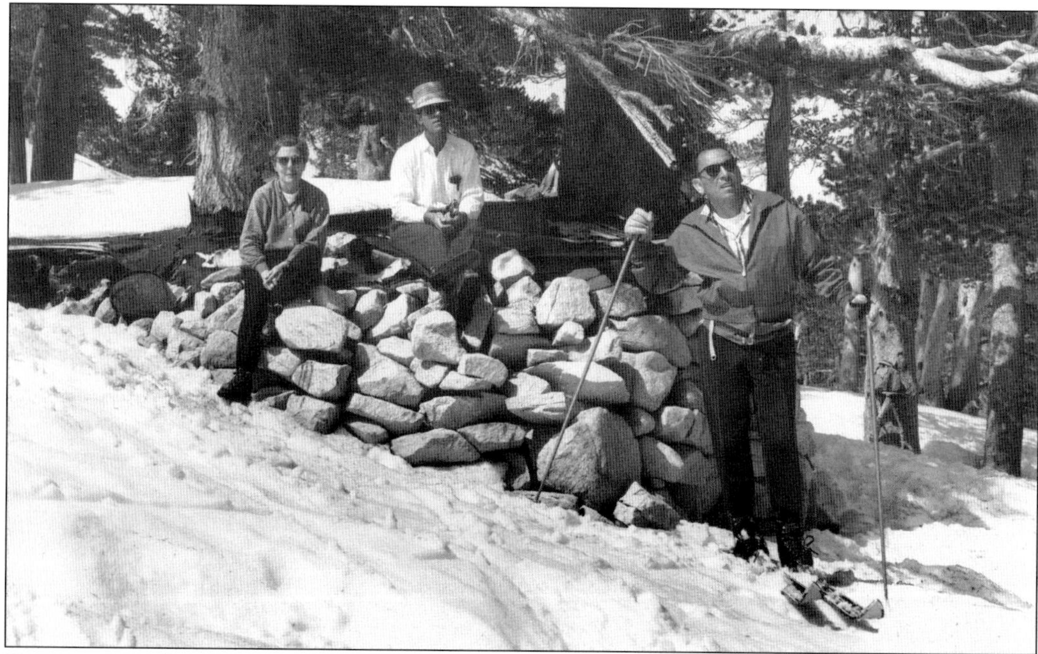

During an exploratory trip in April 1962, Isabel Wade, an unidentified companion, and Alex Deutsch (from left to right) pause for a break at the Edelweiss Hut. Deutsch, an avid skier, made several trips to Washington to express support for the development of ski facilities on San Gorgonio.

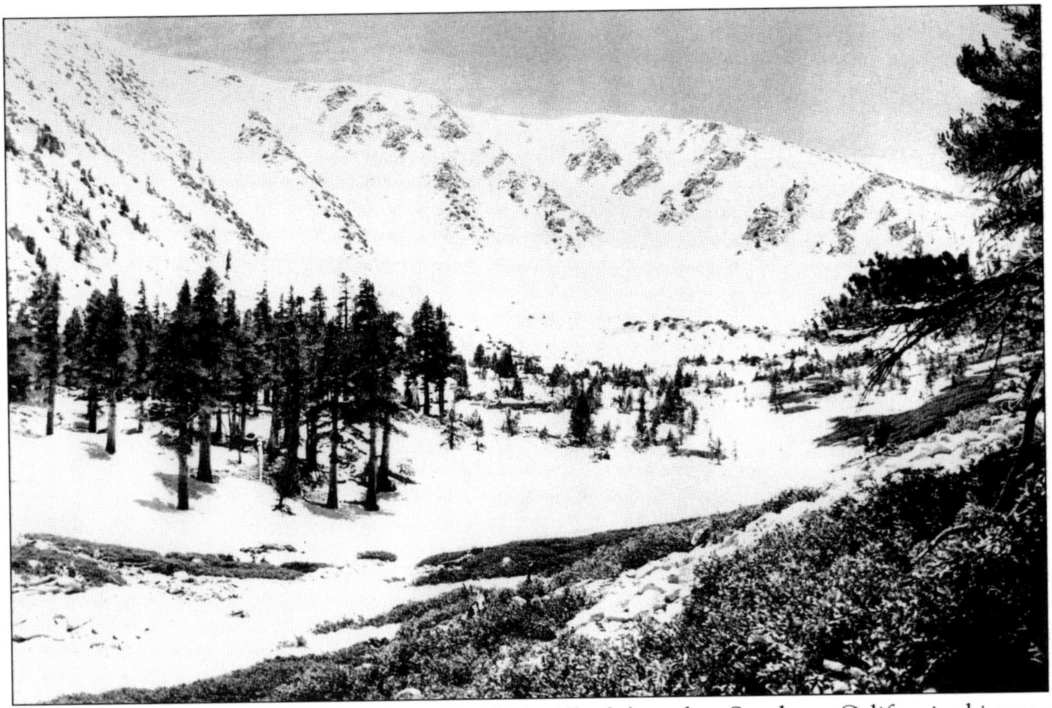

This image shows Little Draw on May 29, 1962. All of the other Southern California ski areas had already been closed for 49 days.

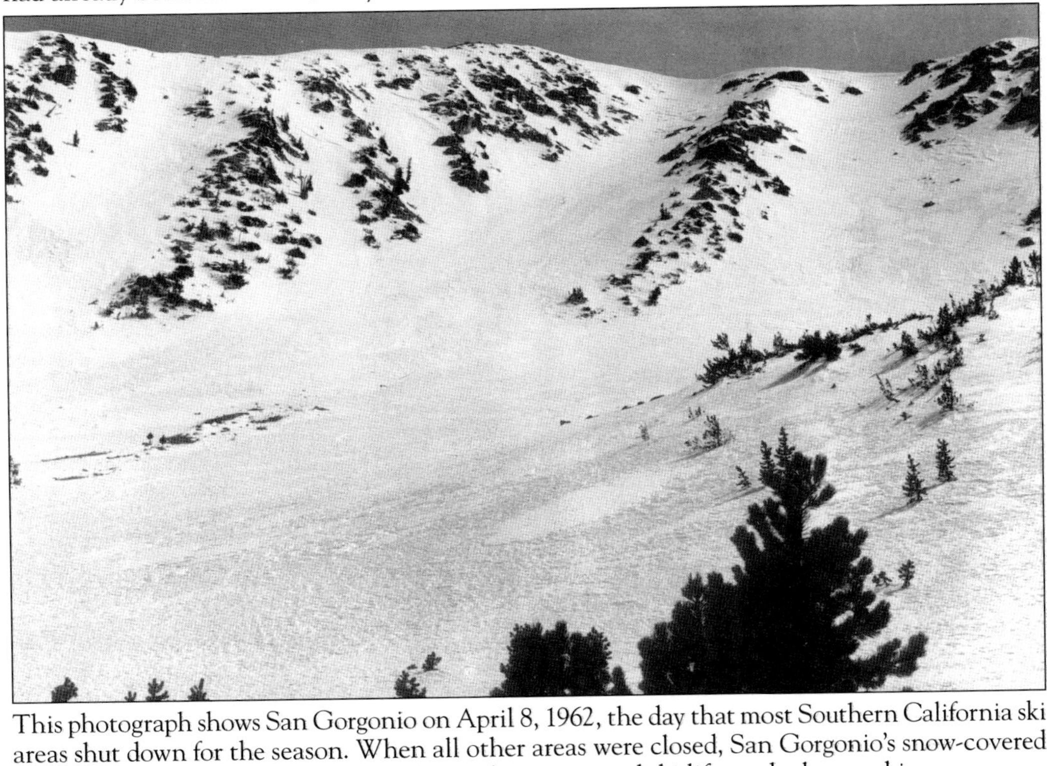

This photograph shows San Gorgonio on April 8, 1962, the day that most Southern California ski areas shut down for the season. When all other areas were closed, San Gorgonio's snow-covered slopes loomed large in the minds of those who envisioned ski lifts and a longer ski season.

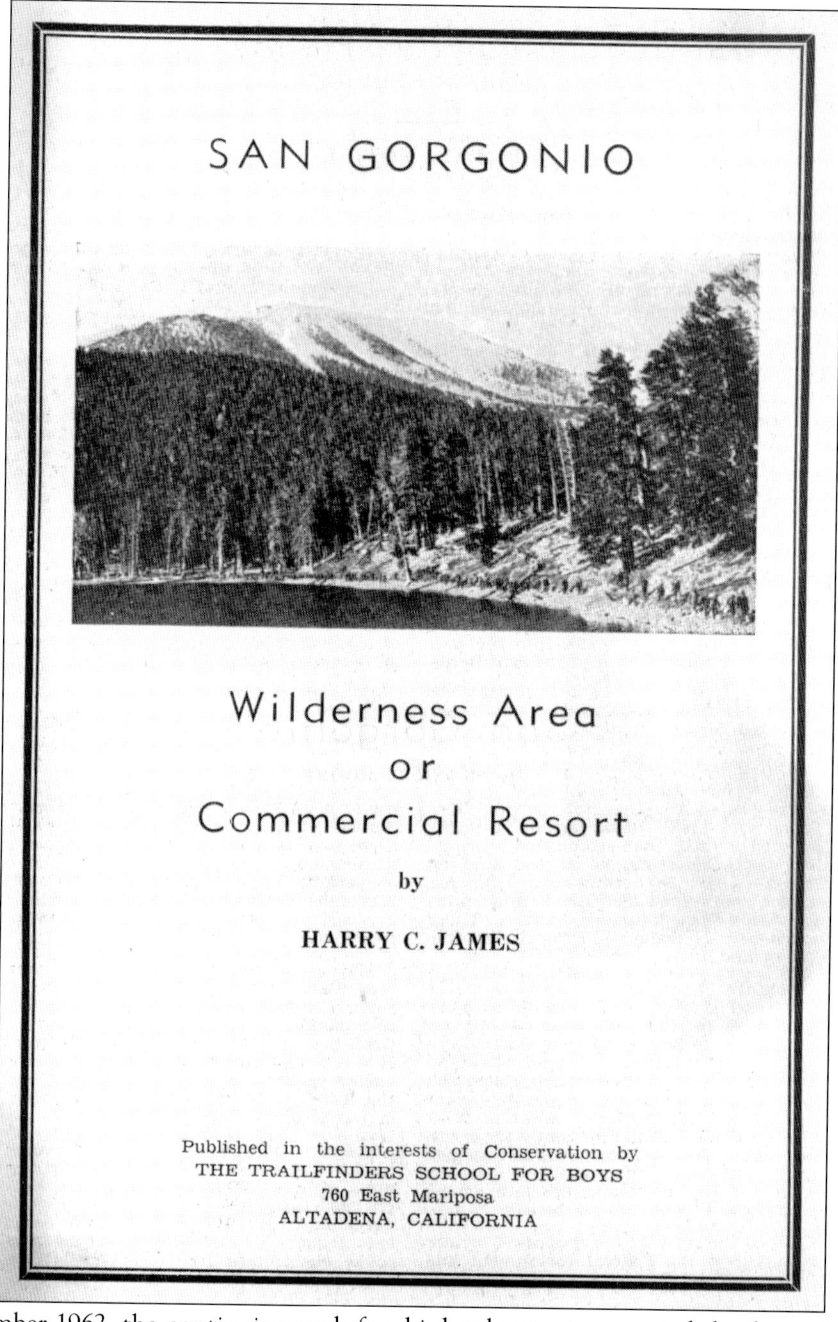

SAN GORGONIO

Wilderness Area
or
Commercial Resort

by

HARRY C. JAMES

Published in the interests of Conservation by
THE TRAILFINDERS SCHOOL FOR BOYS
760 East Mariposa
ALTADENA, CALIFORNIA

By December 1962, the continuing push for ski development prompted the formation of the Defenders of the San Gorgonio Wilderness, a group headed by Harry James, retired San Bernardino postal superintendent Joe Momyer, and secretary Alice Krueper. This brochure was one of many published and circulated by James to promote the protection of San Gorgonio as a wilderness area. Ski-area proponents wanted the area exempt from the new proposed Wilderness Bill, but on July 30, 1964, to the disappointment of developers, the Wilderness Act was passed. Because of the tremendous efforts of the Defenders of the San Gorgonio Wilderness, the Sierra Club, and legions of conservationists, the wilderness still exists.

Nine

Eastern Sierra Skiing

Inyo and Mono Counties are more than 200 miles from downtown Los Angeles, but area promoters were quick to point out that the Inyo-Mono ski areas could be reached in just a little more time than it took to reach the closer areas. Plentiful snow, a wide variety of slopes, and the lack of the usual overcrowded conditions drew many die-hard skiers from Southern California.

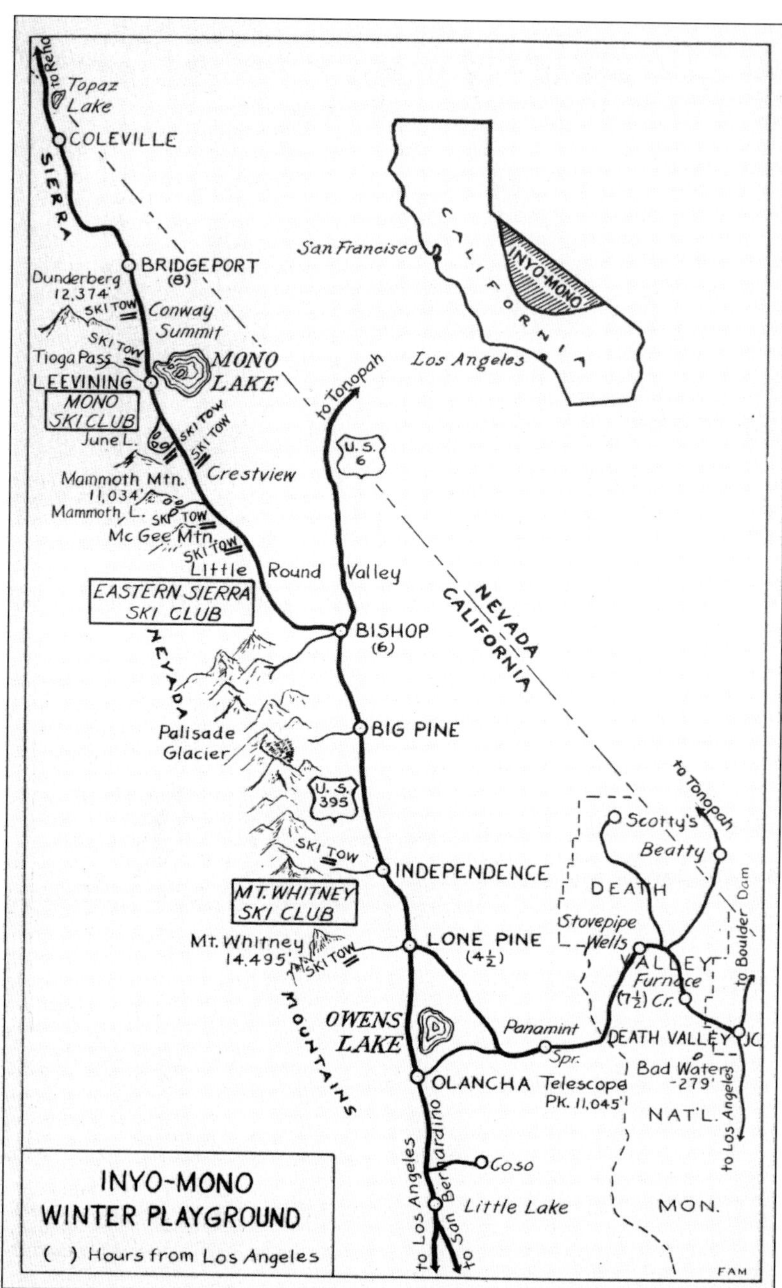

Numerous ski clubs formed along the Eastern Sierra, most having their own ski tows with easy access near Highway 395. In 1947, the clubs formed the Inyo-Mono Winter Sports Association to promote winter sports in the area. Member clubs included the Mono Ski Club, the June Lake Winter Club, the Mammoth Mountain Winter Sports Association and Ski Club, and the Eastern Sierra Ski Club. Any approved and recognized winter sports group in the area could become a member. The major goals of the association were to coordinate ski meets and events, provide a permanent race committee and equipment for events recognized by the association, promote area advertising, create a ski patrol, and encourage standards of skiing as sponsored by the California Ski Association.

ANNOUNCING!

The official opening of the

ONION VALLEY

Winter Sports Area

NEAR INDEPENDENCE, CALIF.

Yes! . . . The roads are open and the snow conditions are mar-velous . . . about 50" of packed snow . . . with enough powder to make superb ski conditions.

GET YOUR GROUP TOGETHER

and make arrangements for a bus trip if you so desire . . . . . .

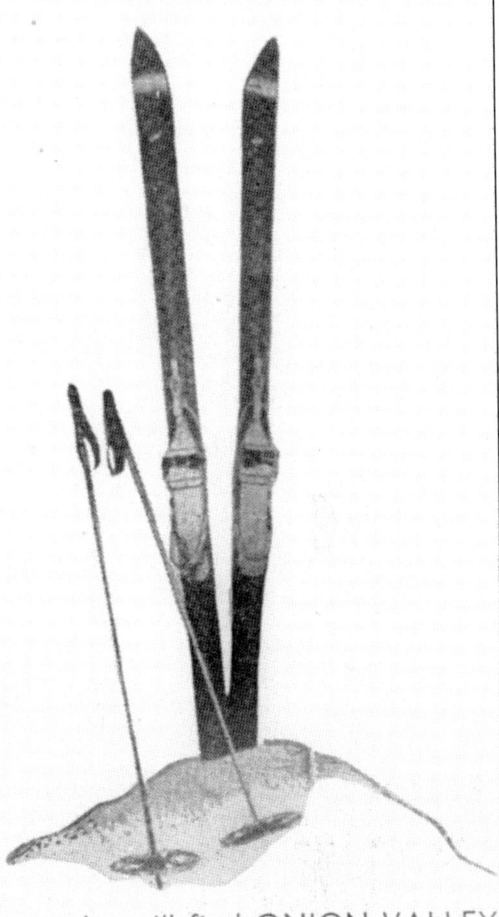

The ski hut takes care of your comforts and you'll find ONION VALLEY a truly outstanding Winter Sports Event . . . .

Reservations, accommodations can be arranged through

EASTERN HIGH SIERRA ASSOCIATION

314 NO. MAIN STREET, BISHOP, CALIFORNIA

Phone Bishop 7811

Onion Valley Ski Area, near Independence, opened in early 1949 with 1,000-foot and 600-foot rope tows. OK and Anne Kelley managed the area. The grand opening also marked the first meeting of the Onion Valley Ski Club, with about 50 members in attendance. The meeting was followed by a party at the newly christened ski hut.

GLACIER LODGE

INYO-MONO'S MOST BEAUTIFUL ALL-YEAR RESORT

LOCATED IN HEART OF INYO NATIONAL FOREST

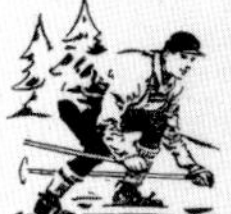

Ski in PALISADE GLACIER SKI BOWL

11 Miles West of Big Pine, California on U.S. 6 and 395 — 250 Miles North of Los Angeles

● SKIING ● CROSS COUNTRY WINTER SPORTS ● SKATING

1200 ft. Ski Tow — 2500 ft. of Downhill Run — Perfect Snow — Cafe
Ski Hut — Mountain Lodge — Heated Hotel Rooms, Cabins, Dormitory

1946 - Glacier Lodge Winter Rates - 1947

All reservations must be accompanied by $5 deposit per person. Accommodations are American Plan, except where indicated that meals are extra.

- Singles without bath $8.50 per day.
- Singles with bath $10 per day.
- Doubles without bath $7 per day per person.
- Doubles with bath $8.50 per day per person.
- Cabins for three or more, $7 per day per person.
- Dormitory, sleeping only, linen and blankets furnished, $2 per day per person. Meals extra.
- Sleeping bag accommodations, $1.50 per day per person. Meals extra.
- Dormitory cabins accommodate from 8 to 12 persons.

SPECIAL RATES TO LARGE SKI GROUPS OF 10 OR MORE

Winter Sports

- 1200 Ft. Tow with 2500 Ft. Downhill Run.
- Perfect Snow conditions at 8,000 Ft.
- Slopes for experts and novices.
- Skating on our own rink near the lodge.
- Paved road 11 miles from Big Pine direct to Lodge. Road open at all times.

CLOSEST HIGH SIERRA SKI LODGE TO LOS ANGELES

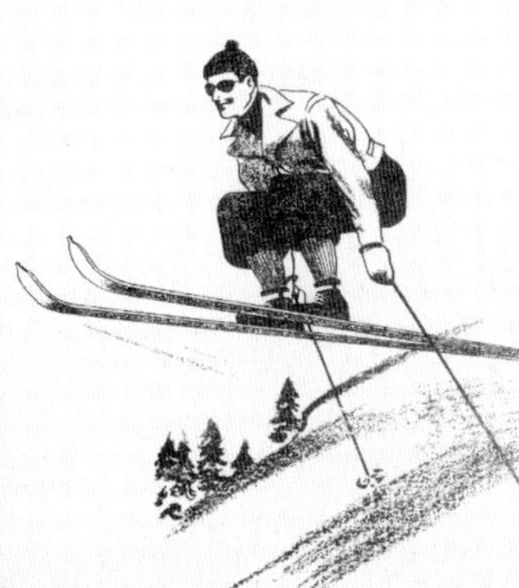

Accommodations

- Hotel Accommodations for 40 Persons.
- Dormitory Accommodations for 80 Persons.
- Modern Heated Cabins, Hotel and Dormitory.
- Lodge Lobby with largest resort fireplace in Inyo-Mono.
- Modern Cafe facilities.

The lodges that sprang up along Highway 395 near ski tows and ski club headquarters provided much-needed food and drink to the hordes of skiers that began to frequent the areas. The slopes at Crestview, as well as those at the Glacier Lodge Ski Bowl, provided excellent practice slopes. Hans Georg and Sigi Engl conducted ski schools at Crestview in 1938. The Eastern Sierra Ski Club, based in Bishop, provided cross-country tours on Mammoth Mountain, led by Chester Jones, Dave McCoy, and Lynn Phelps.

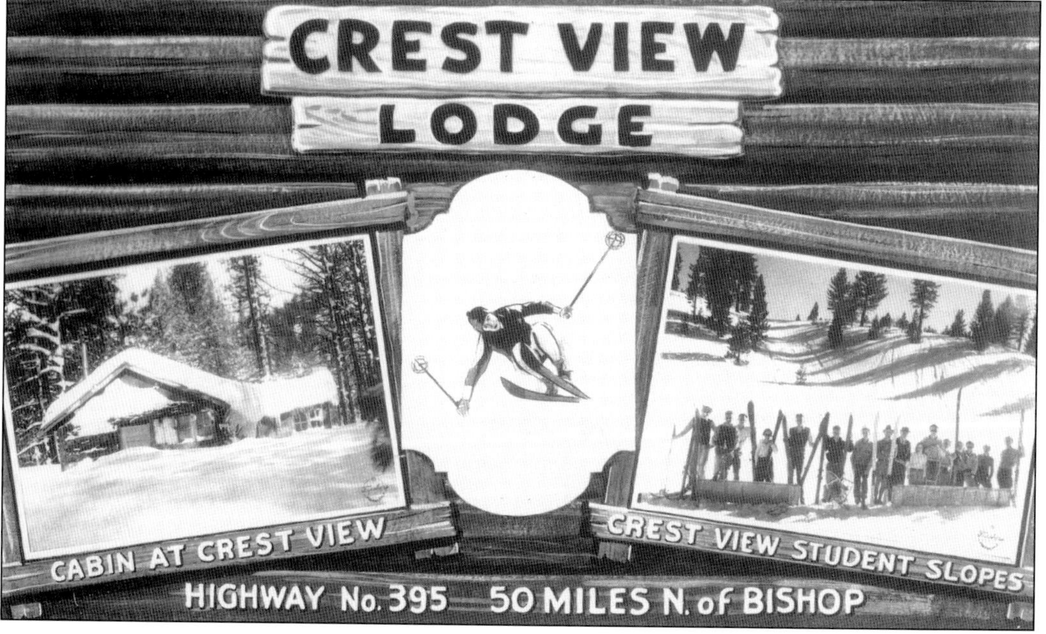

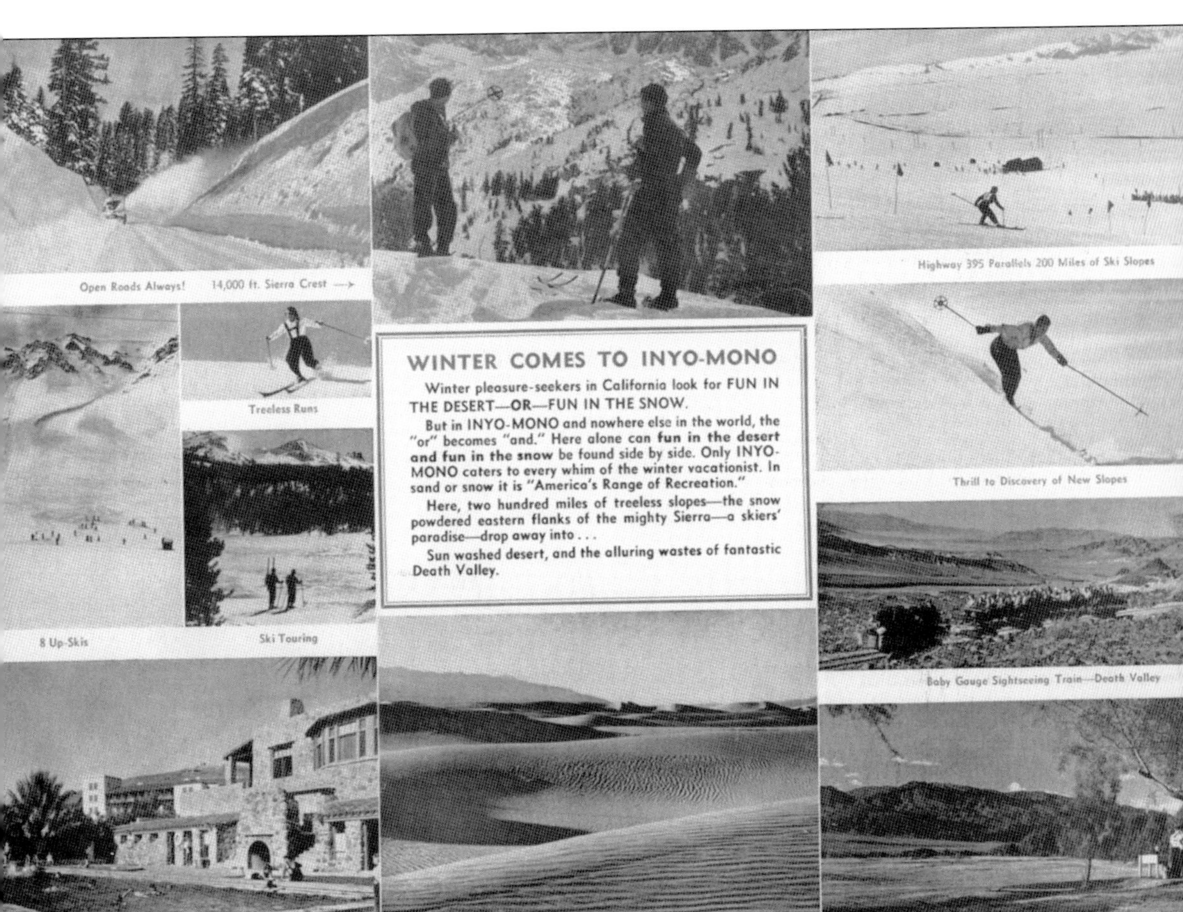

Open Roads Always! 14,000 ft. Sierra Crest →

Highway 395 Parallels 200 Miles of Ski Slopes

Treeless Runs

WINTER COMES TO INYO-MONO

Winter pleasure-seekers in California look for FUN IN THE DESERT—**OR**—FUN IN THE SNOW.

But in INYO-MONO and nowhere else in the world, the "or" becomes "and." Here alone can **fun in the desert and fun in the snow** be found side by side. Only INYO-MONO caters to every whim of the winter vacationist. In sand or snow it is "America's Range of Recreation."

Here, two hundred miles of treeless slopes—the snow powdered eastern flanks of the mighty Sierra—a skiers' paradise—drop away into . . .

Sun washed desert, and the alluring wastes of fantastic Death Valley.

Thrill to Discovery of New Slopes

8 Up-Skis

Ski Touring

Baby Gauge Sightseeing Train—Death Valley

The Inyo-Mono area covers a large segment of Highway 395, from Lone Pine in the south to Conway Summit in the north. By 1939, there were five tows operating along the route. The residents of Lone Pine and Independence built a 400-foot rope tow that was used on the slopes of Mount Whitney and in Onion Valley, west of Independence. The longest tow was at Little Round Valley, north of Bishop. It was a combination rope and steel cable tow, measuring 3,700 feet long and rising 700 vertical feet. On McGee Mountain, the Eastern Sierra Ski Club erected a 1,200-foot rope tow that rose 400 vertical feet. Residents of Lee Vining built a 1,200-foot rope tow on the slopes of the mountains directly behind the town. At Conway Summit, a 1,500-foot rope tow, rising 400 vertical feet, provided skiers with a choice of many delightful runs.

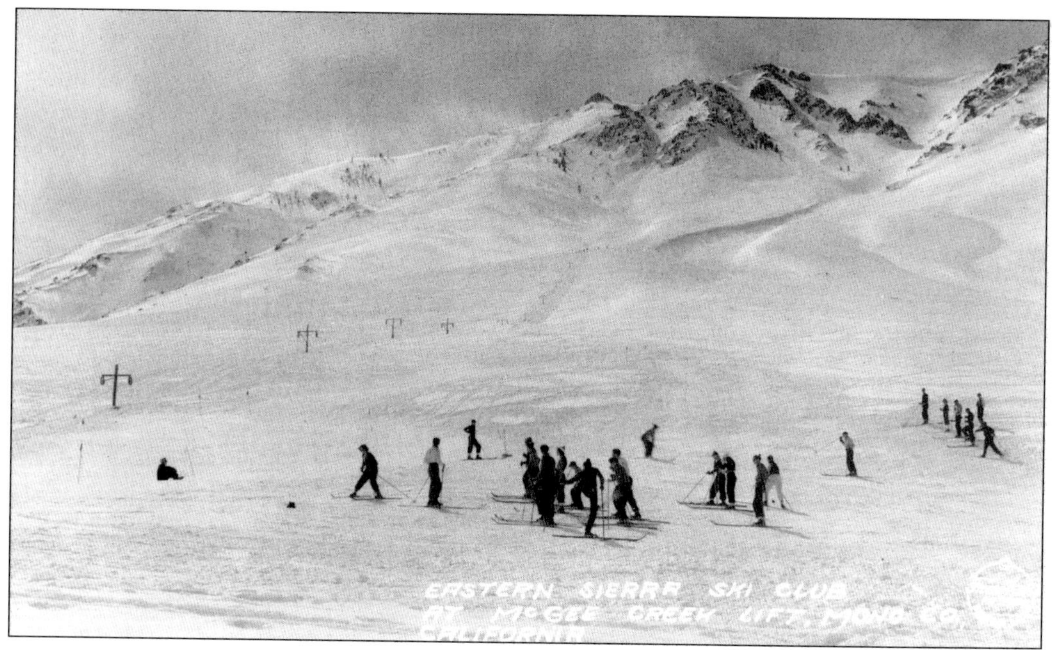

McGee Creek was one of the first Eastern Sierra areas to attract the attention of skiers. It was convenient because of its proximity to Highway 395. The large expanse of open slopes made it one of the most popular ski areas in the 1930s and 1940s.

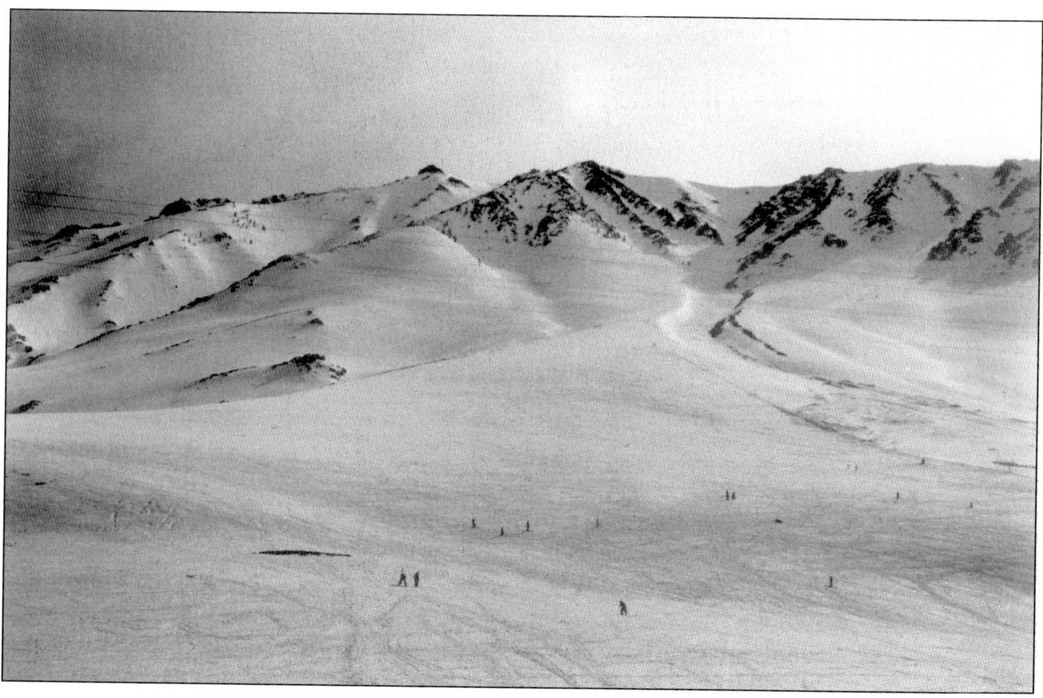

Once skiing became more popular and began to attract more winter sports devotees, a variety of newsletters and brochures were published by some of the ski clubs and winter sports associations. This pamphlet, with its photographic cover, highlighted the lift and slopes at McGee Creek.

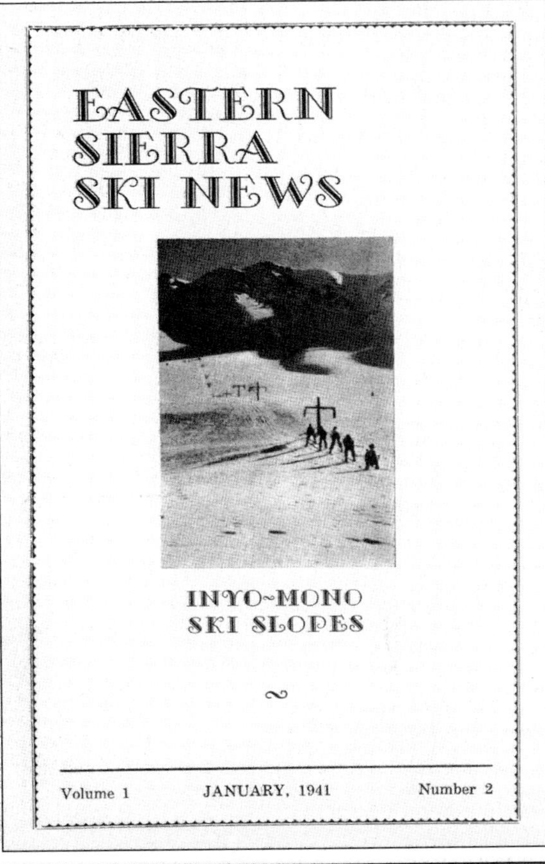
EASTERN SIERRA SKI NEWS

INYO-MONO SKI SLOPES

Volume 1 JANUARY, 1941 Number 2

With its rope tow and warming hut, McGee Creek attracted large numbers of skiers, and it was the scene of the first slalom race on the east side of the Sierra. Cortlandt T. "Corty" Hill organized and sponsored the race, held in April 1937. Hill also financed the lift at McGee Creek, which was planned and built by Tex Cushion and aerospace engineer Jack Northrop.

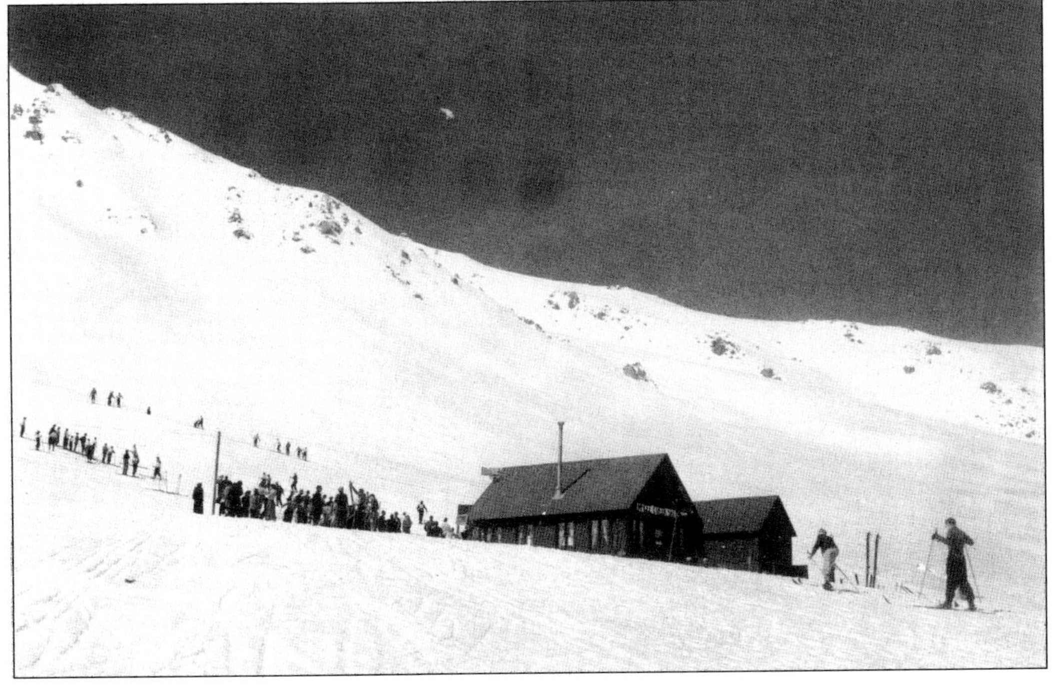

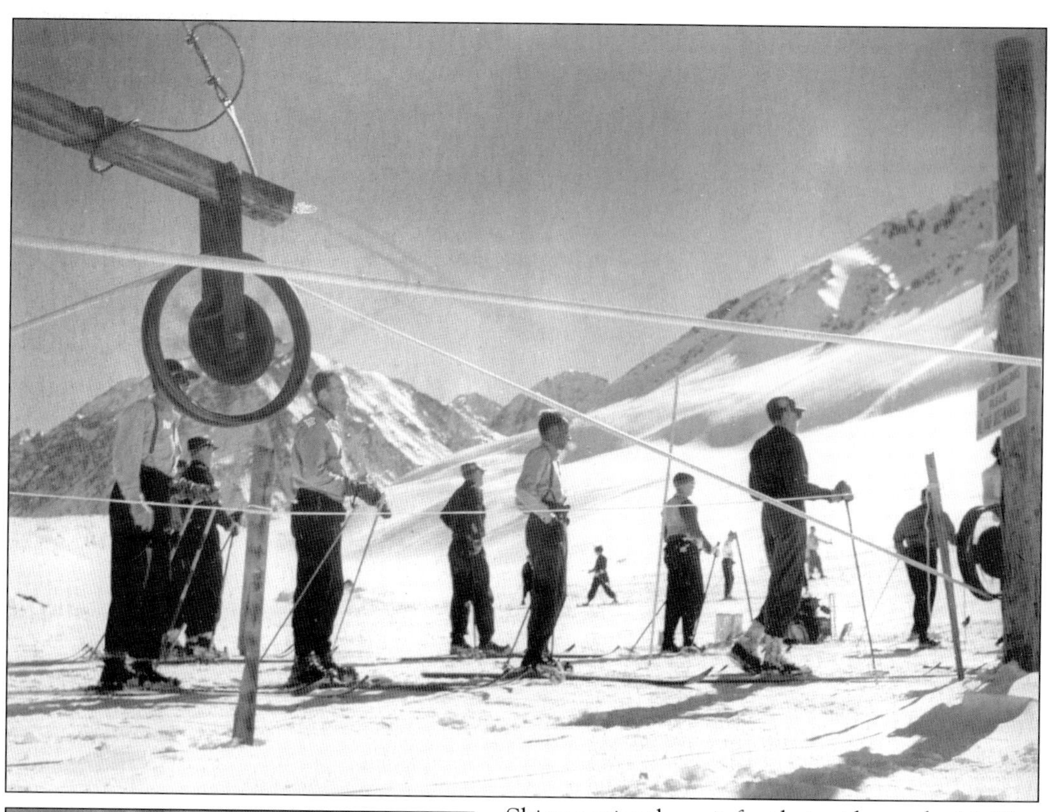

Skiers patiently wait for their ride on the McGee Creek rope tow. (Courtesy Elmar Baxter.)

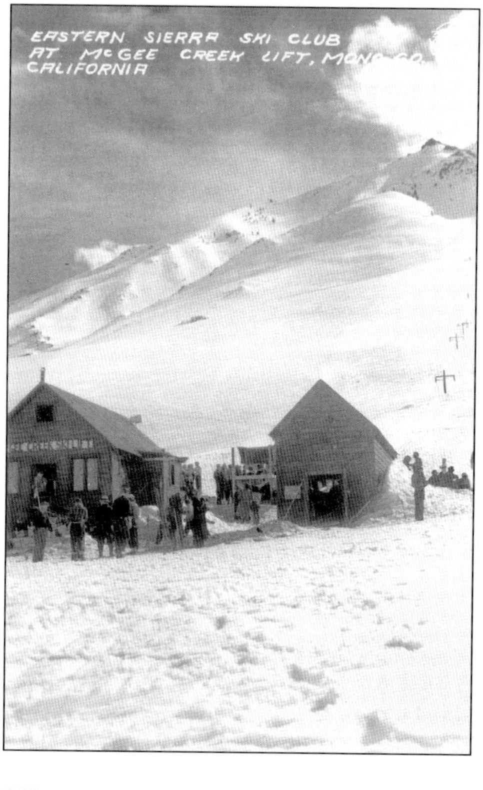

EASTERN SIERRA SKI CLUB
AT McGEE CREEK LIFT, MONO CO.
CALIFORNIA

The McGee Creek warming hut, the base area, and the lower section of the rope tow, located well in view of travelers along Highway 395, attracted the attention of skiers and nonskiers alike.

Hans Georg arrived in the Sierras in the 1930s and operated some of the first rope tows at McGee Creek and Mammoth Mountain. He organized the first summer ski race school in the United States, held at a 12,000-foot elevation on the eastern slope of Mount Whitney.

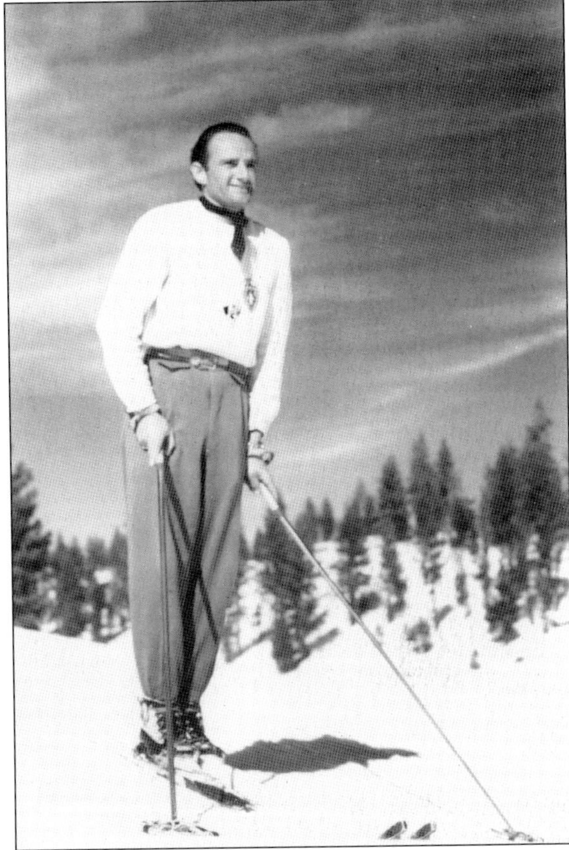

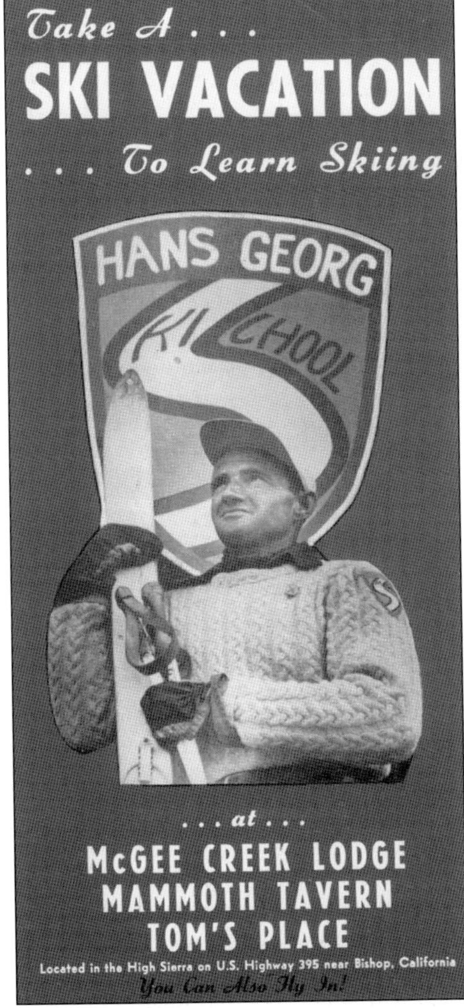

Hans Georg established his ski school in the McGee Creek and Mammoth Mountain areas in 1938. He became well known as an ingenious instructor, and his school grew to be very popular.

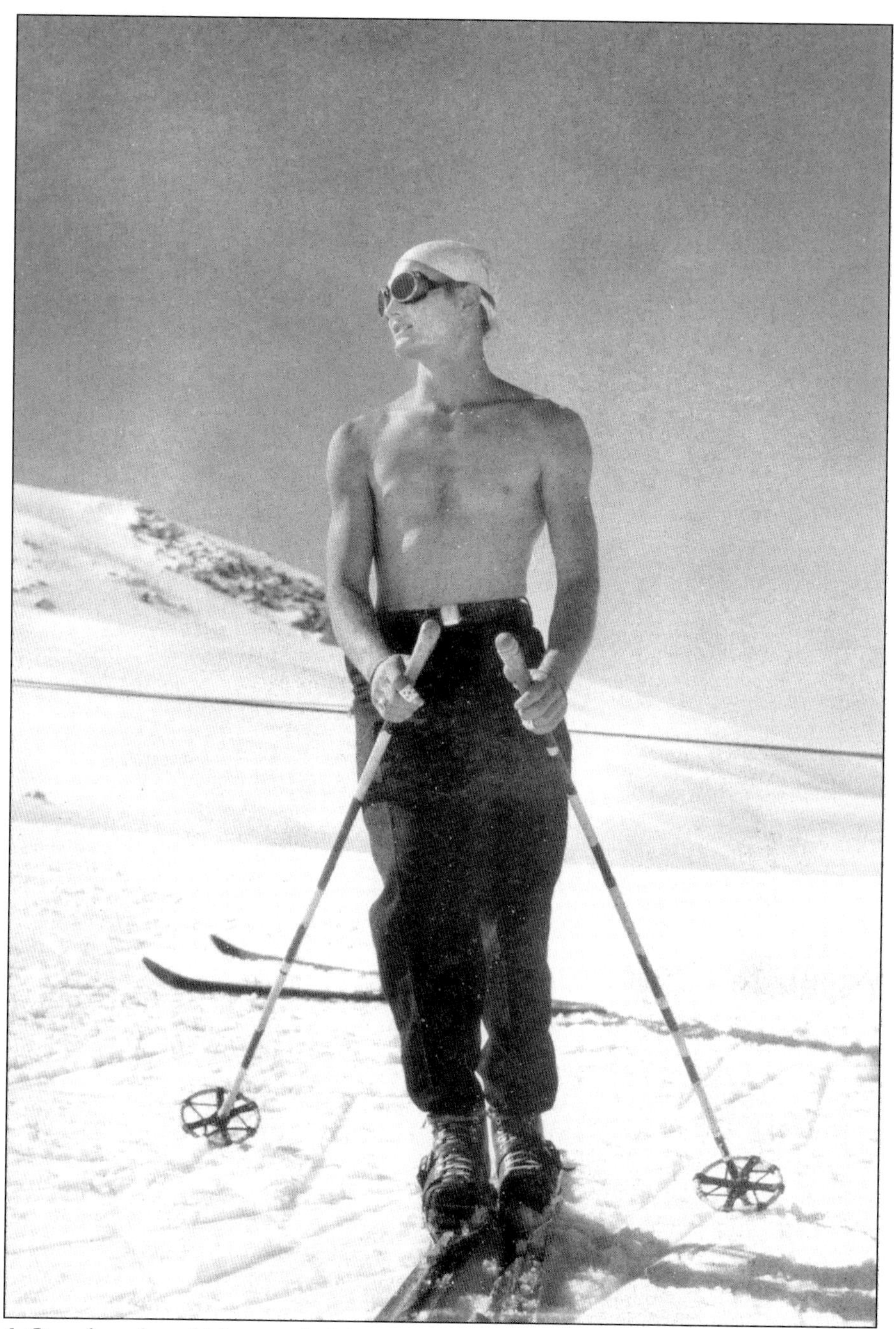

Dave McCoy, founder of Mammoth Mountain Ski Area, arrived in Independence during the summer of 1935. Already a skier, McCoy, along with two friends, erected the first rope tows in the Eastern Sierra. One was a fixed tow at Gray's Meadow, located above Independence. The other was a portable tow that could be moved to any locale that had plenty of snow. In this photograph, McCoy is taking a break during the first ski race in the Eastern Sierra, held at McGee Creek on April 10 and 11, 1937. He won first place for the Class B slalom. McCoy began operating Mammoth Mountain's first chairlift in the fall of 1955. It was the birth of what would become one of America's premier ski resorts and a perennial favorite of Southern California skiers.

In the late 1930s, Conway Summit Lodge was owned by Fred and Gene Curtis. They promoted their area as having the highest elevation on Highway 395. They also ran a ski lift that rose 400 feet, providing a five-mile run down slopes to the highway below. Once at the road, skiers would return to the lift by car.

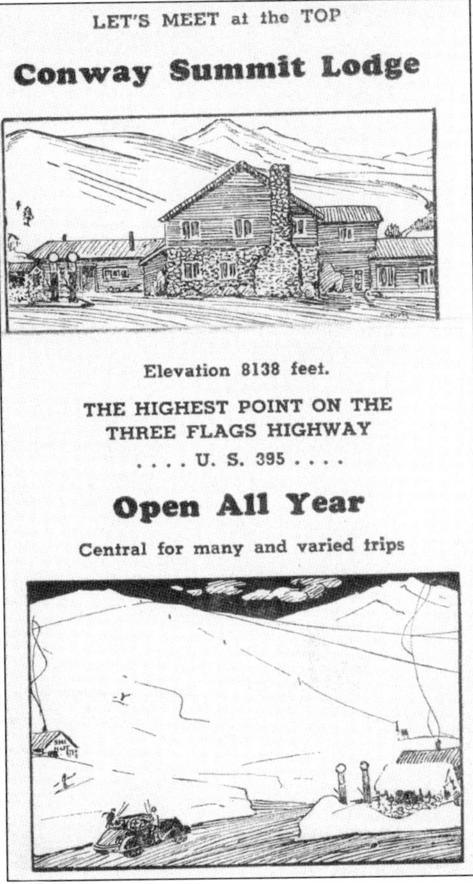

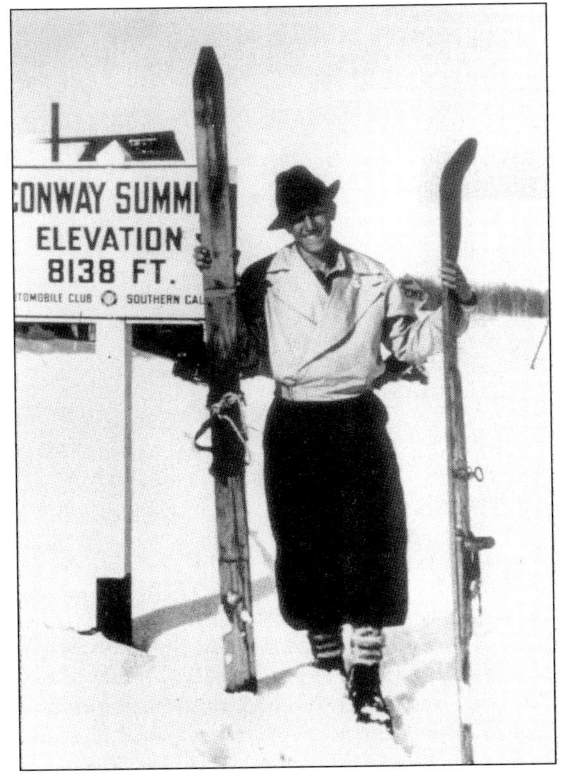

As tourists and travelers pass over Conway Summit today, there is no evidence of those early rope tows or the hoteliers that catered to skiers. In the 1930s and 1940s, the area attracted many die-hard skiers, who were drawn to any slopes holding ample snow. Here Wolfgang Lert pauses for a break at Conway Summit. Lert was a ski coach at the University of California, Los Angeles, a ski mountaineer, a ski writer and photographer, and a longtime partner in Hagemeister-Lert, quality ski importers.

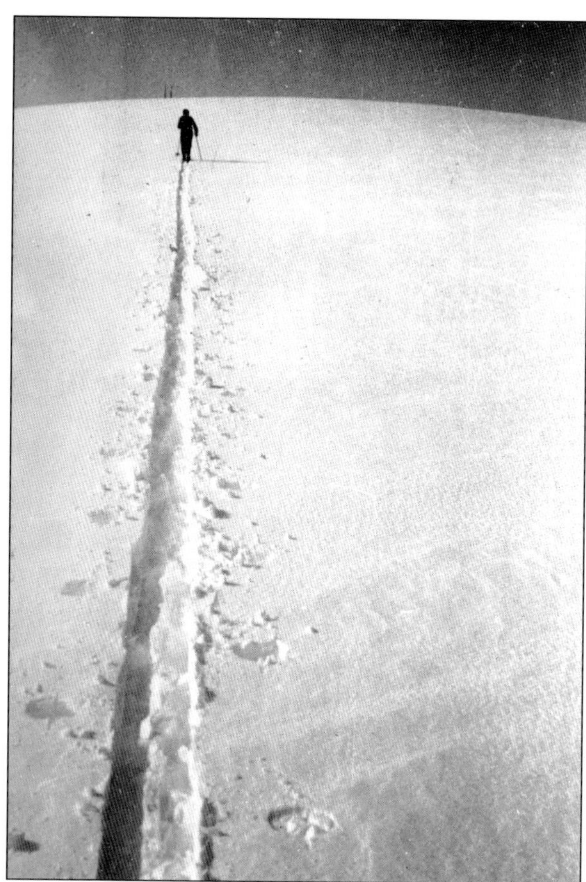

In 1938, Ed Heath installed a rope tow on Conway Summit. Ski ace Sigi Engl and sister Clarita Heath formed the Tyrol Ski School at the area. Lack of snow doomed the operation, which closed after a season or two. When snow was plentiful, the clear, open slopes and acres of rolling ski terrain provided skiers with excellent skiing and unlimited runs. (Courtesy Chris Schwarzenbach.)

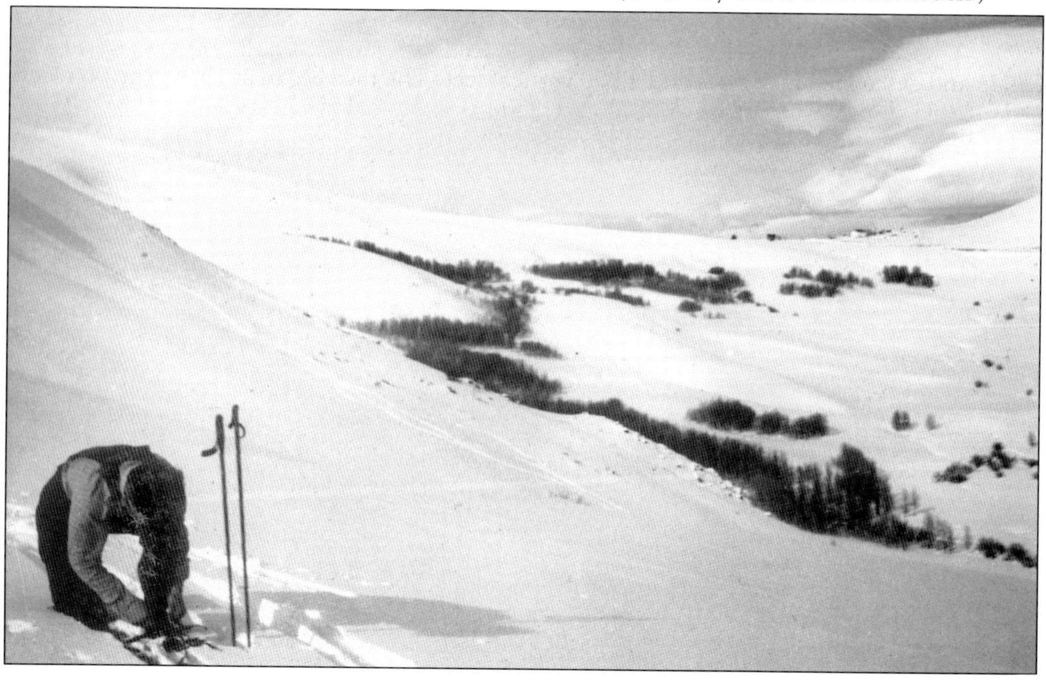

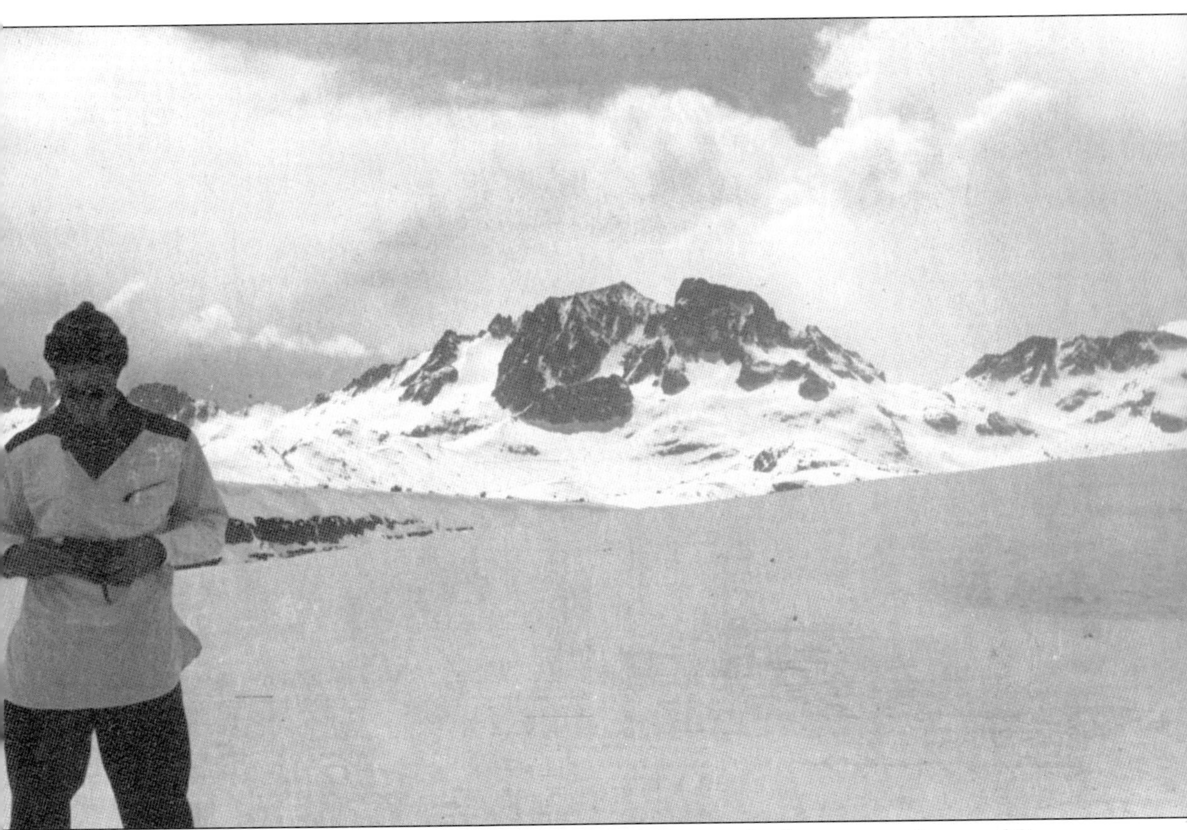

A. K. Pitcher, seen here in a photograph taken by Chris Schwarzenbach, pauses at the top of Carson Peak during the inaugural Flying Skis Invitational Race in 1941. Organized by the Mono Ski Club, it was considered one of the most dangerous races ever held in the Eastern Sierra. It started above 11,000 feet on the steep slopes of Carson Peak. Skiers threaded their way through Devil's Chute and descended five miles and 4,000 vertical feet. The race began at 10:30 a.m., so racers had to begin the climb, which took five hours or more, at dawn. It took racers about four minutes to descend the course. Schwarzenbach won the race. (Courtesy Chris Schwarzenbach.)